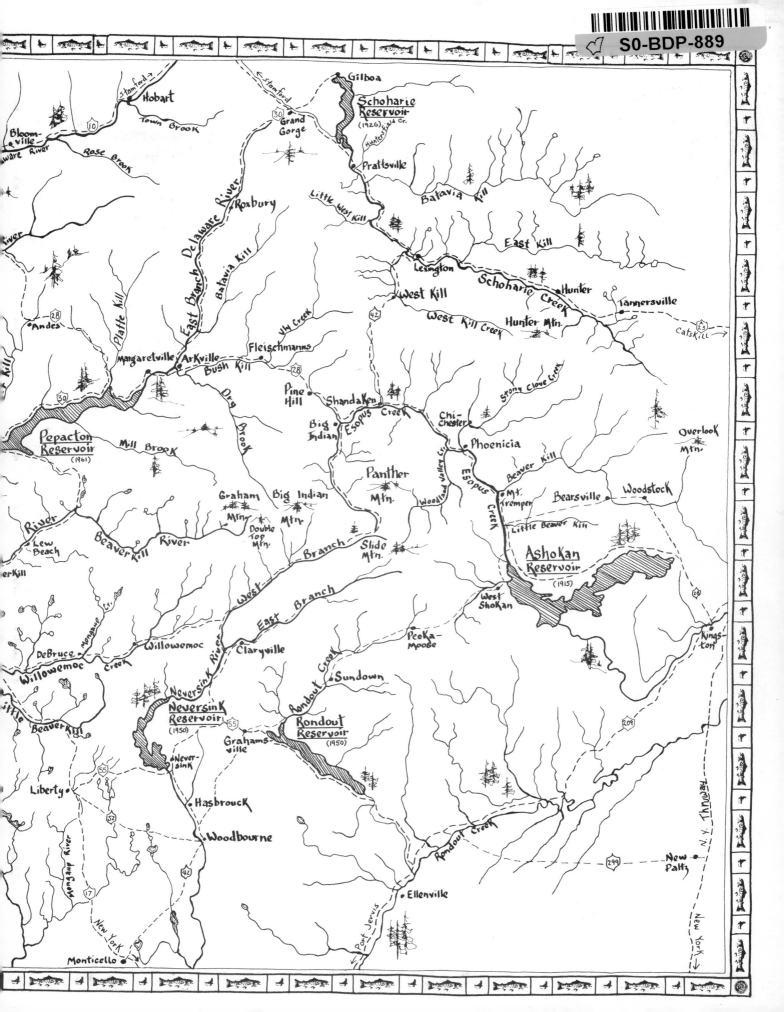

Catskill Rivers
Birthplace of
American Fly Fishing

BOOKS BY AUSTIN M. FRANCIS

Catskill Flytier (*with Harry Darbee*)
Smart Squash
Catskill Rivers

Catskill Rivers

Birthplace of American Fly Fishing

Austin M. Francis

Maps by John Manikowski

LYONS & BURFORD, PUBLISHERS

Printed in the United States of America

10 / 9 / 8 / 7 / 6 / 5 / 4 / 3 / 2 / 1

The Library of Congress has cataloged the hardcover edition of this work as follows:

Library of Congress Cataloging-in-Publication Data

Francis, Austin M.
    Catskill rivers : birthplace of American fly fishing / Austin M.
  Francis ; maps by John Manikowski.
        p.   cm.
    Originally published: Piscataway, NJ : Winchester Press, c1983.
    Includes bibliographical references and index.
    ISBN 1-55821-513-1 (cloth)
    1. Fly fishing—History.   2. Trout fishing—New York (State)—
  Catskill Mountains.   I. Title.
  SH456.F73   1997
  799.1'755—dc20   96-43312
                                                        CIP

Contents

FOR ROSS—

my "best chum"
both on and off the stream

Acknowledgments

One of the major rewards in writing this book has been the opportunity to meet an extremely interesting and diverse group of people. Universally, they have been generous with their time and knowledge and have matched my enthusiasm for the project. There were those also whose encouragement meant a great deal to me in keeping up the momentum, and I thank each of them sincerely if not by name.

For direct and important contributions during the research stages, I am indebted to: Dr. Robert Ahearn, Frederic Banks IV, Gioia and Mitchell Brock, Eleanor and James Cain, Carolyn Capstick, Douglas Carlson, Patricia Carrol, Phil Chase, Frank Connell, Scott Conover, Judie Darbee, Francis Davis, Henry Davis, Winnie and Walt Dette, James Dudley, Wayne Elliot, Bessie and William Erts, Julia Fairchild, Michael Fairchild, Stephen Ferguson, Paul Fitzgerald, Michael Gann, Delano Graff, Gardner Grant, Carolyn and Kenneth Hobbs, John Hoeko, Mabel Ingalls, Adele Jennings, Lazare Kaplan, Walter Kaufman, Walter Keller, William Kelly, Calvin Koch, Walter Kocher, George LaBranche, Jr., Lewis Mack, Ian Mackay, Shaw McKean, Frank Mele, Jim Merritt, Louise Miller, Linda Morgens, Victoria Murphy, Victor Norton, Edward Ostapczuk, Maurice Otis, Guido Pantaleoni, Henry Reed, George Renner, Richard Salmon, Mike Santimauro, Jay Schaffran, Lynn Scholz, Mayzie Scofield, Glenn Seeley, Pearl and Fred Shaver, JoAnna Sheridan, Charles Silbert, Jane Smith, Susan Smith, Montagnie Van Norden, Matthew Vinciguerra, John J. Walters, Dwight Webster, Judd Weisberg, Leonard Wright, Joan and Lee Wulff, and George Yamaoka.

I am indebted to Alf Evers for sharing the "Trout" drawer from the extensive files for his book *The Catskills: From Wilderness to Woodstock.* I could never have covered all the regional libraries, historical societies, and newspaper archives, but he had done it very thoroughly, and its availability was a major research windfall.

For her warm hospitality when I was using the Anglers' Club library as a guest, I am grateful to Mary O'Malley; more welcome even than her coffee and Irish soda bread biscuits was her evident conviction that I was up to something worthwhile.

I would have omitted the important role of the Catskills in early split-bamboo rod-building had not Hoagy Carmichael discovered my graphite-induced oversight and patiently guided me in the ways of the split-bamboo tradition.

The Schoharie comes closest among Catskill rivers to being a one-man river, and that man is Art Flick; I thank him for the careful telling of its/his story and of the legendary fishing hotel he ran, Westkill Tavern.

For thoughtful advice to a fledgling from a veteran angling historian, I am grateful to John McDonald, whose familiarity with the Catskill tradition and incisive editorial comments at the outset and in the closing stages have contributed immeasurably to a better organized, more complete manuscript.

I am grateful to my secretary Tina Getman for typing the manuscript, and perhaps more important, for guarding the door and enduring the long silences while I wrote much of the book at my desk.

For their encouragement and advice in planning and producing the limited edition of *Catskill Rivers*, I am indebted to Judith Bowman, Hoagy Carmichael, James Cummins, Benjamin and Sidney Shiff, Donald Sigovich, and William Sullivan.

John Manikowski, to use Jim Deren's phrase, is "an angler at heart"; if it were not so he would never have gotten through the arduous task of illustrating the detailed river maps in this book. It was truly a labor of love, and I thank him for the considerable value they have added to the book. John and I both acknowledge the influence of Louis Rhead, one of the finest angling artists of all time, whose drawings inspired the title cards on the river maps.

Because they depend on the memories and tales of fishermen, angling histories are partly subjective. I have tried nonetheless to portray reliably the Catskill tradition, and in this regard I am indebted to Paul Schullery, former executive director of The Museum of American Fly Fishing, whose own example as an angling historian and extensive research support have been invaluable.

For their help in tracking down the origins of brown trout in America, I am indebted to Joseph Bergin, Robert Herbst, Dr. William Maxon, Tom Pero, and John Randolph.

I am grateful to Ed Van Put for the many hours he spent helping with the physical descriptions of the rivers. We drove and walked along the rivers together and he talked, as only Van Put can, of the fish and the fishing. Based on his extensive knowledge as a fisheries professional and an insatiable angler, I have given the reader liberal helpings of Ed's effervescence and keys to angling success.

Harry Darbee occupies a special place among those who have contributed to this book; it was he who hooked me into it, unconsciously, and then generously shared his library and the contents of his well-stored mind. When he added his enthusiasm for the rivers and stories from a life filled with angling, I was a pushover; I landed myself.

I am indebted to Sparse Grey Hackle for the high standard of excellence he set and maintained for more than forty years of meticulous research and lively reporting on the Catskill angling tradition. More directly, I thank Sparse for the long sessions in which he regaled me with encyclopedic recall from his vast store of angling lore. Thus elevated to his shoulders, I have been privileged with the view of a giant.

Finally, I thank Nick Lyons and Peter Burford of Nick Lyons Books. I am convinced there is no one else who combines as strongly as Nick does the skills of publisher, editor, angling author, and fly fisherman; a more fitting synthesis for this book could not be imagined. As a small publisher, where the promptness of each author counts, Nick supported me unflaggingly while the making of *Catskill Rivers* consumed five years instead of two. For this, and for his friendship throughout, I am indeed grateful.

Introduction

O ne bright June day in my first full season of angling, the fly I was using floated behind me down the current, over a tiny waterfall and into the mouth of a fifteen-inch rainbow trout. Before that moment I had caught nothing larger than ten inches. Not wanting to lose my only copy of this amazing fly, which had fooled so lovely a fish all by itself, I carefully put it away until I could find some more of them.

Later, seated on the bank, I examined the fly, trying to recall where I had gotten it. The green drakes were hatching and, following Flick's little book, I had tied on the closest thing I could find to a Grey Fox Variant. Then I remembered who had given it to me. The summer before, Ross and I had come up to the Catskills to try our brand-new fly-fishing equipment bought at the urging of two angling uncles shortly after we were married.

We ended up camping on an island in the lower Beaverkill just upstream from the hamlet of Peakville where there was a bar known locally as the "Snake Pit." At the end of our trip we stopped in for a beer and, upon learning that we were beginners, Smitty the owner became very instructive. He told us a number of places to fish, when the best times were, and what patterns to use. Reaching under the bar, he produced one of those big round fly boxes with a pie-shaped opening in the top and started picking out flies. Naming each in turn as he lined them up in front of us, he handed me one of them and said, "Here, keep this one; it's a real killer. Harry Darbee tied it." From his tone it was obvious that any questions about Darbee's credentials would go over like a two-pound chub, so I nodded gravely and we thanked Smitty sincerely as we left to drive back to the city.

Now, sitting there on the bank, having found the key to large trout, I realized that the next step in my accelerating development as an angler would be to locate Darbee and get some more of these flies.

About two weeks later, I got into the car and, leaving Ross and two house guests at the little cottage we were renting for the summer, set out on my pilgrimage. The fly was safely stowed in its own box in my pocket. After a short drive and several inquiries I pulled into a crowded parking area next to the house and fly shop of Elsie and Harry Darbee. As I got out of the car I patted the fly box and, checking for my wallet, discovered I had not brought any money. Nothing to do but go in and at least meet them, having come this far . . .

As it turned out, I could not have paid for what I came away with that day. After two hours of confusion amid the throng of customers and friends clogging the entire downstairs of the house, I left realizing that here was a sport much deeper than I suspected and—though the fly proved a fake—having met a man who was going to enrich my life. Smitty had given me much more than he thought.

I returned often, and Ross and I became friendly with the Darbees; we fished together, yes, but more typically we gathered around their kitchen table for either a meal or bouts of storytelling and conviviality. The aura of the sport began to overpower its actual pursuit. But this seemed natural, even desirable, as long as one fished enough to join in the exchange. And the wonderful thing I discovered was that the level of angling expertise had nothing to do with being welcome around the table.

Harry's stories had a cumulative effect. Often enough he would tell a particularly good one and say, "That's going in my book." Or, he would describe his secret method for dyeing hackles and say, "I'm saving that for my book." One night, to use his phrase, we were "getting as comfortable as possible," and Harry told a story that was going into "the book." I had heard this now for about three years and, realizing he had been saying the same thing to others for at least ten years before that, I offered somewhat forcefully that there was never going to be a book and why didn't he stop talking about it if indeed he wasn't going to write it. Such blunt reality was more than either of us could take, and given our tender condition, we dissolved into choked reassurances of friendship and affection. Progressively shoring each other up, we ended the evening by swearing to write the book together.

The following morning we renewed our vows in the cold light of day and embarked on the joint creation of *Catskill Flytier*, a book full of Harry's stories and advice on his career, tying techniques, raising dun hackles, and fishing experiences.

The next four years were an extended baptism in trouting, immersed in book work with Harry, fly-tying lessons with Elsie, fishing, and chance meetings with expert anglers who passed through the Darbees'. The more I learned the more I was captivated by the Catskills and the rivers. "These rivers are the birthplace of American fly fishing," I was told; and, "Theodore Gordon is the father of modern American angling."

At first I accepted these statements on pure faith; angling is after all a religion. Later, although still a believer, I began to wonder why there was no "bible" to attest these truths and document the beginnings of our sport in this country. Was the case for the Catskills as "birthplace" not strong enough to bear examination? Was this a gap in the angling literature that really needed to be filled?

The desire to answer these questions gave rise to another book. In the early stages, I expected that the work of such famous anglers as Gordon, Hewitt, and LaBranche would easily show why the Catskills were known by so many as the "cradle" and "birthplace" of American fly fishing. And so it did, but I also found that, even without these three men, an overwhelming number of contributions to early American angling originated in the Catskills.

From the 1850s on, the Beaverkill, Willowemoc, Neversink, Esopus, Schoharie, and Delaware were the setting for a continuing series of angling innovations: fly fishermen came to terms with the sophisticated brown trout, newly immigrated from Europe; a whole new angling methodology centered on the dry fly spread quickly throughout the region, affecting fly patterns, rod design, casting, and stream presentation; hatchery science, stream improvement, and fisheries management techniques were perfected and used to rejuvenate miles of neglected trout water; pioneer entomologists and flytiers created a system for identifying stream insects and matching them with effective imitations; rod builders reached the highest level of skill in making split-bamboo fly rods; women fly fishers waded into male-dominated streams and demonstrated a formidable talent for angling.

Those are the highlights in a procession of events, developments, and personalities that constitute one of the world's richest angling traditions. In telling its story I have tried to create more than a fishing history. These are living rivers, every bit as troutworthy and beautiful today as they were in the days of our angling forefathers. With the help of expert anglers, I have also portrayed the rivers as they fish today, with descriptions of their physical characteristics, insect life, trout distribution, stocking practice, access, angling pressure, fishing conditions, and successful angling techniques. In doing so, I hope that I have done more than document the central importance of Catskill rivers in the heritage of American angling; I hope also that I have helped extend the life of these rivers as valued places to fish.

AUSTIN M. FRANCIS

Beaverkill, New York
November 1, 1982

PART ONE

Catskill Angling Heritage

Photo by Larry Madison.

ONE

The Catskill Angling Mystique

I t is dusk and the big browns are rising to Hendrickson spinners in a ledgerock pool on the Beaverkill. The air cools and a mist begins to form as your line straightens and the fly falls just ahead of the last rise. Upstream, in a quiet eddy, a file of baby mergansers paddles along behind the mother, the nearest one of them climbing onto her back for a free ride. Dark and the mist close around the willows as you net your last trout, a good fish, and head back up the hill to the cabin. It is the proper end to another day of Catskill angling.

If you are a sensitive angler, Catskill streams have the power to possess your soul in an altogether benign but permanent manner. They have a captivating mystique that is unique in the world of angling. You come to fish them, and you are taken in not only by their natural beauty and wildlife but also by the realization that you are joining a procession of anglers who have created one of the richest traditions in fly-fishing history.

To comprehend the Catskill angling mystique requires more than time on the streams; it needs also a receptive spirit and a good deal of curiosity. Perhaps a general idea of what is in store for those who succeed can be conveyed by identifying some of the qualities that make up the ambience of Catskill streams and by listening to anglers past and present who have pondered their mysteries.

The Catskills are a small, well-worn range of mountains. They lack awe-inspiring peaks sculpted by deep ravines. Morris Longstreth, a hiker and writer of the early 1900s, observed that the virtue of the Catskills "resides very little in their measurements, but in the serene sweep of their slopes, the harmony of their contours, and the appeal of their covering, whether it be forest, rock, or snow." They are endowed with a humble beauty that soothingly invites the angler to come fish and stay a while. The typical Catskill trout stream and its surroundings were created on a personal scale that intensifies the feelings of privacy and intimacy with nature so highly prized among anglers. They are the perfect size for fly fishing.

Longstreth also noted—he really should have been a fisherman—that his favorite memories were of scenes he had stumbled upon by surprise. "You can follow up any brook only a little way, and you are certain to come upon mossy grottos, cool, damp, and very lonely, where you can have a waterfall to yourself." He cherished these experiences, which he called "minor personal discoveries," and felt that the Catskills were full of such enticing little surprises.

Longstreth was a disciple of John Burroughs, the famed nineteenth-century naturalist and author, who was born on the East Branch of the Delaware River and grew up fishing in the Catskills. Perhaps better than any other angler, Burroughs fathomed the mysteries of these streams.

> I have been a seeker of trout from my boyhood, and on all the expeditions in which this fish has been the ostensible purpose I have brought home more game than my creel showed. In fact, in my mature years I find I got more of nature into me, more of the woods, the wild, nearer to bird and beast, while threading my native streams for trout, than in almost any other way.

His keen sense of observation and talent for articulation enabled Burroughs to create haunting evocations of the stream:

> The creek loves to burrow under the roots of a great tree, to scoop out a pool after leaping over the prostrate trunk of one, and to pause at the foot of a ledge of moss-covered rocks, with ice-cold water dripping down. How straight the current goes for the rock! Note its corrugated, muscular appearance; it strikes and glances off, but accumulates, deepens with well-defined eddies above and to one side; on the edge of these the trout lurk and spring upon their prey.

In the same spirit, contemporary angler Vic Norton looked beyond his flies and the catching of trout to expand his appreciation of the stream. After having fished the Beaverkill for almost twenty-five years, about a dozen years ago he started paying serious attention to the flowers along the stream. For two years, every week from April to September, he spent as much time identifying and photographing wildflowers as he did fishing. Now he can enjoy a different wildflower show each week during the trout season. He says that the trout fisherman who is unaware of this is missing half the fun. "One day," he recalls, "when without my camera, I espied an especially beautiful lavender flower on a bare, leafless stem. I dug it up carefully, transplanted it into a miniature wildflower garden near the house where it promptly died. It was a one-flowered cancer-root, a parasite which requires a piece of rotting wood under the ground in which to root. How does it find such an underground piece of rotting wood?"

Catskill trout streams have a way of leading the fly fisherman rather quickly through and beyond the conventional stages of angling development from catching the most fish, to the biggest fish, to the most difficult fish, and finally to the soul of the stream. Sparse Grey Hackle, a Catskill man to the core, discovered this early in his fishing career. "I learned long ago," he said, "that although fish do make a difference—*the* difference—in angling, catching them does not; so that he who is content to not-catch fish in the most skillful and refined manner, utilizing the best equipment and technique, will have his time and attention free for the accumulation of a thousand experiences, the memory of which will remain for his enjoyment long after any recollection of fish would have faded."

Thus the Catskill angling mystique has several attributes that combine the elusiveness of the subtle beauty of the streams, the inner spirit of fully evolved fishermen, and the trout themselves. It manifests itself also in the rare angling companionships that have grown to fruition on these streams.

In the 1920s, when Roy Steenrod fished with A. E. Hendrickson, he tied a special fly for their trips; it didn't have a name, they called it "the fly." A. E. would ask for some more of "those flies." Only later was the fly named after Hendrickson. They fished "around the world," he, Hendrickson, Jim Payne, and maybe a couple of others. They would go down the Beaverkill, up the East Branch, cross over and fish up the headwaters of the Esopus, connect with the West Branch of the Neversink, fish it down to its closest point to the Willowemoc and fish that on down to the starting point at Junction Pool in Roscoe. They would be gone for a week to ten days when they made the circuit. They could vary that and hit different streams if they wanted, but generally they fished a loop right through the Catskills.

Then there was Thad Norris and his little band of "Houseless Anglers." In the 1850s, he, "Uncle Peter" Stewart, and a small group of like-minded anglers fished the Beaverkill and neighboring streams. One of their favorite pleasures was the gathering at noon, after the morning's fishing, to roast their trout under a dark sugar maple at streamside. They took these small, nine-inch trout, scoured them in sand, washed them clean, opened and gutted them, allowing no water to touch the inside so the blood and natural juices of the fish would be retained as much as possible. Then they cut off the heads, scored them, peppered and salted them well inside and out and stuck them on sweet birch twigs, running the twig along the upper side of the backbone, and held them to the fire. By keeping an eye on the inside of the fish, it was easy to tell when they were done. They disengaged the twig from the flesh with a twisting motion, laid the fish on hot stones, and buttered them while warm. They called this "the noonday roast."

Lying at the heart of the mystique are the emotions of the angler, none of them stronger than his anticipation of spring. The images that populate his mind on the reawakening of the valley and the river were conjured wistfully by

Catskill angler Palmer Baker: "An old phrase evokes the fly-fisher's spring: the sweet of the year. On an April evening the wind comes softly from the south. The angler reaches the countryside with his friends. Stepping from the car, he smells the damp earth and feels the wind. Then suddenly the sweetness is upon him. . . . The morning landscape has its own sweetness. Over the new grass the rays of the sun are soft, diffused by the moisture in the air. The tamaracks and willows are lemon-yellow. . . . The great thing about trout fishing is that it makes the angler part of this young and lovely season."

Catskill winters are long and severe, giving rise to the most powerful yearnings for the arrival of the new season. Theodore Gordon, living year-round on the Neversink in his later years, conveyed through his notes the poignance of a solitary angler being tantalized by the first hints of spring: "I was greatly pleased when I heard the little frogs and peepers so early as April 15, as I presumed that these creatures were instinctively weatherwise, and that their advent heralded continued mild, springlike weather. I am sorry to say that, according to the country wiseacres and ancient superstition, peepers in April foretell frost in May. This is very sad: sad for us and sad for the peepers. They will have to fold up their little air bladders, or whatever the thing is that they blow up and peep with, and go right down into the mud again."

Gordon used to sit by his stove during those lonely Neversink winters and tie flies without a vise because he could not work at the table near the window without freezing. He ached for spring, and as he put on wood he also fueled a continuing fantasy of the stream. "Human nature is optimistic," he said, "and despite experience we are again making plans for a perfect vernal season. We are thinking of fresh yet balmy breezes, clear-rushing streams and deep, dark pools flecked with foam. The widening rings made by rising trout are easily seen if we shut our eyes for a moment. The duns are sailing down like tiny yachts with sails erect, and the little caddis flies are struggling and skittering on the water."

So come with me and we will go with all the anglers who ever fished these streams. Listen to their stories, share their memories and hopes, learn their secrets enfolded now in the mist that hovers around the Willowemoc and Beaverkill. Unlimber your rod and come down to the river. Cast your fly into the pool of a thousand fishermen past and untold thousands of risen trout, feel the take and pull, the rod spring to life as you revel in the Catskill angling mystique.

TWO

Early River Industries

Sometime around 1760 Daniel Skinner came over to the Delaware River from Connecticut and settled near Cochecton. Being an inventive Yankee, he looked at the towering white pines that lined the river and soon figured how he could make some money—by floating the trees down the river to Philadelphia where they would make excellent masts for the seagoing schooners being built there.

Skinner's first attempt involved simply the launching of several trees during high water, and they were smashed to pieces on the boulders in the river before they had run even a few miles of their 175-mile journey. The trick, Skinner decided, would be to *steer* the trees around the boulders, and to do this you would need to tie them together and install a rudder and a steersman. Skinner succeeded beyond his best expectations, and his fleets of log rafts grew so plentiful that he became known as the "Admiral of the Delaware." Newcomers to the rafting industry had to introduce themselves to Skinner and render homage in the form of one bottle of good wine. Thus was born the rafting industry—a cost-efficient merger of Catskill trees and rivers that lasted for more than a century.

Daniel Skinner was the first of the Catskillers whose livelihood depended on the rivers. It was to be several generations before these streams would win their fame as trout waters. Until that time, the Catskill rivers were the province of a hardy race of men whose everyday feats are the stuff of legend.

They ran rafts to Philadelphia and walked home carrying heavy oars and ropes. They felled two-hundred-foot hemlocks, skinned them, and hauled the bark to streamside tanneries. They built dams and erected water-powered mills. They chopped hardwood by the cord for twelve to fourteen hours a day. And when they were done they drank, fought, laughed, and drank some more. Frank Curtis Pelton brought them to life in his epic poem "Eel Rack":

> Partridge, deer, black bear and panther,
>   roaming all this wild domain
> Since God gave birth to creation,
>   have coursed o'er its jumbled main.
> Few but mountain whites the meanest,
>   —no accounts, on murder bent—
> Here, the generations drifting,
>   drunken, cursing years have spent.
>
> Berry pickers tanned and brazen;
>   basket makers—low-down whelps—
> Scoopers, trappers, guides and brawlers;
>   gatherers of furry pelts:
> Swappers of their worn-out women—
>   for a jack-knife, like as not—
> With a pint of rot-gut whiskey
>   you could buy the pesky lot.
>
> Outlaws—ignorant and vicious—
>   bark-wood peelers, raw and tough!
> Rafting bulldogs, cured with red-eye;
>   greaser bandits in the rough:
> Hell-bent roustabouts and fiery:
>   hawk-eyed lappers at the bar—
> Poker-playing tavern bullies
>   on the hemlocked Delaware.

Rafting on the main Delaware, its two branches, and the Beaverkill and Willowemoc supplied much more than masts for schooners. It supplied the fast-growing East Coast cities with lumber for houses, huge timbers for docks, and the underpinnings of early skyscrapers. The pine rafts carried top loads of cherry, maple, oak, and other low-buoyancy hardwoods, which became floors, paneling, and furniture.

In the mid-1800s, when the pines ran out and it looked as if the rafting industry would end, someone cast an eye on the stark carcasses of the hemlocks that for many years had rotted unused after their bark had been peeled off by the tanneries. Although knottier, ruddier, and less clear of grain, hemlock lumber found a ready market and kept the rivermen in business for several more decades. But as both the lumbermen and the tanlords bore down on the hemlocks, in time they too gave out. The rafting industry shrank with the diminishing supply of its raw materials until the late 1800s, when only a few scattered trees and diehards were left. The last known Beaverkill log raft was run from Spooner's Eddy at

Rafting began in the Catskills around 1765, making it the region's earliest "river industry." This log raft and crew, under command of the steersman (foreground), are headed down the Delaware to a sawmill. *Courtesy Eleanor and James Cain.*

Horton to a Callicoon sawmill on the lower Delaware in July of 1904.

In rafting times, Catskill rivers were not thought of as places to fish. The famous pools of today were without names. Raftsmen had no time to think of trout as they sped above their holts on the crest of a spring freshet. Their minds were on the "danger places," and for these they had names: The Jaws, Whitney's Rocks, Totten's Gut, Mulnick's Bend, Foul Rift, Shaver's Turn, Goose Bar, Tim's Turn, Sucker Bars, Anlizer's Twist, Jane's Gut. A gut was a straight, narrow, deep run through which the raft got sucked so fast in high water that the best one could do was position for its center and pray he would miss the sides.

Occasionally, the rafters caught fish whether they wanted to or not. In 1877, three rafts going through Foul Rift struck a school of shad coming upriver to spawn. As the rafts dipped, hundreds of shad weighing five pounds and more swam on board and were trapped. The men ate the shad and sold what was left for a nice extra profit on that particular trip.

Rafting never developed on other Catskill rivers. The Schoharie flowed north, away from the lumber markets. The Esopus joined the Hudson, which would have been ideal, but it was blocked with the dams of many busy mills. The Rondout was too flat in its lower reaches to provide the flow required by log rafts. And the Neversink, well, that's another story.

Otto William VanTuyl settled in Bridgeville in 1811 and built a house and store on the banks of the Neversink. At that time lumbering was a principal means of livelihood in the Neversink valley, but the river's waterfalls and boulder-filled gorges were too treacherous for rafting. Lumbermen were forced to cart their lumber over the mountains into Orange County.

So VanTuyl conceived the plan of making the Neversink navigable for rafts. He saw in it great wealth in tolls for himself and prosperity for the lumbermen. He got a $10,000 loan from the state, giving as his security a mortgage on the river, and worked for two years building aprons over falls and removing rocks. The state's commissioners pronounced the river "safe and navigable for rafts." Toll rates were set: $1.50 per thousand board feet for

Otto VanTuyl tried unsuccessfully to run log rafts down the Neversink in the 1830s; this obstacle near Fallsburg was one of the causes of his failure. *Courtesy Department of Environmental Conservation.*

lumber, 10¢ for each log, 2¢ per bushel of charcoal, and so on.

On a spring day in 1831 with a good "fresh" running in the river, the first attempt was made. A raft was launched near Fallsburgh, and as it passed Bridgeville, VanTuyl had visions of the tolls pouring in. The raft passed safely through the rapids, but was wrecked and lost in the "Dive Hole" at Denton Falls. VanTuyl didn't give up. He made more improvements in the river, and the following spring he hired experienced Delaware River raftsmen, and launched another raft from Bridgeville.

VanTuyl was so confident this time that he let his sixteen-year-old son, William, go along for the ride. The raft had almost reached the point of the previous disaster when it too smashed into the rocks and was torn to pieces by the swift currents. Two of the men were drowned. The steersman and young William were thrown clear onto a rock and marooned for twelve hours before they could be rescued. Just as they reached shore, a gigantic tree swept across their rock and careened downriver. They had been saved by moments from

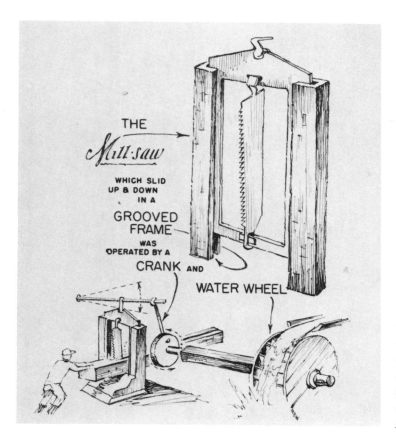

THE *Mill-saw*

WHICH SLID
UP & DOWN
IN A
GROOVED
FRAME
WAS
OPERATED BY A
CRANK AND

WATER WHEEL

Up-and-down saws, powered by water wheels, were the centerpiece of countless Catskill sawmills in the early 1800s. "They are at work," said Theodore Gordon, "on or near every stream in whose neighborhood any trees worth cutting are to be found." *Drawing by Manville Wakefield.*

sudden death. This ended any further attempts to navigate the Neversink. VanTuyl was a ruined man.

Except for VanTuyl's abortive scheme, Catskill rivers were free to all. Another mountain industry to exploit them as a source of free power was the sawmills. Closely linked to the rafting industry, some sawmills shipped their planks and timbers on the rafts; the larger ones below the Delaware Water Gap bought the rafts from the rafters and "buzzed" them up into boards.

Sawmills were set up anywhere that six to seven feet of head could be achieved by damming up the stream to turn a water wheel. The wheel powered an "up-and-down" saw that traveled vertically to saw the logs into boards. It was not until after 1860 that steam power and the circular saw began to revolutionize the sawmill industry.

The Catskill water-wheel mills were never very big and rarely employed more than ten men. During their peak days, seventeen Beaverkill sawmills operated in the fourteen miles from Rockland to Jones Falls. "They are at work," said Theodore Gordon, "on or near every stream in whose neighborhood any trees worth cutting are to be found." Water wheels also powered grist mills that ground flour from local grains, mills that carded wool into roves, and wood-turning mills that created several subindustries of their own.

Wood lathes powered by the water wheels of Catskill streams enabled the founding of numerous chair and bedstead factories, many at the sites of tanneries whose hemlock bark resources had been used up. The wood for the chairs came

Many water-powered mills were situated along Catskill streams in the 1800s. This woolen mill, already falling down in a photograph taken around 1895, operated at Palenville on Kaaterskill Creek. *Photo by Lionel DeLisser.*

from the maple, cherry, beech, and ash groves that had replaced the virgin stands of pine and hemlock.

Other wood-turning mills made bowling pins, porch pillars and balusters, Indian clubs, dumbbells, rolling pins, bowls and trays, policemen's billies, belaying pins, baseball bats, and the little covered wooden boxes in which druggists dispensed ointments.

One upper Beaverkill community, Turnwood, was named after its turning mill, whose reputation came in part from the quality and variety of its peg legs. The hard maple leg, rugged and coarse grained, with an iron ferrule shrunk over the business end of the peg, was preferred for work and everyday use, although for socials and Sunday use the light and fine-grained basswood leg was very much in vogue.

Of all the early Catskill river industries, tanneries were undoubtedly the most complex, colorful, and far-reaching in their effect on the environment.

Schoharie Creek, which had escaped the effects of rafting and lumbering, bore the brunt of the tanning. There, on its banks at Edwardsville (now Hunter), sat the largest tannery in the Catskills, five hundred feet long, with four towering chimneys spewing sparks and smoke from the fires that heated the vats full of hides.

Workers pose for a company photograph at the Wurtsboro Tannery on the Basher Kill, a tributary of the Neversink. Hemlock bark is stacked in the foreground left and right; across the center, hides are hanging to dry. *Courtesy Sullivan County Historical Society.*

In the spring, when the sap was running, the barkpeelers fanned out from the tannery, felling and peeling the bark from every reachable hemlock. Only the prime bark from the butt to the first limbs was taken. Many trunks were hauled away to sawmills, but far more lay to rot where they had fallen. Everywhere you looked, the hillsides were covered, as a local newspaperman put it, "with their prostrate trunks and branches glistening white in the dying light of day, like the bleaching bones of some army of giants fallen in mortal combat."

Wagonloads of cowhides arrived from nearby Hudson River towns, where they were shipped from South America. The bark to tan a single hide far outweighed the hide, hence the economy of bringing the hides to the trees.

The hemlock bark, stacked in squares by the cord (a good man could peel and stack two cords a day), was ground to chips in a water-powered mill similar to a huge coffee grinder, then taken to a leaching house where it was mixed with boiling water and steeped for a week. The tanning liquor was then ready to be piped to the tanyard vats.

The raw hides were soaked for about a week, pounded until soft, and split into "sides." The sides were placed in sweat-pits for another week, then pounded again to remove hair. At some tanneries the hair was removed with ground limestone from the base ridges of the Catskills. The waste, a hair-and-lime paste,

Barkpeelers going after the big hemlock trees that once covered the Catskills. They skinned the bark and hauled it to tanneries where it was used to tan hides. Illustrated News, *May 17, 1853.*

was thrown into the river to be carried off downstream. Decomposed flesh and any remaining hair had to be "flensed," or scraped, from the hides before the tanning could begin; all of this, along with ashes from the furnaces, spent tannin-and-bark slurry from the vats, and ruined hides, was dumped into the stream.

The clear waters from upstream were piped into the tanning vats, where layers of prepared hides were separated by freshly ground bark and mixed with increasingly stronger solutions of tannin over a period of several months while the hides acquired the softness and rich red color typical of hemlock-tanned leather. The stream was also harnessed to pump the tanning liquors from vat to vat and to run the finishing rollers and beaters.

In the final stages, the hides were placed in lofts to dry, rubbed with fish oil, hung again to dry, and then rubbed with tanner's oil before being rolled and packed for shipment. It is probably unnecessary to point out that only tannery workers could stand the company of another tannery worker.

The Schoharie Creek tannery at Edwardsville was built in 1817 by William Edwards. That same year, twelve miles up the valley, Gilbert Palen built another and Palenville was born. Two years later, Zadock Pratt put one up seventeen miles downstream and Prattsville was born. Pratt's tannery, though slightly smaller than that of Edwards, consumed many more hemlocks. Over a period of twenty-five years, Zadock Pratt's tannery shipped an average of 60,000 sides of leather a year, and in the process probably consumed well over a million hemlock trees.

At the time these three tanneries were founded, more than seventy-five tanneries were already operating in Greene, Delaware, and Sullivan counties. How many more existed throughout the Catskills is not known. On the Esopus, Shandaken—its name derived from the Algonquin words for hemlock—was the site of a busy tannery taken over by James Simpson and a partner in 1843. Simpson later built an even larger tannery downstream. It was called the Phoenix Tannery and gave its name to the town of Phoenicia.

When the Erie Railroad was completed in 1851 along the Delaware, it attracted tanneries from Greene County because their hides could be shipped in and their leather out by rail. In 1856, a 35,000-acre contract for hemlock bark resulted in a tannery at DeBruce, rough roads throughout the woods, and many isolated camps. The enterprise opened up the country considerably. By 1860, there were 157 tanneries operating in the Catskills, 39 of them in Sullivan County alone.

The War of 1812, the Mexican War (1846–48), and the Civil War (1861–65)—with their great demand for leather boots, harnesses, saddles, gunslings, belts, and bandoliers—stimulated the growth and continuity of the tanning industry. Following the Civil War, the price of leather fell at the same time that the last of the accessible hemlocks were being taken, and within the next fifteen to twenty years, all the tanneries had gone out of business.

The legacy of the rafting, tanning, and sawmill industries was substantial and pervasive. An early complaint of their effects on the fishing appeared in the July 1859 issue of *Harper's New Monthly Magazine*:

> The banks of the Beaverkill and the Willerwhemack, tributaries of the Delaware, twenty years ago were famous for brook trout, and were once favorite places for the lovers of piscatorial sports. These haunts, where genius once found leisure from the toils of city life, with thousands of others which a few years ago abounded in game, are now deserted, and fret their way on to the ocean, stained by tan and thickened by the refuse wood that tumbles from the teeth of the grating saw.

"How we detest a sawmill on one of our favorite streams!" said Theodore Gordon a full fifty years later. "The sappy, heavy sawdust not only floats on the surface, but sinks to the bottom and permeates the entire river. The trout will not rise; in fact, I do not believe that natural flies would be noticed, even if they would come up through the trash, and hatch out on the surface. Those sawmills are responsible for many muttered bad words, and for several melancholy days."

The rivers, fouled and barren below the tanneries and sawmills, gradually cleared, but their water temperatures were permanently raised because the protective canopies of the hundred-foot-plus hemlocks never grew back, especially in the broader valleys and along the principal rivers. The brook trout were eliminated from all but the smaller, colder headwaters and feeder streams. Only

Jones Mill on the upper Beaverkill was typical of the early sawmills that harnessed the waterfalls for power; today, all that remains is the falls of the same name. *Courtesy Pearl and Fred Shaver.*

the warm-water tolerance of the newly introduced European brown trout saved the lower rivers as trout fisheries.

The bare hillsides could not hold rain as they had before, the snow melted sooner, and there were more flooding, erosion, and silting of the streams. When the trees finally grew back they were mainly hardwoods whose leafed-out canopies shaded the streams less than half the year.

Mother Nature in the Catskills had given much to support her children through the years, sacrificing great store of river and woodland resources. Now, in her unstinting bounty, she heaved her bosom once more and flexed into life the wood-acid industry.

Catskillers, including the idled barkpeelers, did not take long—after the first crude acid factories appeared along the rivers around 1880—to become expert choppers of "four-foot wood." Cherry, maple, ash, birch, beech, and other hardwoods cut to four-foot lengths and as small as three inches in diameter were the raw materials of the acid factories. Their kilns and retorts, through the process of destructive distillation, devoured thousands of acres of hardwood to make wood alcohol, acetate, and charcoal.

The acid factories depended on the rivers almost as much as had the tanneries. A common method of transporting wood was that of the Leighton Acid Company at Elk Brook on the lower Beaverkill: the wood was floated downriver to be hauled in by the combination of a deflecting "cricket" dam, a boom, and a bankside backwater scooped out right next to the factory.

River water was also diverted to flush the retorts and carry away the wastes and unusable by-products of the distillation process. And, unlike the residue from the tanneries, it was not mere putrefaction; it was highly corrosive and deadly to the fish and bugs in the stream.

The Forest, Fish and Game Commission of New York revealed in its 1900 annual report:

> Acid factories in Sullivan County were running acids into the trout streams in quantities injurious to the fish. The foreman at Beaver Kill Hatchery was sent to Spring Brook, the point complained of, and investigated. He dipped out some of the water, placed in it a six-inch trout, and the fish died in four minutes.

The offending proprietor was forced to remove the poisonous acids by erecting holding vats far enough from the stream to prevent contamination by seepage. Nevertheless, acid pollution of the streams was a chronic problem throughout the life of this industry.

The Luzerne Chemical Company factory at Horton on the Beaverkill (foreground), the last wood acid factory in the Catskills, closed down in 1955. Stacks of four-foot wood can be seen at far left. *Courtesy Glenn S. Seeley.*

Interior of the G.I. Treyz Chemical Plant, a wood acid factory located at Cooks Falls on the Beaverkill. Large iron doors set into the brick wall are the retorts where hardwoods were processed by destructive distillation into wood alcohol, acetate, and charcoal. *Courtesy Glenn S. Seeley.*

Acid factories opened on most of the Catskill rivers but they were not as plentiful as the tanneries. They combined capital and labor intensity as they operated around the clock and kept the wood choppers busy from dawn to dusk. It was a common sight before 1900 to see the factory wagoneers descending a steep hillside on their drays, a front bobsled with stout trailing poles supporting two cords of four-foot wood. The driver perched high atop his load, feet well braced, the weight and strength of his body keeping a taut rein on his team several feet below him. The rut-way, as it was called, was often so steep that the horses actually sat in their breechings, and with their hooves firmly planted in the dirt or snow, they and the load of wood literally slid to the bottom of the mountain.

There is a story about the time Harry Darbee cut four-foot wood. In the summer of his eighteenth year, already an accomplished fly fisherman and quite handy in the woods, he signed on with a crew of wood choppers for a local acid factory. At daybreak, the men all piled onto the company truck and were driven to the wood lot where they set to with four-pound, double-bitted axes.

The pay was by the cord stacked in four-by-four-by-eight-foot piles, and it was the accepted practice to stack your wood as loosely as possible to make the cords build up more quickly. The saying was, you weren't a good man if a dog couldn't chase a rabbit into your cord and out the other side. Harry didn't know this. So he started chopping and stacked a very tight cord with the ends all carefully lined up. He called the foreman over when he figured he had a full cord, and asked him if he should start on a second pile.

The foreman took one look at the pile and yelled: "Hey, Lew, Gene, you fellows come here and see if you think this boy has a cord yet."

When the men saw Harry's cord, one of them winked at the foreman. "Well, Jake, she's pretty close, maybe eight or ten more good pieces'll do her." So off Harry went to chop a few more trees, but suspecting that something was up, he detoured past one of the other men's work areas and immediately saw what was happening. Without a word, he cut a good dozen lengths more, stacked them neatly on his pile, placed his axe on top of that, and walked home. He never cut another stick of four-foot wood.

The height of the acid factory business was reached during World War I when their owners profited heavily on the munitions-related use of acetate, charcoal, and other wood derivatives. Truce and the development of synthetic processes brought an end to another Catskill river-and-wood industry, for which the growing ranks of fly fishermen gave thanks. The last acid factory closed on the Beaverkill at Horton in 1955.

THREE

Birthplace of American Fly Fishing

Fly fishing was "born" in America, not with the cast of a "first" fly but with a series of interconnected events and discoveries occurring predominantly in the Catskills over the approximate 50-year period from 1865 to 1915.

No one knows exactly where the first fly was cast; nor the first *dry* fly. These events may never have been recorded. Fly fishing is such an old and private sport that the earliest occasions of its pursuit could well have been unheralded outings on unsung rivers by fishermen who never became central to its history. The only way to document the birth of American fly fishing is to examine the broader development of the sport and the era from which it emerged.

A rare view of early American fly fishing that did get recorded appears in "The Angler," one of the essays by Washington Irving included in *The Sketch Book of Geoffrey Crayon, Gent.*, published in 1819. Irving had by then returned from England, where he had been tutored in "the gentle art," and in company with several American friends had studied Walton's *Compleat Angler*, whereupon they were "all completely bitten with the angling mania." He described an outing they took on a brook that drains the eastern Catskill Mountains:

> It was early in the year; but as soon as the weather was auspicious and that the spring began to melt into the verge of summer, we took rod in hand and sallied into the country, as stark mad as was even Don Quixote from reading books of chivalry.
>
> One of our party had equalled the Don in the fulness of his equipments, being attired cap-a-pie for the enterprise. He wore a

broad-skirted fustian coat perplexed with half a hundred pockets, a pair of stout shoes and leathern gaiters, a basket slung on one side for fish, a patent rod, a landing net, and a score of other inconveniences only to be found in the true angler's armory. Thus harnessed for the field, he was as great a matter of stare and wonderment among the country folk, who had never seen a regular angler, as was the steel-clad hero of La Mancha among the goatherds of the Sierra Morena.

"Regular anglers" in America were few and far between in the early 1800s, as were the writings of their whereabouts. In August of 1838, *The American Turf Register and Sporting Magazine* published the following report on fishing in the New York area:

> The largest proportion [of anglers] are whipping their flies over the placid ponds of Long Island, where the run of trout this season is of unusually fine size. Two or three parties, made up principally of 'old hands,' have lately made a descent upon the rivers of Sullivan and Montgomery counties, in this state, and with immense success. The Williewemauk, Calikoon, and Beaver-kill, are three of the finest trout streams in this country; they are comparatively unknown to city anglers, and are less fished than any others of like pretensions within our knowledge. The trout are large, very numerous, and of the most delicious flavour.

Fly fishing in America, as in England, grew out of the Industrial Revolution. And, as American industrialization trailed England's by a good half century, so did our coming of age as anglers. Before 1850, in keeping with an agricultural economy, most fishing in the United States was done not for recreation but for subsistence. Incidentally, Catskill agriculture peaked in the middle of the nineteenth century, when the largest number of cleared acres existed. A good part of the demand for farm products was internally generated by thousands of hungry barkpeelers and hoop shavers.

Soon after the Civil War, with the effects of industrialization accelerating in American society, big cities got dirtier, noisier, and more crowded. Significantly, they were also the source of increasing wealth and leisure to escape these harassments. Getting out of the city and back to nature became the ideal pastime for millions of urban Americans. They flocked to the country for long summer vacations, and eventually—when the transportation improved—for weekends. They were the guests at the countless hotels and boardinghouses that sprang up in the late 1800s, especially in the Catskills. Their pastimes included hiking, picnicking, porch sitting, vista viewing, and—for the more adventuresome—hunting and fishing.

Fly fishing gained momentum as newly monied urban industrialists, using English angling techniques and equipment, spread out from Boston, New

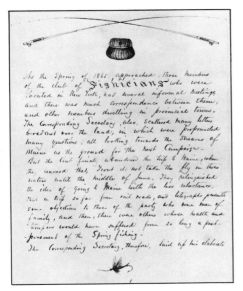

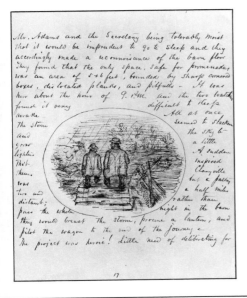

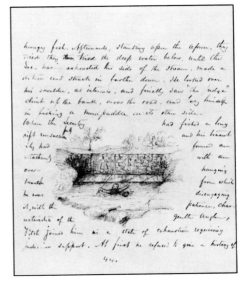

Pages from the outing journal of the "Fishicians," a small group of anglers—mostly doctors from New York and "provincial towns"—whose excursion to the Neversink River in 1865 was detailed by their "Secretary," Walter DeForest Day, with illustrations by fellow member Dr. Otis. Judge James Fitch, shown on page 28, was one of the group. In ten days of fishing the main river below Claryville and up both branches, the three men who kept a tally caught 1,535 brook trout, none heavier than a pound. *Courtesy The Museum of American Fly Fishing.*

York, and Philadelphia to the lakes and streams of Maine, the Adirondacks, the Poconos, the Catskills, and Long Island.

Before 1850, Long Island drew greater numbers of New York anglers than did the Catskills, mainly because it was easier to reach. "I love Long Island, and venerate its trout streams," said Genio Scott, author of *Fishing in American Waters* (1869). "Their value to New York City is inestimable, for each one of them is approachable by railroad in a few hours."

Robert Barnwell Roosevelt was a trendsetting angler, and in his book *The*

Game Fish of the North, published seven years before Scott's, he had already witnessed the move to the Catskills:

> The brooks of Long Island, especially on the southern shore, abound with trout. But they are few in comparison with the hordes that once swarmed in the streams of Sullivan and Orange counties, and in fact all the lower tier of counties in this State, before 1851 when the Erie Railroad was built, and opened the land to the crowd of market men. I am proud to say I have travelled that country when it took the stage coach twelve hours to go twenty-four miles, and when, if we were in a hurry, we walked, and sent our baggage by the coach. Now you are jerked along high above our favorite meadows, directly through our wildest hills, and often under our best streams, at the rate of forty miles an hour, and yet people call that an improvement. As well might you lug a man out of bed at night, drag him a dozen times round his room, and fling him back into bed, and say he was improved by the operation. No one wants to be lugged out of bed, precisely as no one wanted to travel beyond Sullivan County; the best shooting and fishing in the world was to be found there.
>
> When the railroad was first opened, the country was literally overrun, and Bashe's Kill, Pine Kill, the Sandberg, the Mon Gaup and Callicoon, and even Beaver Kill, which we thought were inexhaustible, were fished out. For many years trout had almost ceased from out of the waters, but the horrible public, having their attention drawn to the Adirondacks, gave it a little rest, and now the fishing is good.

Roosevelt noted in an 1884 edition of this same book that "Many of Long Island's waters have been depleted, and they have been so thoroughly preserved that there is hardly a free pond or stream from one end to the other of it."

Once the Catskill streams were discovered as "boss places for trout fishing," their proximity to the largest metropolis and the arrival of rail transportation attracted thousands of aspiring Waltons into this paradise of trouting. The Catskills became, in the words of one outdoor writer, "the merry stamping ground for those whose wont it is during the heated term to shake the dust of business from their shoes and change the rappings of the 'ticker' for the clickings of the reel."

*   *   *

It was the natural outcome of throwing city and country fishermen together that contrasting perceptions and behavior should arise. The rituals and precepts of "the gentle art" were both blinding to the practitioner and amusing to the beholder. *The American Angler's Guide*, the first American book completely about fishing, appeared in 1845. In it, John Brown observed that the "scientific and graceful art of throwing the artificial fly" was not so difficult as generally imagined, for he had seen such "untutored examples" as the raftsmen and lumbermen from the Delaware River in the fishing tackle stores of New York "selecting with the eyes of professors and connoisseurs the red, black, and grey hackle flies, which they use with astonishing dexterity on the wooded streams of their mountain homes." This he said was reason enough for anyone who hesitated to make the effort required to master fly fishing.

If the country angler was a bumpkin, the city angler was a bungler. Any countryman could tell you:

> I seed a feller, sort o' stylish chap, down ter the bridge yesterday, an' he didn't have a fishin' pole no thickern my finger, with a little clock onto it, and when he hooked a fish, thar' the darned fool stood turnin' the handle o' that little clock, and the fish runnin' roun' an' roun', an' the little fishin' pole bendin', an' I sw'ar if he didn't monkey an' monkey for purty nigh half an hour with that 'ere fish afore he got his flippers onto him. Now that's wot I call cussed nonsense. None o' yer monkeyin' with a trout when he gits aholt o' my grasshopper. I yanks him out if I loses a leg.

Transportation played a major role in the development of American fly fishing. All the money and leisure in the world would not have mattered had there been no practical way to reach the rivers. The biggest role in opening up the trouting regions and introducing the masses to the sport was played by the railroads. They carried fishermen to the rivers, provided free transportation for hatchery trout, and publicized boardinghouses and hotels throughout the region. Before their arrival, it took a really hardy and determined soul to go by steamer up the Hudson and by stagecoach over the old turnpike roads into the mountains.

After the Erie Railroad was opened in 1851 along the Delaware, it was possible to fish that river conveniently, but it was still difficult to get into the heart of Catskill trout country.

In 1872, two new railroads came through just ten miles on either side of the headwaters of the Rondout, Neversink, Esopus, Willowemoc, and Beaverkill rivers. From that year forward Catskill trout fishing began to change radically. Even though the combination of railroad and buckboard took travelers up to twelve hours from New York to reach the rivers, the Catskills' choicest concentration of brook-trout waters were now accessible to "rodsters" from the city.

To the north, the Ulster & Delaware line ran from Kingston, which was reached by the Hudson River Dayliner or excursion trains up the river's west shore. From Kingston the U. & D. climbed the gradual grades of the Shawangunks, up through the valley of the Esopus, stopping at Mt. Tremper,

Phoenicia, Shandaken, Big Indian, Arkville, Roxbury, Stamford, Hobart. A spur of the U. & D. ran from Phoenicia up through Stony Clove notch to Hunter, connecting the Esopus and Schoharie creeks. Its bed was cut into the sides of this deep notch, and the grade in some places was a formidable 187 feet per mile. A local traveler of the day, in his awe, exclaimed: "So this little narrow gauge, puffing, snorting branch of the Ulster & Delaware railroad has to do a heap of climbing, in the Catskills, like the rest of us."

To the south, the Ontario & Western line left Weehawken, New Jersey, went up the Hudson to Cornwall, then headed into the mountains with stops at Liberty, Livingston Manor, Rockland, Cooks Falls, East Branch.

From these stations the visiting anglers went by horseback or wagon to their final destinations. Some roughed it in the woods. Some fished around, stopping for lunch or overnight at farmhouses along the river. And some were just beginning to buy stretches of river on their own or with small groups of friends.

The arrival of railroads marked the peak days of Catskill brook-trout fishing. By the early 1870s, there were still many miles of unexplored wilderness trout streams, largely recovered from the tannery days, which had not yet been overrun by the increasing number of eager new anglers.

A feeling for what it was like is given in this reminiscence, which appeared in the April 11, 1896, *Pine Hill Sentinel*:

> There have been many changes in the fishing grounds within the memory of the writer. The Catskills were a paradise for fishermen when the old stage coach ran between Kingston and Delhi. There was not then an influx of visitors in the mountains. The streams were full of trout, so that anyone who could afford the time could have a successful outing any time during the season. It was the custom to consume at least three days on a fishing excursion, and some of the old timers spent several weeks every year enjoying their favorite pastime. Trespass signs were unknown. Those who lived in the vicinity of the streams heartily welcomed the fishermen, and were always glad to board them for a reasonable compensation. The fad of clubs of city people was unknown. For miles and miles it was a place of solitude, and a man could fish all day without meeting a human being. How restful it was to the tired brain to be thus alone with nature and mosquitoes.

Those were the days before the Catskills' economic base shifted from agriculture to recreation. How this transition unfolded, from about 1870 to 1900, and how it affected the fishing, is a fascinating story.

From the time of rafting and tanning down to the present, the Catskill economy has depended largely on external consumers. When the forces of industrialization put an end to the old river industries and to many of the farms, these same forces created a leisure class that supplied new consumers in the form of weekenders, vacationers, and sportsmen. For the native Catskiller, however, this was a period of hardship and uncertainty. Consider the fate of one little Neversink community, described around 1900 by Lionel De Lisser:

> DeWittville cannot be said to have had any particular occupation since the tannery located there ceased to operate and the tidal wave of prosperity, which that business brought into the place, retreated, leaving the little hamlet high and dry on the top of the mountain, 22 miles from the nearest railroad, or to be truthful, anywhere else.

Many thousands of acres owned by the tanning, lumbering, and wood-acid operators were abandoned after the trees were gone and the industries displaced by more modern processes. When taxes on these properties remained unpaid long enough, the lands came up at tax sales. Small farms also became available, such as those that had grown hay to feed loggers' oxen, and those tucked away in narrow, cul-de-sac valleys of the sort that give rise to trout streams.

Absentee owners began appearing on the Catskill tax maps where formerly the landowners had been almost entirely local residents. In fact, the Catskill Forest Preserve, owned by New York State, got its start in 1885 when no one would buy a huge chunk of abandoned acreage in Ulster County.

With increasing competition for elbow room on the trout streams, it was natural that many of these new owners should be wealthy New York fishermen establishing their own mountain retreats and private trout preserves. They were further stimulated by the growing recognition that fly fishing was a sport for gentlemen and was enjoyed by members of England's nobility, who were so admired by socially climbing Americans.

Anthony W. Dimock, author of *Wall Street and the Wilds*, located his haven at Peekamoose on upper Rondout Creek, one valley over from the Neversink. In the introduction to his book, he created a vivid picture of the conflicting forces in a city-based angler's life:

> It was the dream of my life to live in the wilds and even during my greatest activity in business I was looking forward to a time when my taste could be gratified. The opportunity came in the seventies, for while on a fishing trip I found a valley in the Catskills so surrounded by mountains and shut in by trees that it promised all the seclusion I could ask. From the nearest railroad station but ten miles of mountain road remained, and as I travelled it my troubles fell away.
>
> I ran a telegraph wire through the woods from the nearest

Judge James "Fitz" Fitch, early Catskill angler, posing in 1883 with his securely harnessed and commodious basket. Fitch lived in Prattsville, maintained law offices at 7 Warren Street in New York City, and fished with Cornelius Van Brunt; he was particularly fond of the upper Neversink. *A. N. Cheney Collection, courtesy Dr. Charles H. Townsend.*

station and the sounder in my room was a comfort when it didn't sound. My family was happy in their sylvan surroundings but they came to hate that sounder, for they learned its language and knew when it called me to the city in tones not to be disregarded.

On one such occasion I started in the blackness of a rainy night for a ten mile tramp over a dangerous road to the little village of Shokan. It was near midnight when I arrived, the town was asleep, and I had to arouse several people before I could find one who would drive me to Rondout, eighteen miles away. At that place I hired a negro to commandeer a boat, in the owner's absence, and row me across the Hudson to Wheatsheaf, where I hired another man to take me to Poughkeepsie, reaching that town in time to take the owl train for New York.

One of the larger and more elaborate Catskill hunting and fishing preserves was that of George J. Gould, son of railroad magnate Jay Gould, located at Furlough Lake on Dry Brook, a headwater stream of the East Branch of the Delaware. Starting in 1890, when he was still in his twenties, Gould bought 550 acres and within several years had expanded his holdings to over 3,000 acres. Centered on the 30-acre lake, he built a 26-room, 2½-story log house, log stable, and boathouse. There was also an enclosed "deer park" stocked

Cornelius Van Brunt, founding member and first president of the Balsam Lake Club on the upper Beaverkill, standing on clubhouse porch around 1883. *Courtesy Balsam Lake Club.*

with Colorado elk, Virginia and black-tailed deer, outside which roamed the native, white-tailed deer. One of the sights most intriguing to his visitors was "a dovecote with 2,000 doves and pigeons of every sort and kind, harmoniously living together in a many-storied, handsome building that looks like a first-class New York apartment house."

Over on the Neversink, numerous small farms were bought and combined into the "country seats" of well-to-do city sportsmen. The larger preserves, of several thousand acres each, were established by Clarence Roof in 1882 on the West Branch and by Raphael Govin in 1898 on the East Branch.

On the Willowemoc, there was the Ward estate at DeBruce, and the Van Norden property farther up on the headwaters at Lake Willowemoc (now Sand Pond). The Van Nordens and their relatives the Van Brunts started the Willowemoc Club, which also owned, over in the Beaverkill valley, Balsam Lake, Thomas Pond (now Beecher Lake), and several miles of the stream. The club members used to walk back and forth across the three miles of mountaintop separating the two rivers and their lakes.

In addition to the single-owner estates, groups of wealthy anglers began forming clubs in the Catskills shortly after the railroads opened up the region. These were "club corporations," established under New York State law, with the right to issue stock, contract debt, limit liability, and in particular, to own river mileage and fishing rights. In a larger context, fishing clubs were patterned on the many other social clubs being formed mainly by urban businessmen in the late 1800s. There were city, suburban, and rural clubs for dining, athletics, golf, polo, yachting, shooting, hunting, and fishing. An article in the *New York Sun* on May 18, 1890, called attention to this trend as "a modern novelty," and stated that an average of ten groups a day were filing papers for incorporation as clubs with the secretary of state's office in Albany.

Salmo Fontinalis was the first of the Catskill stream clubs. It was formed in 1873 on the upper Beaverkill and for the next ten years was the only club on the river. In 1883, it was joined upstream by the Balsam Lake Club, whose founding members included the Van Nordens and Van Brunts of Willowemoc Lake. The Fly Fishers Club of Brooklyn was incorporated in 1895 by a group of wealthy Brooklyn brewers and fishermen, and it set up its headquarters between Beaverkill and Roscoe in Ben Hardenburg's log cabin. A full-page article in the March 20, 1904, edition of the *Brooklyn Daily Eagle* included this tidbit: "James Rice, Jr., a founder of the Brooklyn Fly Fishers, was for years a very successful bait fisher at Henryville. When he discovered this famous section of the Beaverkill and the club was organized, he swore off bait and has ever since been a fly caster of great skill." Chancellor Levison and Charles Bryan, both charter members of the Brooklyn group, and several of their clubmates, are credited with instrumental roles in the 1906 founding of The Anglers' Club of New York.

In 1900, the Beaverkill Fishing Association was organized at farmer Voorhess's homestead just below Lew Beach. Ten years later one of its members bought out Voorhess, and the group merged into the newly formed Beaverkill Trout Club. In 1913, Whirling Dun Camp opened officially downstream from the Salmo Fontinalis Club and, through several stages of individual or club ownership, emerged in 1955 as Quill Gordon Associates. And, in 1959, Clear

Founding fathers of The Fly Fishers Club of Brooklyn gathered on the porch of their Beaverkill clubhouse around 1900. From the left: James Rice, H. B. Marshall, Richard "Pop" Robbins, B. J. Scholerman, E. J. Allen, Frank Perkins, and a guest, George M. L. LaBranche. *Courtesy The Fly Fishers Club of Brooklyn.*

"J. M. Johnson telling a fish story on the Beaverkill." An 1880s photograph from the Mary Orvis Marbury Collection. *Courtesy The Museum of American Fly Fishing.*

Lake Club was formed out of the old Marble estate on the river opposite the lake of the same name.

On Mill Brook, a tributary of the East Branch of the Delaware, a group of New York businessmen formed the Tuscarora Club in 1901 by purchasing a bankrupt farm, boarding house, and sawmill. At the source of Esopus Creek, several Kingston and Albany sportsmen founded Winnisook Lodge in the late 1800s. On the Neversink, Ed Hewitt converted his river property into the Big Bend Club in 1947. And, on Willowemoc Creek in 1936, having incorporated as the Woman Flyfishers Club four years earlier, a group of pioneering female anglers set up their first headquarters, later moving briefly to the Rondout before settling down on the West Branch of the Neversink. Farther down on the Willowemoc, a group of fishing friends who frequented Ward's DeBruce Club Inn organized the DeBruce Fly Fishing Club in 1959 when the inn went out of business.

All these clubs are still in existence. Others that were formed and did not survive include: on the Beaverkill, the Beaver Meadow Fly Fishing Club, Colchester Fisheries Club, Saugerties Club, Alder Lake Club, Beaverkill Flyfishers, Beaverkill Trout and Skeet Club, Iroquois Club, Jersey Trout Club; on the Willowemoc, the Willowemoc Club; on the Esopus, Jocelyn Country Club ("an active angling club"); on the Rondout, the Peekamoose Fishing Club, which was started in 1880 and disbanded fifteen years later; and on the East Branch of the Neversink, of the same vintage, the Hamilton Club, which was described in the 1890s as "going to seed and the tender mercies of the porcupines."

That so many clubs have survived the varied threats to their continuity is testimony to the durability of the institution. The appeal most often cited by fishing-club members is the congeniality of their clubmates followed closely by the serenity and beauty of their surroundings. Fly fishing and trout are taken for granted; these exist with or without the club privilege.

Catskill fishing clubs range in size from seven to 63 members; in later years membership rolls have tended to increase in order to support rising taxes and upkeep. Stream mileage owned or leased by the clubs ranges from about 1½ to seven miles. Women guests, anglers or otherwise, are welcome in varying degrees; some of the clubs are set up to accommodate couples and families; however, a few are very tenacious about their long tradition as fraternal retreats.

The first Catskill fishing clubs were more social than sporting, combining the virtues of a wilderness camp, a quiet pond, and gentlemanly recreation. Indeed, three of the four earliest clubs were situated on small lakes, up away from the stream. Theodore Gordon was unknown to these men; for them the art of angling had not yet begun its technical revolution. Recalling the founding members of his club, who fished in the late 1800s, one Balsam Lake member wrote:

> Few, if any, professed to be skillful fishermen. They loved the woods, the birds, the beauty of the place, and as they could catch all the small fish they wanted, but no large ones no matter how they tried, no one studied the angler's art. They were men of affairs, exceptionally well read, and enjoyed the company as well as the fishing.

Outsiders, especially those who might once have fished the water now monopolized by the clubs, viewed these gentlemen in a different light. One of them said: "You can generally tell the health of the stock market by the number of fancy-pants fishermen along the Beaverkill; they vary in direct proportion to the Dow Jones averages." Others were not so kind:

> Not many of them were fishermen but were leaders, tycoons of business, and political bigwigs who devoted most of their time at the Lodge with Old Crow and Canadian Club and were seen strutting about the lawn in their Prince Alberts and derby hats, twirling their canes or twisting their mustaches as suited their vanity, not knowing that in nature a pauper is as good as a prince.

From the moment that the streams were posted by clubs and individual owners, the "paupers" and the "princes" were adversaries. A few local residents benefited from caretaker positions and fishing privileges, but the majority of those who had fished these streams were now closed out forever.

Letters of outrage and editorials appeared in angling journals and newspapers protesting that "a few privileged men should shut down the streams that have made this region celebrated among anglers. The native who has lived within

Gentleman angler of the 1890s relaxes beside a pasture trout brook in the southern Catskills. *Courtesy Alf Evers.*

sound of their waters and fished them at will all his life, as well as the city angler who has been in the habit of spending his vacation along their banks, can now only steal to their pools and cast their lines as poaching outlaws."

And so the poaching instinct, a human trait from the earliest days of protected game, was nurtured in the Catskills. As the incidents proliferated, poaching became the number one concern among clubs and private owners. It was standard procedure to post and patrol one's stream.

Some owners were quite imaginative: one of them had his trout pond guarded by a gamekeeper installed in a tower; another enclosed his streamfront and let loose "a splendid Jersey bull, about as vicious and ugly as any ever turned into a bull-fighting arena in old Spain." One owner hid in the bushes, and when a

Poaching was not limited to local anglers exercising their "ancestral rights"; as often guilty of the deed were city anglers trespassing on a farmer's water, as portrayed here at the moment of confrontation. *(Artist unknown.)*

poacher showed up, fired off his shotgun yelling, "Did I get 'im, Bill?" Pausing, he altered his voice and yelled back, "Naw, Jack. Give that gun here and I'll learn ye how to shoot!"

George Renner recalled a novel poaching defensive tactic used by the predecessor club to the Clear Lake Club: "When Marble had it, it was known as the Iroquois Club. They never took fish, but they all had to carry little yellow baskets; that way he could sit on his porch and identify who belonged on the river. If a guy didn't have a yellow basket, he couldn't fish, and Marble went right out and got him."

The poachers were every bit as creative. Pete Rose of Roscoe raised the art of poaching to its highest level. He enjoyed fooling the stream owners more than he did catching their fish. Rose would fish a well-known club's home pool at night right out in front of the clubhouse as the members were playing cards inside, and if he got a big fish on he would simply stick his reel underwater and play the fish without a sound.

On one occasion, Rose was fishing his favorite club water in broad daylight and, rounding a bend, he ran into a member. Seeing the member first, Rose began thrashing the water repeatedly with his rod and a short length of line. He "fished" right down opposite the member, beating the water into a froth, and yelled in a screechy little voice, "You catchin' any, mister?"

"Why no, uh . . . no, I'm not. How about you?"

"Nope! They just ain't bitin' today." Without letting up, Rose thrashed his way on downstream and out of sight as the member hurried into the lodge to tell his clubmates about the demented angler he had just witnessed.

Of the mainstem mileage in the trout zones of the Catskills' six major trout streams, less than 25 percent is private and posted. Fishing clubs and individual owners were attracted to the more protected upper valleys of the Neversink, Willowemoc, and Beaverkill rivers. The Esopus, Schoharie, Delaware, and lower Beaverkill are almost entirely "open" water, where at most a fisherman should ask permission to fish, just as it was in the old days of buckboards, farmers, and boardinghouses.

*   *   *

The gradual emergence in the Catskills of a distinctively American style of fly fishing can be traced in its evolution: the dominant fish went from bass, to brook, to brown trout, while the dominant lure went from bait, to wet, to dry flies.

When sport fishing was still in its rudimentary stage, Catskill fishermen favored the black bass that had been imported first from Ohio and planted successfully in lakes and lower elevations of the larger rivers. They fished out of boats and used such live bait as hellgrammites or lamprey eels. The black bass was a wonderful fighter, very strong and very acrobatic, and as luck would have it, a ready taker of flies. So the bass performed missionary services by converting bait fishermen to flies. One such incidence occurred in 1878 when Robin Ruff, outdoor writer for *The American Angler*, was flat-boating on the upper Delaware with a friend.

Starting at Hancock, they had reached Lackawaxen where the Delaware and Hudson Canal Co. had a dam that raised the river and formed what raftsmen called "The Pond." Here is what happened:

> The supper bell was ringing, but I had an idea that the bass might rise, so supper bells had no charms for me, and I pulled down to the dam and found there ten or twelve of the natives sitting on the piers and walls, all bait fishing, and "nary" one had caught a fin. I think that none of them had ever seen bass caught with the artificial fly; anyway, some of them were having a little audible fun at my expense. In a short time I found where the fish were, and on the second rise fastened to two bass, one of which weighed one and one-half pounds, which was the largest that I have ever caught with the fly in that river; the other weighed three-quarters of a pound. During an hour's fishing I caught twenty-eight bass, between thirty and forty sunfish and a few chub. I did not see one fish caught with bait. It was my turn to laugh, but I did not.

The transition from bass to brook trout was the natural outcome of contiguous habitats of the two fishes. There was some overlap but not much; when the water got too cold for bass, it was just cold enough for brook trout. And both fish shared an appetite for gaudy wet flies. So, as more anglers took up fly fishing it often happened that a bass fisherman on the larger rivers would run into a lovely, seductive little feeder stream and, before he realized what was happening, would have made a few casts and been hooked by the thrill of brook-trout fishing.

Kit Clarke fished the upper Delaware in the late 1800s and came back with glowing descriptions of the many fine trout brooks that entered the river every mile or so:

> I recall wading along the shore casting flies for bass, and in the back-cast my hooks became entangled on a low limb. In detaching the hooks I discovered, much to my amazement, the outlet of a fine brook completely hidden by a heavy bunch of willows, and promptly explored it for perhaps a hundred yards. The following day this obscure stream yielded a full basket of handsome trout, many of ten and eleven inches in length, and since then it has repeatedly been visited with excellent results.

The classic style of fly fishing in the heyday of the brook trout was a cast of two or three brightly colored wet flies quartered downstream. All-American wet patterns favored by anglers at the time included Parmachenee Belle, Montreal, Professor, Brown Hackle, and Grizzly King. Colonel Francis Sayre Pinckney, born in Catskill, New York, was a leading brook-trout angler and fishing writer in the 1880s under the pen name "Ben Bent." "He was never so happy," said a fishing friend, "as when wading down one of our beautiful mountain streams, casting with an ease and grace peculiar to himself a gang of flies to entice and lure the brook trout."

Seduction is a proper concept for what happened to many of the early brook-trout fishermen. They were virgins, lacking any idea of conservation, new to the sport, and high with ecstasy over the ease with which they could wade into a stream and fill a basket with three- and four-ounce trout.

"It was the custom," wrote Sparse Grey Hackle, "on returning to one's rural hotel or boardinghouse, to lay out the day's catch on the grass of the front lawn for the ladies and guests to admire and envy. They were laid in a neat rank, running in diminutiveness from flank to flank and including everything larger than the smallest fingerling; a four-incher was a 'nice fish.' "

There are many stories out of the 1870s and 1880s of the "fish hogs" and "trout butchers" whose voraciousness almost eliminated the brook trout from the Catskills. This one, from an 1889 issue of *The American Angler*, is typical:

> The two largest catches truthfully reported this season were made a day or two ago in the upper waters of the Neversink River by three young men of Liberty, who do not claim to be experts. In one day's fishing Charles Humphrey and James Theobald took 470 trout, weighing altogether more than forty pounds. F.M. Lamoreaux, fishing alone for nine hours, took 478 trout, weighing altogether thirty-three pounds. Catches of ten to fifteen pounds weight are matters of every day occurrence.

As the brook-trout population dwindled from these abuses, loud wailings went up throughout the angling community. City and country fishermen blamed one another as the sole perpetrators. They were both guilty, sometimes even as accomplices: "natives of the Beaverkill are catching trout under legal size and selling them to rodsters from the city who want to be proud of their scores." Theodore Gordon noted that some of the city anglers would sit in a barroom all day after hiring local anglers to fish for them, returning home with baskets full of trout to show their admiring friends.

Fish hogs were known to use extreme methods in their assaults on the streams. Some of them "fished" with sledgehammers; they would find a pool with a ledgerock shelf extending out over the trout's lair, pound the top of the rock and scoop out the stunned fish as they floated downstream. Others poured caustic liquids into the heads of pools and seconds later gathered up the gasping fish. The most destructive of the trout butchers were those who dynamited the streams; they killed hundreds of fish with each blast, reducing those nearest the charge to "mere fish skins filled with jelly."

By about 1890, the combination of overfishing, thoughtless slaughter, and logging had all but wiped out the brook-trout fishing. Without the glimmer of a doubt, lamented angling writers of the day, fly fishing was a doomed sport. Then the "Germans" invaded the Catskills and saved the day.

The first brown trout to arrive in this country, in the form of eighty thousand impregnated eggs, were received on February 24, 1883, by Fred Mather, superintendent of the Cold Spring Harbor Hatchery on Long Island. They were sent by Herr F. von Behr, president of the Deutsche Fisherei Verein, whom Mather had met in 1880 while attending the International Fisheries Exposition in Berlin. During his stay, Mather had fished the Black Forest streams near Baden, and was thrilled with the fighting qualities of the German browns. Von Behr promised to send him a shipment of eggs, and when they arrived Mather forwarded half of them to Seth Green, his counterpart at the Caledonia hatchery, which supplied the stocking needs of Catskill streams.

The following year, 1884, some of the fingerlings escaped from the Caledonia hatchery, and they are supposed to be the first brown trout ever to be stocked in American waters. The first purposeful stocking of browns in the Catskills was at Aden Brook, a tributary of the Neversink, in 1886. Thereafter, more brown-trout eggs arrived from Germany, and then some from Loch Leven in Scotland, sent by William Marston, editor of the *Fishing Gazette*. Seth Green got some of the Loch Leven eggs and the fry got mixed in with the German trout fry. It didn't make much difference because the various subspecies of *Salmo trutta*, the European brown trout, are so similar that very few anglers can tell them apart.

What mattered was how the angling fraternity, most of them hidebound traditionalists, perceived these alien fish. It would be an understatement to say they felt threatened, and not just by the browns. In 1875, eight years before the browns arrived, several varieties of rainbow trout had been imported from

California by the Caledonia hatchery. There were so-called mountain trout, sea-run trout or steelheads, and some the Indians called Noshees. These fish also were stocked in various Catskill streams.

So, even as the brook-trout fishing was "playing out," the imported species were beginning to be caught. One outcome of this was a new familiar name for the brook trout. Before, they had been called "speckled beauties" and "spotted darlings," but now they became "natives" to distinguish them from the "Californians" and "Germans." Because it was literally a foreign fish, the brown trout was singled out by many anglers as a target for bad-mouthing and resistance. Their fighting and table qualities were maligned, and they were blamed for cannibalism and decimation of the native trout. Recalling an incident on the Willowemoc from the 1890s, Frederick White wrote in The Anglers' Club *Bulletin*:

> One morning Mr. Schultz, a kindly, mild mannered gentle-man, caught his first Brown—a six-inch fish—and, to my surprise, threw it on the stones and stamped on it with expressions of extreme distaste and anger.

White, on the other hand, was more tolerant and, upon evidence of the large browns being caught over on the Beaverkill, transferred his allegiance from the DeBruce Club Inn to Jay Davidson's boardinghouse on the Beaverkill and fished that river almost exclusively for the next twenty-five years.

Brown trout remained a controversial topic for quite some time. Fred Mather waited several years after the first eggs arrived in his hatchery before insisting on being given credit for what was actually a brilliant piscicultural coup. In the 1886 annual report of the New York State Fisheries Commission, he became adamant: "This fish which has become a favorite wherever known, was introduced into this country by me in 1883 . . . I have been thus particular in stating this as I see that others, with whom I have divided my eggs, have claimed they imported them direct." In the same report, printed in 1887, Mather mentions "a small shipment made to W. L. Gilbert, of Plymouth, Mass., from some person in Europe," but gives no date for the shipment. Gilbert was a commercial fish culturist primarily interested in raising fish for market. The State of Massachusetts gives 1887 as the year brown trout were first introduced to its waters, as reported by Cecil Heacox in *The Compleat Brown Trout* (1974).

Others in the angling community reacted strongly for or against the European brown trout:

> "Owning to the size of the brown trouts and the practice of putting them in comparatively small and shallow streams, where they can ravage at will on *fontinalis*, planting of them should be discountenanced and discontinued." —William Harris, editor, *The American Angler*.

"I must say they are a grand fish. They are beauties. I was going to say the most beautiful, but I am afraid some people would call this treason and I will take it back. On account of their being such good feeders I think they will be a favorite with the fly fisherman; they certainly will after the fisherman lands the first one of them as they are great fighters."—James Annin, Jr., Caledonia Hatchery Foreman, 1886.

"On the whole I think the outlook for the success of the German trout in the waters of this country is very favorable, and as they are a very beautiful and gamy fish, and equal to any of the trout family of this country, as a table fish, it is earnestly to be hoped that there may be no pull-back to their thorough establishment in our waters." —Seth Green, Caledonia Hatchery, 1887.

"These German trout are fearfully voracious fish, and such a monster as Mr. Josclyn caught on the 29th of July would breakfast on a half-pounder along with ten or a dozen six-inchers, pick his teeth with a No. 4 Sproat hook, and be ready for lunch promptly at 11 o'clock. If every large pool in the Beaverkill harbors a scaly old Dutchman, it is no wonder that the trout fishing was poor this last season." —G.L. Plumley, N.Y.C. angler, 1892.

In one of angling's more ironic coincidences, Englishman Louis Rhead arrived in America in 1883, the same year as the brown trout, and 20 years later had edited what still stands as the most profusive paean to the native American trout, *The Speckled Brook Trout*. In keeping with his artistic, romantic outlook on life, Rhead quoted Benjamin Kent:

Comparisons are generally odious, but they are especially so when you compare a brown trout to a native. In appearance the brown is scaly, flat, greenish-yellow, irregular in form, bad eye, homely all over. In the native the scales are invisible; he is gold and silver, round and symmetrical, and as beautiful an object as lavish nature produces.

Perhaps understandably, the makers of trout-stocking policy for the state were the most hesitant in accepting brown trout as the fish of the future. The following comments appeared as late as 1920 and 1923 in the annual reports of the state's Conservation Commission:

There are many kinds of fish which the Commission propagates, but none is more popular among anglers than the brook trout—the gamy inhabitant of our cold, clear streams, which non-indigenous species have failed to supplant in favor.

It is not the intention of the Conservation Commission to introduce brown trout into waters where there is even a remote possibility of continuing the native species. Applications received by the Commission for brown trout have nearly doubled in recent years; but the greatest care is exercised in alloting these fish to see that they do not come in contact with the far more desirable native species.

Consistent with his innovative spirit, Theodore Gordon was one of the first to recognize and promote the virtues of brown trout. Looking back over the marvelous fishing he had had since his first brown in 1889, Gordon wrote in 1903:

Fifteen years ago, in many of our best New York trout streams, a one-pound native trout was a big fish. In all my experiences of waters easily accessible from New York, I took but one fish of sixteen inches. Since the introduction of the brown trout, all this is changed. The average size of trout taken has much increased, and many fish of two pounds are caught every season with fly. Not only is this the case, but not a year passes that a number of immense fish are not (at least) hooked by fly fishermen. I mean fish weighing from four to six pounds. These usually escape, owing to the light tackle used, but they afford a man a sensation that he is in no danger of forgetting to the last day of his life.

Many miles of Catskill fishing, no longer prime habitat for brook trout, were rejuvenated by the introduction of brown trout. They are hardier fish, living up to twelve years, three times longer than brook trout. With that much more time to grow, they are bigger fish, as Gordon observed. Browns of over ten pounds have been caught on flies in Catskill streams. They are superb fighters. Browns are more tolerant of today's shallower, warmer water in most Catskill lower- and middle-river reaches. They are less gullible than brook trout, requiring the mastery of more sophisticated angling techniques. And, happily for the final evolutionary phase of early American fly fishing, browns rise more readily to the dry fly.

The first mention of "dry" fly fishing in America appeared in 1864 in Thad Norris's *The American Angler's Book*:

It occurred at a pool beneath the fall of a dam on the Williwemock, at a low stage of water—none running over. The fish were shy and refused every fly I offered them, when my friend put on a Grannom for a stretcher, and a minute Jenny Spinner for a dropper. His leader was the finest gut and his flies fresh, and by cracking the moisture from them between each throw, he would lay them so lightly on the glassy surface, that a brace of Trout would take them at almost every cast, and before they sank or were drawn away. He had tied these flies and made his whip especially for his evening cast on this pool, and as the fish would not notice mine, I was obliged to content myself with landing his fish, which in a half hour counted several dozen. Here was an exemplification of the advantage of keeping one's flies dry.

Theodore Gordon had prepared himself for the coming of the dry fly. He had grown up with *The American Angler's Book*, and from it he had learned to face upstream and fish his wet flies dry. He had fished through the demise of the brook trout into the rise of the brown. And he was well connected with England and the rest of the angling world through his correspondence and readings. So it was natural that he should hear of Frederic M. Halford's crusade for the dry fly in England and his trend-setting books, *Floating Flies and How to Dress Them* (1886), and *Dry Fly Fishing in Theory and Practice* (1889).

Gordon devoured both of Halford's books and wrote to ask him for more information on this new phenomenon. Halford's reply is now fly-fishing history; on February 22, 1890, he sent back a letter offering to help Gordon create new floating patterns specifically for American waters. Clipped to his letter, each identified alongside, were approximately fifty of his favorite dry flies. And thus, wrote John McDonald, "the dry fly winged its way to the New World."

This event has come to symbolize the arrival of the dry fly in America partly because it involved a dramatic, documentable exchange between two angling giants, but mainly because Gordon used Halford's flies and advice to create the first *American* dry-fly patterns. Actually, Gordon was one of a growing number of Americans who knew of Halford and were experimenting with English dry flies and wets fished dry beginning with Thad Norris in the early 1860s. Dry-fly articles had already appeared in American periodicals of the 1870s, and the first American books to mention dry-fly tactics and tying were published in the 1880s. The thing that sets Gordon apart from the other early American dry-fly enthusiasts is the fact that he scrutinized English dry flies and dry-fly tactics and found them unsuited to American trout streams. So he started from scratch to identify native insects, design new patterns, and perfect his own presentational techniques. Where the others accepted what was available, Gordon was inquisitive, skeptical, and innovative.

When Gordon brought Halford's letter home from the post office, his hands must have trembled as he opened it and viewed the famous dry-fly master's creations—Pale Watery Dun, Little Marryatt, Orange Bumble, Jenny Spinner, Welshman's Button, and all the others. "The bacilli or microbe which infects the dry fly entered my system," wrote Gordon, "and the attack which followed was quite severe." He went all-English with imported rod, dry flies, gossamer silkworm gut, and "all other prescriptions which I presumed necessary

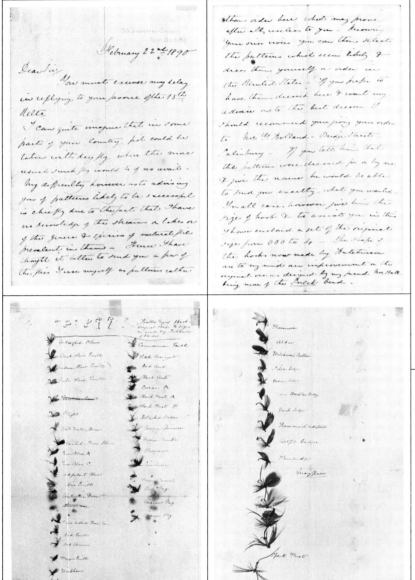

Frederic M. Halford's historic letter and enclosure of personal favorite dry-fly patterns sent to Theodore Gordon in 1890. "And thus," wrote John McDonald, "the dry fly winged its way to the New World." *Photos by Matthew Vinciguerra. Courtesy Roy Steenrod.*

to effect a cure," but soon discovered that the English equipment and even their dry-fly tactics were not working to his satisfaction. Their insects, on which Halford patterned his flies, differed from ours, and the placid chalk streams of Hampshire were nothing like the tumbling, freestone streams of the Catskills.

Gordon realized that he was now confronted with both a great opportunity and a difficult challenge. Undaunted, he started with the basics, using the English theories as a general guide, and created dry-fly patterns that worked on American streams. For this he had to devise a crude system for classifying stream insects before there was ever an American stream entomology. He bemoaned the lack of such, and the fact that "an angler will often be at a loss in trying to identify an insect which he finds is attractive to the fish." But he persisted in his conviction that "a copy of the natural fly upon the water will often give one a good basket of trout when all other artificial flies are nearly, if not quite, useless."

One day, in May of 1906, M. T. Davidson met Gordon for the first time while both men were fishing the Beaverkill. Davidson had raised an exception-

Theodore Gordon's fly box. Soon after Gordon received Englishman Halford's dry flies, he discovered that their insects, on which those flies were patterned, differed from ours. He thus had to start from scratch, using English theories as a general guide, and create patterns that worked on American streams. Many of the flies in this box are the result. *Photo by Matthew Vinciguerra. Courtesy Roy Steenrod.*

ally large fish and, casting repeatedly, had been unable to hook it. Seeing from Gordon's tackle that he was a real fisherman, Davidson told him where the big trout was, but Gordon would not fish for it. Instead, he gave a brilliant lesson in matching the hatch, described by Davidson a few years later in a letter to *Forest and Stream*:

> Along the banks grew some willows, and in these Mr. Gordon found several fine specimens of the fly. After securing a large one, Mr. Gordon produced a box of feathers, gut and No. 12 fly hooks. In a remarkably short time he had tied a beautiful duplicate of the original and, handing it to me, insisted that I make another try at the old trout.

Nervously, Davidson tied on Gordon's imitation, cast for, hooked, played, and landed a 20¼-inch, three-pound, eight-ounce trout. The two fishermen went back to Trout Valley Farm where they ate supper together and where Davidson christened the new fly "Gordon's Fancy," even though "fancy" flies were not supposed to be imitations of real insects.

Creating successful imitations of American stream insects was only half of Gordon's problem. The other half was working out a dry-fly construction for American streams, where the flies, quoth McDonald, "are always being ducked by white caps, froth, converging currents, and all the movements of the stream." Halford could afford to use softer hackle, for he and his countrymen fished to the rise in quiet water, but Gordon sought a stiffer hackle and tied it as sparsely as the conditions would allow. In so doing, he gave birth to a typically American style of dry-fly tying, later perfected by his Catskill followers into the "Catskill style," described vividly by Harry Darbee:

> Its characteristics: a good-sized hook, typically size 12 Model Perfect, a notably lean spare body, usually of spun fur or stripped quill of peacock herl; a divided wing of lemon-colored, mottled

barbules of a woodduck flank feather; and a few sparse turns of an incredibly stiff, clean, glassy cock's hackle, mostly either blue dun or ginger. The wings and hackle are set back from the eye of the hook, leaving an unusually long, clean "neck" at the expense of a slightly shortened body. This puts the sustaining hackle so close to the point of balance that the fly rides over broken, turbulent water like a Coast Guard lifeboat, so nearly balanced that often the tail of hackle whisk (originally, a little curlicue of several woodduck barbules) doesn't touch the water at all.

The perfections in style that postdated Gordon in the creations of Christian, Cross, and Steenrod were the divided wood-duck wing (Gordon rolled his wood-duck fibres and tied them on in a single, upright stalk), and the ratio of long, clean neck to shortened body (Gordon's wings and hackle were rather compressed right behind the eye of the hook followed by a longish body).

The consistent and most prominent characteristic of the Catskill style from Gordon until the present day is sparse, stiff hackle. Soft hackle was a pet peeve with Gordon. Because he ordered so much of his tying material by mail he could never be sure of the quality until he opened the envelope. Harry Darbee examined many of Gordon's old envelopes then owned by Roy Steenrod: "The English envelopes, of heavy hand-made paper, were addressed with a quill stating 'feathers, no value.' Although this notice was meant for the customs inspector, Gordon occasionally agreed as to their worth for tying purposes. One

Theodore Gordon used this thumb vise to tie flies on the stream by putting the ring on his thumb or by screwing it into a tree or post. As did most of his possessions, it passed into the hands of Roy Steenrod when he died. *Photo by Matthew Vinciguerra. Courtesy Roy Steenrod.*

envelope hadn't been touched, but on the outside he had written, 'Examined one packet of duns, not six hackles in it that are fit for flies. On the outside a *good* hackle, on the inside *trash*.' "

Gordon helped popularize dry-fly fishing among American anglers with his articles in the sporting journal *Forest and Stream*. Beginning in 1903, he reported regularly on his insect discoveries and fly-tying experiments, although he avoided explicit tying instructions and dressings. In the April 3, 1909, issue he presented a discourse on the theory and tactics of the dry fly, entitled "A Little Talk About the Dry Fly." He also gave addresses on dry-fly fishing at angling-club dinners as far back as 1897.

In spite of his preeminent role as a pioneering dry-fly fisherman in America, Gordon never gave up other methods of fishing. His hero, Francis Francis, "one of the greatest British anglers, practiced all three methods of fly-fishing, dry, wet and sunk, also up and down streams, as the occasion necessitated, but he belonged to no particular school." For Gordon and the fishermen of his day, fishing "wet" meant casting wet flies upstream, free-drifting them down in the film, whereas "sunk" flies usually referred to a gang of wets quartered downstream.

Even though Gordon respected Halford and numbers of other English and American dry-fly experts, he had little patience with the fast-growing "cult of the dry-fly purist." He could be temperate and smile at them: "A few ultra dry fly men may assume airs of superiority, but they are mostly good fellows. I have never known one of them to kill too many trout." Or, he could be intemperate as when he wrote to Halford's wet-fly rival, G.E.M. Skues: "Mr. Halford is like many another. He has become an authority on dry-fly fishing and has been tempted in 'Ethics of the Dry Fly' to speak authoritatively on wet-fly fishing of which he knows nothing. How any man can be such an unmitigated ass as to 'flog' a slow clear river like Test or Itchen downstream, I cannot imagine." Halford had ignored the refinements of wet-fly fishing and characterized the wet-fly man as a "flogger" of the stream, which insulted Gordon's sensibilities.

Three months before he died, Gordon wrote to Steenrod, still fretting over the Skues-Halford rivalry:

> Mr. Skues did rather a plucky thing some years ago. He worked out a system of wet fly fishing for the chalk dry fly streams, and killed many trout when the dry fly would not work. Then he published a book on "Minor Tactics of the Chalk Streams" that stirred up all the prejudice in the dry fly ranks. Mr. Halford was particularly fierce, and gave Skues (of course not mentioning him) the devil in his last book. I was very sorry as Halford had always been so fair for over 20 years, but he was growing old; for years he had fished only certain preserved lengths of the Test and Itchen. He was recognized as *the* great authority, and had become a bit prejudiced and dictatorial.

As John McDonald has observed, Theodore Gordon performed in this country the joint services of a Skues and a Halford. He arrived on the scene when Americans were fishing only wet flies and the English were going through a dry-fly revolution. In having brought about the juncture of these two great traditions, Gordon fully deserves to be known as "the father of modern American angling."

The decade from 1905 to 1915 saw the American dry-fly movement turn into a full-scale boom. At its 1907 annual casting tournament at Harlem Mere, The Anglers' Club of New York began sponsoring classes for dry-fly fishermen; at luncheons they held formal debates on dry versus wet flies. And, along with Gordon's articles on the subject, other dry-fly writers began appearing in print.

In 1912, the first American book on the dry fly, *Practical Dry-Fly Fishing*, was published. Its author, Emlyn M. Gill, fished almost exclusively in the Catskills, particularly the Willowemoc. Like Gordon, he took most of his inspiration from Frederic Halford; but unlike Gordon, Gill confined his observations to the tactics of dry-fly angling. Interestingly—for he must have been aware of Gordon's articles—he dismissed the need for American patterns by saying, "there seems little doubt that many of the duns found upon the streams of England also exist on American waters." He added that it was moot whether English dry flies imitated American insects because there was no American stream entomology with which to check this out. In other words, where Gordon became intensely curious, Gill glossed over the whole subject of matching the American hatch.

Gill's position was typical among early American dry-fly purists, and understandably so; for beyond the flies of Theodore Gordon, the only dries being sold in this country were of English origin. Therefore, our first "dry-fly men" concentrated on proper casting form and stream tactics. Said Gordon of America's leading dry-fly purist, "LaBranche is a very expert fisher, but manual dexterity is his chief pleasure."

Gill's book preceded George M. L. LaBranche's *The Dry Fly and Fast Water* by two years as the first American work on dry-fly angling. The nearness in time of these two books is a basis for some interesting observations.

Gill and LaBranche knew each other—both were habitués of the Ward stretch on the Willowemoc—and they were certainly rivals, perhaps even friendly, in their goal to write the first American book on dry-fly angling. Both men were also members of The Anglers' Club of New York, but Gill, curiously, resigned the same year his book came out. The history of the Anglers' Club says that Gill resigned "after figuring in some sort of controversy."

In June of 1914, the year his book was published, LaBranche told Theodore Gordon that he had "entirely recast his book since he first wrote it, before the publication of Dr. Gill's book." One can only speculate on why LaBranche felt this was necessary. Both books naturally covered similar topics, for example, the creation of an artificial hatch by repeated casts over the same lie, a technique that Gill attributed to Englishman H. D. McClelland.

Gill in his book paid homage to LaBranche's "profound knowledge of dry-fly methods and of the habits of the trout," and in one chapter set up a rather elaborate teacher-student situation in which his "bad judgment" on a Willowemoc pool was corrected by LaBranche months later while the two of them were reliving the experience together on a train.

The Gill-LaBranche rivalry became an extension of the hare-and-tortoise fable, for *The Dry Fly and Fast Water* ended up being the American classic on dry-fly angling. As Sparse Grey Hackle observed in 1961 in writing LaBranche's obituary:

> George, more than any other man, revolutionized the great American sport of fishing with the fly, for he was the creator and prophet of what is still the distinctive and unique American school of dry-fly angling.

LaBranche earned his fame with several developments in angling technique adapted to America's faster, more turbulent streams. He shifted the emphasis from the physical aspects of the artificial fly to the manner of its presentation—its exact placement on the current which is the fish's food lane. He cast his flies to the places where fish should lie rather than waiting for a fish to begin rising to natural flies, as preferred on the chalk streams of England. And he popularized the "artificial hatch," making cast after cast until a trout could no longer resist the procession of his flies.

All these developments depended on precision casting, and LaBranche was a champion tournament caster. He excelled both in accuracy and in distance events, but his stream casting has been described as "incredible" by Sparse, who

George M. L. LaBranche, author of *The Dry Fly and Fast Water*, about whom Sparse Grey Hackle said, "He was the creator and prophet of what is still the distinctive and unique American school of dry-fly angling." *Photo by Henry G. Davis, courtesy Carolyn Capstick.*

goes further and dissects LaBranche's casting technique:

> George LaBranche had the most delicate presentation of any angler whom I have ever observed. In his books, George speaks repeatedly of checking the fly in the air to get a delicate delivery, but what he did was really more than that. He made each cast, short or long, with a deliberate powerful stroke; checked the line hard so that the fly whipped down until it was only an inch above the water, with its headway killed; and then seemed to lower it gently, through that remaining inch, onto the water. On short casts, he could put his fly on the surface before line or leader touched the water.

One's understanding and appreciation for LaBranche's casting abilities are enhanced by a small piece of fishing gossip from an inquiring fellow angler who confided that he had examined the contents of LaBranche's handcrafted cedar fly box:

> I wish you could see them! I never saw so many rotten flies in my life. I was literally astounded. You know the stuff—Mills' best, and a bunch of English flies. Of all the miserable soft hackle, lathered on in bunches! It is no wonder that he became such a magnificent caster. If he hadn't learned to put those flies down so carefully they would not have floated.

Devotees of the dry fly were not limited to the decade of ferment and agitation when the art was being perfected by Gordon, Gill, and LaBranche. In 1932, Malcolm Whitman, a Beaverkill angler and nationally ranked amateur tennis player, wrote a short parody called *Fly Fishing Up to Date*, in which he carefully explained that, just as flies are not flies until they are hatched,

> If someone asks me whether I prefer fly fishing with a "dry" fly, or a "wet" fly, I answer simply that I prefer fly fishing and put the accent somewhat suavely on the word "fly."

And thus was born the sport of fly fishing in America; from bass, to brook, to brown trout, from bait, to wet, to dry flies. Only the master, George Michel Lucien LaBranche, could capture the spirit of this achievement:

> The dry fly fisherman has passed through all of the stages of the angler's life, from the cane pole and drop-line to the split bamboo and fur-and-feather counterfeit of the midge fly. He has experienced throes of delight each time he advanced from the lower to the higher grade of angler. Let him who doubts put aside his prejudice long enough to give the premier method fair trial, and soon he will be found applying for the highest degree of the cult—"dry fly man."

FOUR

The Catskill Professionals

S ix disciplines were essential to the birth of American fly fishing, each embodying a main current in the emergence of our sport. They were the "ancestors" of our angling tradition: the fishermen, the flytiers, the rodmakers, the entomologists, the riverkeepers, the publicists. These were the men—almost every one of them connected with the Catskills—who discovered and preserved a distinctly American style of angling.

Most of these pioneers would be classed today as professionals, but some of them were amateurs whose livelihoods, and even families, often competed with fishing for attention. In their commitment and dedication to the sport, they were the principal contributors to the Catskill—the American—fly-fishing tradition.

The Fishermen

The best-known American fly fisherman of the nineteenth century was THAD-DEUS NORRIS, author of *The American Angler's Book*. John McDonald said of Norris: "He knew about everything there was to know in his time, put it all down in 1864, and thereby established the school of early American fly fishing with a rounded theory and practice."

Norris fished extensively in the Catskills. One of his favorite places to start from was the Boscobel, a hotel in Westfield Flats, now Roscoe, not far from famous Junction Pool where the Beaverkill and Willowemoc meet. The Boscobel was owned by Harry Darbee's great uncle, Chester Darbee. Norris dedicated his book to "the little club of Houseless Anglers," a small group of friends organized around 1852, including himself and Chester Darbee, who fished mainly on the

Beaverkill and neighboring streams. In describing the club Norris said, "All the members (their number never exceeded ten) were fly-fishers, some of whom had met for the first time on the stream and had become acquainted without any conventional introduction. We chose the unassuming name of the 'Houseless Anglers' in contradistinction to the old Fish-House clubs—associations rather of a convivial tendency than that of pure angling."

THEODORE GORDON would have been welcome among the Houseless Anglers. Indeed, much of his angling philosophy was gleaned from his readings of *The American Angler's Book*. It was his first fishing book, his "book of books." Why he never wrote a book himself can be inferred from his feelings about fishing that emerge from the thousands of articles and letters he wrote. Rarely did he preach a doctrine or impose his views on the reader as so many angling authors were primarily motivated to do.

Gordon's message was direct and intimate, as if the reader alone were receiving a daily communiqué from the stream:

> With three figs in my pocket in lieu of dinner, I began work last Thursday, about 10:30 A.M., quite near the house, and enjoyed every minute of the day until 4:30 P.M. Where trout were not in evidence I caught big chub, which gave the same sport for a moment; in fact, they fooled me beautifully. One is quite sure that he has a fine trout until something queer in the play, or the glimpse of a silver side, undeceives him. Before returning home, I washed the slain in an ice-cold spring, then placed the chub in the basket first, with eight fine trout above. This you must confess, was much the best

Theodore Gordon and his dog in a photograph that appeared with his obituary in the June 1915 issue of *Forest and Stream*, a sporting periodical he contributed to regularly from 1903 until his death. *Courtesy The Museum of American Fly Fishing.*

arrangement. Would you have shown the chubs on top? Why, man, you would have received credit for chubs only.

He was a private but lonely man with few fishing companions. He kept himself balanced psychologically by sending out from the Neversink a steady flow of "little talks" and observations:

> It is rather annoying to have spectators overlooking our sport. We prefer to be alone with nature, with perhaps one good friend somewhere in the same stream. It is pleasant to have a chum to lunch with and to share the homeward tramp. Then perhaps we realize for the first time that we are weary and the miles are not so long if we can chat and rehearse the striking events of the day.

Gordon can best be understood by realizing that he subjugated everything to his fishing. In spite of his superior talents as a flytier and reporter, he shunned attention on both and focused them rather on enhancing his fishing pleasure. The innocent excitement in his reflections over time draws you in and makes you want to be with him on the stream:

> The only safe and sensible plan is to make other things give way to the essentials, and the first of these is fly-fishing. . . . In January we begin to think about fly-fishing, and to look forward hopefully to the season which is not very far away. . . . We wish to be as keen as mustard when the trout streams are open to us at last. . . . The spirit of the boy lies dormant in many of us, and only needs to be released by just going fishing.
> Good luck!

GEORGE LaBRANCHE was every bit as dedicated a fisherman as Gordon, but he had a different philosophy about fame. He sought it and he won it for his abilities and theories as a dry-fly angler. His achievements and authorship of *The Dry Fly and Fast Water*, covered in the preceding chapter, established him as the country's leading expert on dry-fly techniques. It all began in 1899 when he cast his first dry fly at the mouth of Mongaup Creek, a tributary of the Willowemoc.

In a letter to the *Fishing Gazette* following Gordon's death, LaBranche said, "I had hoped that he would give his ideas to the fly-fishing public in permanent form, but it seems that was not to be during his lifetime." His observation underscored the difference between these two men, one who fished for fun, the other also for achievement. Or, as Gordon put it, "It is just as well to remember that angling is only a recreation, not a profession."

For HERMAN CHRISTIAN, fishing was an integral part of living, along with hunting, trapping, and subsistence farming. He was born on the Rondout and reared on the Neversink, and he lived to be one of the all-time greats among

Herman Christian with the E. F. Payne rod given to him in 1912 by Theodore Gordon who said, "I don't know of anybody who would appreciate it as much as you would." Christian fished with it for another forty years before the Payne rod company acquired it for its museum. *Courtesy The Anglers' Club* Bulletin.

Catskill fishermen. Fred White, writing on Beaverkill history in a 1923 article in The Anglers' Club *Bulletin*, almost seemed to be describing Christian:

> Formerly, the average native fisherman was a bait man, but, today, some of the best fly fishermen I know are natives, with an almost uncanny knowledge of fish and water conditions, and often, too, they tie their own flies.

Christian was Theodore Gordon's most constant fishing companion and the only man Gordon truly envied as an angler: "Christian is a great expert, and has more patience and perseverance than any other man I ever met. This is the secret of his big fish. That and going for them *at the correct time*. I think he deserves the big trout he catches and am glad to see them when he brings them to me to show."

The admiration was mutual, as evidenced by Christian's recollection in an interview after Gordon's death:

> Mr. Gordon was a very fine fisherman. He did not cast a particularly long line in spite of the big rods he used, but he cast a particularly nice line and he could put the fly right where he wanted and put it down just the right way.

Whenever Christian located "a nice big fish," he took Gordon there the next day to fish for it. On one occasion, Christian saw "a couple of good trout in a hole about a mile below Neversink."

> I took Mr. Gordon down there and he got one fish, a 16-inch fish, and I think I got the other one later, in the middle of June, at night on a No. 6 dun fly. It was 29½ inches long and weighed 8 pounds 4 ounces.

The Flytiers

THEODORE GORDON first learned to make flies when he was thirteen from reading Norris: "Body first, hackle next and wings tied on last. This, I suppose is the oldest method of tying flies. I know that I killed many trout with my rough flies." His next major influence was Englishman Frederic Halford's *Floating Flies and How to Dress Them* (1886): "I was fortunate enough to secure one of the first copies that were imported. I learned all the methods described in that magnum opus and from that time read all the articles on fly tying that I could find."

American fly tying was very primitive before Gordon. Robert Barnwell Roosevelt, in his 1884 edition of *The Game Fish of the Northern States and British Provinces*, described the state of American fly-tying art:

> Few people in this stage of civilization dress their own trout flies. . . . It is to be regretted that there is not more uniformity and pride in, or practical acquaintance with, the subject among our principal tackle-makers. With the English makers it has always been an especial care that their flies should be dressed well and with uniformity; but here, anything that can be palmed off on an ignorant or indulgent public, or a barbarous country trade, is all that is desired.

Mary Orvis Marbury, daughter of Charles Frederick Orvis, founder of the Orvis Company, echoed Roosevelt in the opening pages of *Favorite Flies and their Histories*, 1896 edition.

> At one period nearly all the tackle-dealers in America were of Scotch, English, or Irish birth, and had brought with them to this land their knowledge of the implements used in the "old country;" the flies they sold were all imported, and so the fishermen of this country came to know and use the flies most favorably known abroad.

Gordon created many original dry-fly patterns. Some he named and they survived into modern times; some were nameless and may have been used for only a season. "I fussed after a fly for two years," he wrote, "and named it after a well-known angler," whom he did not identify. There was the Orange Grannom, worked out in 1909, and its close relative the Dark Grannom, "a favorite of mine, also an earlier riser and smaller, that carries a bag of orange colored eggs (dark) at the end of the body."

In many cases, Gordon took the standard American wet-fly patterns and tied them "in dry-fly fashion." The Light Cahill was one of these. The Beaverkill, a wet fly descended from the British Silver Sedge, had been used in this country for about forty years before Gordon picked it up and turned it into a floater.

There was the Gordon, known then as the G.B.S. or Gold Bodied Spinner, which has survived, and of course the Quill Gordon, then called the Gordon Quill, which he tied in a variety of shades and sizes. He described it in a 1906 letter to G.E.M. Skues:

> I would like to have you try the following. Body plain quill, peacock, light color, hackles and tail, light blue hackle, wings wood duck plain, mottled from a good sized finely mottled feather, using double strips for each side the stem. I usually varnish the foundation to strengthen the quill. It is a light blue quill, with wood-duck wings and I will gamble on it killing, if dressed to suit the water, also try same fly with dubbing of pale blue (dun) wool. This fly has been killing wherever I have used it, and is now doing great execution on the Beaverkill.

Sometime around 1900 Gordon became a professional flytier. He sold his flies mostly by mail although he had a few friends and customers who got their flies directly from him at his residence or on the stream. They included Abe Snedecor and Dick Robbins of the Brooklyn Fly Fishers, George LaBranche, Guy Jenkins and his father Henry, Willard Spenser, Fred White, and Alfred Caspari. In 1935, Jenkins recalled the Gordon flies they used:

> In the early days Mr. Gordon was the only source in this country of an Honest-to-God dry fly, except the English flies in some few tackle stores. I cannot emphasize too strongly that flies tied by him on eyed hooks, as far back at least as the middle '90s, or earlier, were as delicate in construction, as stiff in hackle, and practically as varied in pattern, as flies of the finest tiers today. They were not just a first step—a crude beginning of the art in America—but the fully formed and finished product.

Whenever HERMAN CHRISTIAN came to visit Gordon while he was tying flies, Gordon would take the unfinished fly out of the vise and lay it on the table and talk about fishing or something else besides flytying. Said Christian, "He never taught anybody to tie; he never showed anybody anything, not even me." Christian should have known that Gordon did teach one man to tie flies—Roy Steenrod of Liberty. Rube Cross also claimed to have learned under Gordon's tutelage, but on this Christian was adamant: "Gordon never spoke to Rube in his life." It would be understandable if Christian, so close to Gordon as a fishing chum, were jealous over being excluded from his flytying advice.

Secretiveness, typical to some extent of many professional craftsmen, was contagious among flytiers. Christian caught it from Gordon; when his grandson asked to be shown how to tie flies, he said, "Find out the way I did." He untied and figured out in reverse how Gordon had tied his flies, just as Walt Dette, Harry Darbee, and later generations of Catskill flytiers did in order to learn the professional secrets of the old masters.

One of Gordon's patterns "dissected" by Christian was the Bumblepuppy. It had been designed originally as a bass fly and to use at night for the biggest brown trout. Gordon used to send one with an order of delicate Quill Gordons and Light Cahills, as a startling gift to his customers. Christian changed the pattern slightly and made it even larger, tying it on a 1/0 hook. A Christian Bumblepuppy is credited with a thirteen-pound, four-ounce brown trout taken by Waldemar Kesk in the Delaware below the mouth of Mongaup River. The trout won a *Field & Stream* national contest.

Christian tied professionally but with some indifference. He once left a flyless Vanderbilt sitting in his kitchen bidding up the price of a few yet-to-be-tied Christian specials while he went out to hoe potatoes in the garden. However, he did for a short period in his life manage the fly-tying department at Pfleuger's in Akron, Ohio. There were more than thirty female flytiers under his supervision.

The notorious Bumblepuppy, designed by Theodore Gordon as a bass fly and as a night fly for big browns. This particular fly was tied by Herman Christian who was forced to untie Gordon's flies to learn how to duplicate them. *Courtesy Louise and Alfred W. Miller.*

In the last ten years of Gordon's life, ROY STEENROD was probably his closest friend. They fished together often, and Gordon singled him out as his protégé in flytying. Interestingly, in contrast to Herman Christian, Steenrod went on to become the best-known flytying instructor in the Catskills. He taught at the DeBruce conservation camp, at Boy Scout meetings, or anywhere there was a handy vise and materials. He was more responsible than anyone else for passing on the distinctive features of the Catskill style.

Steenrod's biggest claim to flytying fame lies in his having originated what today may well be the most popular brown-trout fly in America, the Hendrickson. This pattern was named for his friend and fishing companion A. E. Hendrickson, trucking magnate, backer of rodmaker Jim Payne, and a constant angler in Beaverkill waters.

As recalled by Steenrod, it was the spring of 1918 when he and Hendrickson were fishing at Ferdon's Pool on the lower Beaverkill and they encountered a tremendous hatch of the mayfly *Ephemerella subvaria*. At lunch-time, Steenrod tied up some imitations which were murderously effective. It became their favorite pattern but remained unnamed. After several years, Hendrickson finally remarked that the pattern ought to have a name. "All right," said Steenrod, "it's the Hendrickson." In recounting the experience years later to Sparse Grey Hackle, Steenrod said, "I could see that A.E. was pleased."

The only man Theodore Gordon instructed in flytying, Roy Steenrod, demonstrates the master's secrets to youngsters at the DeBruce State Conservation Camp. *Courtesy Harry Darbee.*

Whether or not RUBE (REUBEN R.) CROSS was taught how to tie by Gordon, he certainly tied his flies in the Gordon manner and, through his book *Tying American Trout Lures* (1936), was a major influence on American flytiers of the thirties and forties. Cross was a huge man endowed with a wonderful flytier's combination of great manual dexterity, keen eyesight, and an incredible sense of color. New acquaintances were consistently amazed "that such a massive individual could produce those tiny specimens of dry-fly perfection." Eugene Connett, fishing writer and owner of Derrydale Press, called Cross "the best professional tier of dry flies in America." He is best known for his Cross Special, Catskill, and Blue Honey Dun patterns.

As good as he was, Rube Cross had to combine a mixture of trades in order to make a living. Besides flytying, he drove a taxi, worked on the town roads, and held the combination job of janitor and bouncer at the Lew Beach dance hall. One night, as recalled by Harry Darbee, "Rube threw Benny Leonard the movie fighter out of the dance hall when Leonard got boisterous; Rube was like a cat on his feet." Another night, he returned home from a dance and found his house in flames, managing to save only a pair of snowshoes. His friends and a group of distraught anglers got together and donated clothing, household items, and about fifteen hundred dollars, but he never really recovered from his loss. Shortly after he had reestablished himself farther

Rube Cross at work tying his perfectionist dry flies for customers all over the country. Cross studied Theodore Gordon's flies, improved their buoyancy, and through his book *Tying American Trout Lures*, influenced numerous American flytiers of the 1930s and 40s. *Photo by Edwin Way Teale, courtesy* Outdoor Life.

downstream near the Craigie Clare bridge, conservation officers paid an unexpected visit and fined him for possessing woodduck and golden pheasant feathers without a license. He developed ulcers and moved to the Neversink, where he continued to tie flies while writing two books on flytying.

In the early forties, when seven miles of the Neversink River were condemned and preparations begun on a new dam, Cross moved to Providence, Rhode Island, where he supplemented his tying income by working in a munitions plant and then a realty company. He stayed in touch with his fellow flytiers in the Catskills, occasionally calling for help as he did in this instance from a letter to Harry Darbee:

> Geezus Keerist, Harry, just when my ulcer and other infirmities start kicking up, this hermorphedite sends in an order of half-assed streamers that I just hate like hell to tie. And I suppose he is strictly a purist. Will you please tie them up as soon as convenient and send them to me at your regular price? My stomach really rolls when I have to tie those patterns.

PARKER EMERY FOOTE came down to the Catskills from New Hampshire in the 1930s. He set up shop as a flytier in the village of Neversink at the same time he and his wife worked for an elderly woman whose house they helped run as a fishing hotel. Foote originated no patterns of his own, but Harry Darbee called him "one of the best tiers I knew." He and Rube Cross were great fishing friends, certainly in part because Foote was such a colorful character. He was one of the best trout-talkers around. "I was coming up dry below the village one evenin'," he would say, "and somethin' took hold. It wa'n't much of a rise—just sucked in the fly; browns'll do that sometimes, especially the big ones. But I set up on him, and mister I knew I had a fish." He called the big browns "old raunchers" and "old soakers," and for the strike he would yell "KA-SLAWSH!"

ED HEWITT enjoyed experimenting with new fly patterns, but he employed other tiers to make production copies for his fishing and to give to friends. Hewitt was very influential as a fly designer and theorist on the use of his favorite patterns. In a pamphlet on nymph fishing he wrote:

> Most of the nymphs of our eastern American streams are brown on the back. They vary in the color of the belly, with various shades of yellow the most common. Nearly all are flat, because they spend their lives adhering to stones and gravel, and are built to have the least water resistance in current.

Based on this theory, Hewitt designed his flat-shaped Hardbacked Nymph and in an experiment on his Neversink water, performed by one of his resident "rods," the flat nymph outfished a round one 165 to 35. He also designed the Brown Bivisible, a palmered brown-and-white fly that both he and the trout could see. This pattern is still very popular today.

Ed Hewitt at his fly vise, where he created such famous patterns as the Neversink Skater, Brown Bivisible, Hardbacked Nymph, and his favorite, the Yellow Stonefly, about which he said, "I can skin the water with this fly if I want to." *Courtesy The Anglers' Club* Bulletin.

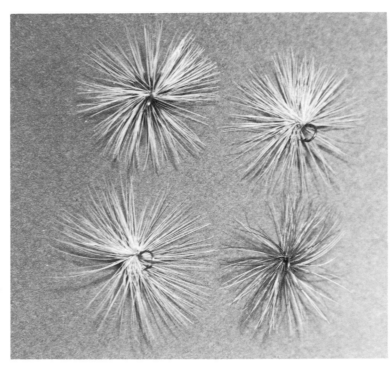

Neversink Skaters, designed and popularized by Ed Hewitt. Tied on a #16 hook, they are patterned after the butterflies Hewitt saw being taken by large trout in broad daylight. *Courtesy The Museum of American Fly Fishing.*

Another Hewitt design, and one of his personal favorites, was a #16 Stonefly with yellow body and pheasant wing about which he remarked: "I find that this is much the best fly for our waters all the time. When I want fish I always put this on, but you must know just how to fish it—wet with a long leader. I can skin the water with this fly if I want to."

It is the Neversink Skater, however, for which Hewitt was best known. This fly is patterned after the butterflies he saw being taken in broad daylight by large leaping trout. It is a #16 spider with no tail, tied with extra wide and stiff spade or saddle hackles to make a fly two inches or more in diameter. The fishing method, prescribed by Hewitt, required great casting precision to keep the fly moving on the water, high—and dry—at all times. The moment it got soaked or taken by a fish, Hewitt put on a fresh one.

WILLIAM A. CHANDLER sold flies at William Mills & Son in New York, and for health reasons moved to Liberty, where he fished the Neversink and tied experimentally for his own fishing. Chandler preferred the dry fly and used it almost exclusively, the one in particular for which he achieved notoriety being his version of the Light Cahill. A modification of Theodore Gordon's Light Cahill, Chandler's pattern had lighter colored hackle and twice the number of tail whisks. The Light Cahill design is also attributed to Dan Cahill of Port Jervis, New York, a brakeman with the Erie Railroad, and to Rube Cross, who tied it with an "almost whitish body." In any case, it is a Catskill pattern that has become an all-time favorite dry fly.

WALT DETTE moved to Roscoe when he entered the seventh grade and immediately fell in love with fly fishing. He and Harry Darbee fished together

Walt Dette, Winnie Ferdon, and Harry Darbee in their carefree angling days of the late 1920s. They trooped around together, made pocket money by winding rods and tying flies, but mostly they did a lot of fishing. *Courtesy the Dettes.*

The Dettes of Dette's Flies—Walt, Winnie, and their daughter Mary—through their more than fifty years of continuous output have made the most sustained contribution of anyone to the Catskill flytying tradition. *Photo by Lawrence Robins.*

almost daily in their school years. When he was about twenty, Walt scraped together fifty dollars and offered it to Rube Cross in return for flytying lessons. Cross turned him down, and Walt joined the Catskill line of self-taught flytiers. He began selling flies shortly after his marriage to Winnie Ferdon in 1928, and by 1933 felt enough confidence to formalize his business as "W. C. Dette, Dry Flies," inviting Harry Darbee to join him. The business consisted of Walt, Winnie, Harry, and then Elsie Bivins until 1935 when Harry and Elsie were married and went out on their own as "E. B. and H. A. Darbee, Flies and Fly-tying Supplies."

Walt and Winnie Dette celebrated their fiftieth anniversary of marriage *and* professional flytying in 1978. Dette designed the Corey Ford pattern and, with Ted Townsend, originated and named the Coffin Fly.

In his first year of business, HARRY DARBEE put out a catalogue listing 232 patterns, including two new designs he originated "to give us something special to offer our customers." One of them, "H.A. Darbee's Mid-Summer Special," was a tiny fly made only from hackle-tip wings, palmered, bare hook shank, and tail—all feathers of the same bird. Said Darbee in the catalogue, "These flies will take any rising fish nine times out of ten when correctly presented."

The other fly he called "H.A. Darbee's Special Mayfly." It was conceived as a hybrid of the deer-hair bassbug and a large trout fly, and indeed came to be known as the Beaverkill Bastard, to be fished when the big mays and drakes were on the water. It was tied on #10 3XL hook, had three hackles, a clipped deer-hair body, and double hackle-point wings. Percy Jennings, one of the Darbees'

Elsie and Harry Darbee, whom Sparse Grey Hackle called "the world's best flytiers," standing below their home, in Willowemoc Creek. *Photo by Francis W. Davis.*

customers, tied it smaller and renamed it the Rat-faced McDougall, turning it into one of the best all-round trout flies to come out of the Catskills. It went through one more evolution when another Darbee customer, Otto von Kien-busch, requested that the wings be changed to white hair so he could still see them with his failing eyes. With this change, the pattern stabilized and the Rat-faced McDougalls became a staple of the Darbees' business. Said Harry, "I cranked out the bodies, Elsie trimmed them to shape, and either of us winged and hackled them. It was the only way we could turn out such a fussy pattern and price it competitively."

Other patterns developed by Darbee include the Shad Fly, an early-spring caddis imitation, and the Spate Fly, a large, dark salmon fly to be fished in high, discolored water.

When ART FLICK came to Schoharie Creek in 1934, the valley had no fly-fishing professionals. In order to succeed as an innkeeper catering to fly fishermen, he also had to become a guide and a flytier. His first teacher in flytying was Clarence Banks, a half-Indian hunter and fisherman who lived on the stream above Lexington. Ray Bergman came up from Nyack and he too helped Flick with his flies. It was Preston Jennings, though, who introduced Flick to natural dun hackles, judged his tying efforts, and cheered him on to become a flytier of extraordinary capability. Jennings himself was responsible for creating the American March Brown from its English counterpart, and for the Grey Fox Variant.

Because Art Flick never tied on a commercial scale, few fishermen besides his Westkill Tavern guests could buy flies from him. "Dana Lamb could get flies out of him when nobody else could," recalled Sparse Grey Hackle. "I remember the night Dana's fishing vest was stolen down in the Antrim Lodge bar, off of a coat hook. They got his fly boxes and everything, but the only thing he wept about to me was his Flick flies."

Flick originated the Red Quill to imitate the male *Ephemerella subvaria*.

A typical Catskill-style dry fly, the Red Quill, designed and tied by Art Flick to imitate the male *Ephemerella subvaria*, the female of which is imitated by Steenrod's famous Hendrickson. *Photo by Cook Nielsen, courtesy* Rod & Reel *Magazine*.

Roy Steenrod had matched the females about twenty years earlier with his Hendrickson. The dressings of these two flies are identical except for their bodies. "I had such success with this fly," said Art, "that I decided to put my same old favorite red quill on Jennings's Blue Variant, Gold Body." The result was Flick's Dun Variant, a killer fly during the *Isonychia* hatch. He also modified Jennings's Grey Fox Variant body from a gold tinsel to a ginger quill and it became the continuing favorite among the fishermen at Westkill Tavern. Flick liked quill bodies because they were quicker to tie, more durable, and easier to keep dry while fishing.

Other patterns developed by Flick include the Blacknosed Dace bucktail and the Hendrickson nymph. From 1939 to 1944, Flick kept a record of his dry-fly inventory. Listing the aggregate number he tied of each pattern in those six years provides an index of their popularity among Schoharie anglers:

Grey Fox Variants	1731
Dun Variants	930
Quill Gordons	899
March Browns	753
Hendricksons	732
Grey Foxes	728
Light Cahills	722
Red Quills	608
Cream Variants	578

Ask an Esopus fly fisherman to name a famous flytier, and invariably he will say RAY SMITH. Smith lived in Phoenicia, was active from the thirties through the sixties, and had the undisputed reputation of being the best guide and flytier in the valley. He originated the Red Fox and Brown Turkey patterns.

Many other flies were originated and fished in the Catskills. Some passed on with their creators; some were adopted more widely and are fished on the rivers today. George Cooper, a local blacksmith and storekeeper, originated the Female Beaverkill; when he first tied it in the 1890s, it was known as the "Nice Nelly." Scotty Conover of the Brooklyn Fly Fishers created the enduring Conover in the 1920s. Mahlon Davidson, of Lew Beach and then DeBruce, tied a fly similar to the Light Cahill with fox-fur body dyed pale green with willow bark, called the Davidson Special. Other Catskill patterns include the Spent Wing Woodruff, Neversink, Catskill, Bradley Special, Kattermann, Campbell's Fancy, Murray's Favorite, Christian Special, Petrie's Green Egg Sac, Quack Special, and Pink Lady.

The Entomologists

ROBERT BARNWELL ROOSEVELT proclaimed as he set out in 1862 to write *The Game Fish of the North* that American trout stream insects had "never been properly described and classified." However, he did not get very far in his pioneering effort before admitting that the job was too much for him:

> When commencing this work, it had been my intention not only to describe the artificial flies in general request, but to give the habits, periods and names of the natural ones of which they were imitations, without which latter information the former would have been far from complete. But the obstacles in my way were so numerous, the confusion existing as to names, localities, and times of appearance was so utter, the difficulty of finding any satisfactory work on the natural insects so great, that I was almost in despair. . .

Because Roosevelt sat back and did his research in books instead of the New York streams where he fished, the end result is a textbookish treatment of the divisions, classes, and families of bugs of interest to trout and anglers. As for the imitations, he gave them lip service and concluded that "the well-known flies should be dressed after Ronalds as far as practicable." Englishman Alfred Ronalds wrote *The Fly Fisher's Entomology* in 1836 strictly as a guide to his native trout stream insects, which Roosevelt acknowledged were very different from ours, so this was in effect a total surrender.

The next work on entomology for American anglers came in 1876 with the appearance of SARA J. MCBRIDE's newspaper article, "Beside the Singing Stream, A Study of the Insect Fauna of Caledonia Creek." McBride was a professional flytier following in the footsteps of her Irish father John McBride, and her field laboratory was none other than the stream where twelve years earlier Seth Green had established the first American trout hatchery. Green's hatchery was primarily responsible for the restocking of Catskill trout streams after the demise of the tanneries and sawmills.

McBride's article was republished in the sporting journal *Rod and Gun* the following year under the title "Entomology for Fly Fishers." It was a noble effort, combining diligent streamside work with aquarium experiments and microscopic observations, but it failed to become the foundation for future angling entomologies. As one of the earliest Americans to advocate tying imitations of the natural insects, McBride confused her readers. On the one hand, she stated that only winged insects attracted feeding trout and were therefore of sole interest to the fly fisherman; on the other, she tied and described only wet patterns and most of them were "fancy flies" of English origin, not intended to match any kind of insect. She also made such basic errors in nomenclature as mixing up caddis and stoneflies. In 1880, after just four years of insect studies and writing, Sara McBride was never heard from again.

After reading two books by Robert Roosevelt, THEODORE GORDON wrote in an article for English angling readers, "I think these are the first books which indicate any study of the natural by an American angler." Continuing, he said "A few papers have been written on the subject," a seeming reference to

Sara McBride, but concluded, "No one can regret more than I do the absence of a standard work on the natural flies of American waters . . . The work required of the author of such a book would be great, for we have many more insects than the equivalents of your English species."

Gordon's lament was heartfelt because throughout his fishing career he was constantly experimenting with imitations of the natural insects he found along the streams. The irony is that although he was the first American to gain a practical knowledge of trout stream insects and the fly patterns to match them, he did not share his understanding of entomology. When it came to the core of experience that underlay his success as a creator of new American fly patterns, Gordon considered this a professional secret.

It is unlikely that Gordon was much influenced by biologist James J. Needham's 1903 work *Aquatic Insects in New York State* when it came along. A strict empiricist, Gordon based his studies solely on the stream: "Some years ago there was a great rise of the dark American Grannom on the Beaverkill after June 3, and I tied six patterns before I got one that would kill."

LOUIS RHEAD, a highly talented artist and the first angler to attempt an American stream entomology, was also an empiricist, emphatically so: "I deem it wise to brush aside the science of entomology, which is of no actual service to our purpose, and to lay before the angler a plain, simple plan." That was the way he introduced his *American Trout-Stream Insects*, published in 1916. In his book he presented for each month from April through August the main insects on which the trout fed. He had collected specimens of ninety-five species during seven fishing seasons on the upper Beaverkill, painted their likenesses, and designed a fly pattern to imitate each of them.

One could read into the face of Louis Rhead the ambition and idealism that fueled his prodigious outpouring of illustrations, articles, and books on stream insects, fish, and fishing. Rhead and George LaBranche are purported to have debated "imitation of the natural" one evening at the Anglers' Club with the result that "George clobbered him unmercifully." *Culver Pictures*.

In spite of his prodigious efforts, Rhead failed to win the respect of his fellow anglers. His system of identification was too informal, relying mainly on color and shape, as befits an artist's eye. The reader encounters a procession of "needletail duns, brown buzzes, nobby spinners, little mauves, short-tails, long-horns, gauze-wings, glossy-flies, and fluffy spinners." Such names provoked William Chandler, a contemporary of Rhead's, to write: "I have never been able to identify any of Mr. Rhead's Female Green Eyes, Lemon Tails, and Pink Tails. It is possible that things looked very different when he collected his specimens before the Eighteenth Amendment."

Several other obstacles prevented the acceptance of Rhead's theories by the angling community. All his artificials were strict imitations of the natural trout foods at a time when impressionistic patterns were gaining favor. "Rhead is such a copyist," said Theodore Gordon, "that I have doubts about him." Rhead actually approached Gordon to tie his "nature flies," according to Herman Christian, but Gordon refused.

Moreover, Rhead claimed that his systematized method of fishing ensured success. Said a book reviewer: "Mr. Rhead is dogmatically certain that his own system of angling is the one scientific, artistic, non-refillable, unbreakable, unshrinkable, and blown-in-the-glass method of extracting game fish from their favorite haunts and transferring them to the angler's creel."

In addition to the fly patterns, Rhead created a series of "Nature-Lures" to imitate minnows, crawfish, hellgrammites, lamprey eels, frogs, grasshoppers, caterpillars, and dragonflies. His "feather minnows," "shiny devils," and "artificial frogs that wiggle their legs and float" seemed ready to crawl and jump right off the pages of his book. All these devices were patented, and were commonly called "patent bait." Said an outdoor writer of that era about an angler taken with these newfangled lures, "he provided himself with a lot of patent bait which looked like a string of tarantulas afflicted with the jim-jams."

Rhead's biggest error in judgment appears to have been his attempt to corner the American dry-fly market with his series of new fly patterns available only through approved tiers and licensed agents. For all his minutely detailed renderings and elaborate descriptions of the ninety-five species, he carefully omits any fly dressings. As one angler/reviewer wrote of *American Trout-Stream Insects:* "It is to be regretted that the author's frequent reference to 'my line of lures' makes the book more suggestive of the sporting goods emporium than of the stream-side."

The need for a reliable angling entomology went unfilled until 1935 when PRESTON JENNINGS completed *A Book of Trout Flies*. Jennings went about his task in the exact opposite manner from Rhead. Recognizing that many fly patterns by the mid-thirties were well entrenched among anglers based on their effective imitation of natural insects, Jennings selected the most popular imitative patterns and began collecting insects during the hatches when these patterns were most effective.

Beginning on the Esopus, and concentrating in the Catskills, Jennings

Preston Jennings, author of *A Book of Trout Flies*, the first American book to provide a reliable correlation of natural trout-stream insects and their imitations. *Courtesy Adele F. Jennings.*

enlisted the help of local anglers in collecting insects during the major hatches on their streams. Among them, Roy Steenrod helped on the Neversink, Art Flick on the Schoharie. Collections were made over three fishing seasons starting in 1933. Specimens were identified by five academic entomologists including Dr. Herman T. Spieth and Dr. James J. Needham.

When he had sorted out this massive amount of information, Jennings classified each of his insects according to accepted scientific methods, gave its emergence dates on the different streams he had surveyed, and correlated each insect with its most popular imitation and dressing.

A Book of Trout Flies was received enthusiastically as a major contribution to fly-fishing intelligence. G.E.M. Skues, the English angling authority, wrote to Jennings: "May I say how gladly I welcome your book as a sound effort to do for anglers on your side what Ronalds did for us over here a century ago."

The next advance in bug science overcame the fact that Jennings had limited his coverage to those insects which had already been effectively imitated by flytiers. The first *comprehensive* as well as scientifically sound American stream entomology, CHARLES WETZEL's *Practical Fly Fishing*, appeared in 1942. As Sparse Grey Hackle observed, "This trail-breaker appeared under severe handicaps. It was put out by a publisher of religious books, with so little promotion that it wasn't even listed in the catalogs consulted by booksellers; and since it appeared in wartime it had no colored plates, which obviously are a requisite for any such book. Nevertheless it sold an edition of 1,900 copies and went into a second printing." Wetzel collected his insects outside the Catskills, from the limestone streams of Pennsylvania, but he is included here as an important bridge between Preston Jennings and Art Flick.

For the majority of fly fishermen, there was still something missing in these entomologies. They were fine for the off-stream reader dedicating himself to a coming season of improved, scientific angling. On Opening Day, he strode onto the stream with bug net and nymph strainer, turning over stones, swiping at invisible targets in the air, examining naturals, searching through his fly box for the one perfect imitation. Sometimes it worked but most often there were simply too many species and patterns to remember.

What was needed was a simplified system giving the angler "all he needed to know about trout-stream insects and their imitations." And that's exactly what ART FLICK came up with. Inspired by the work he did for Preston Jennings, Flick continued his stream studies and flytying until he became an expert in his own right. In 1947, based on three more years of Schoharie Creek research—and after years of prodding by Ray Camp—Flick produced the *Streamside Guide*. It was immediately hailed by anglers as a "practical classic."

The distinguishing achievement of the *Streamside Guide* was its substantial reduction of the "must" patterns a fisherman had to have in his fly box. With this little book and its simplified emergence tables, identification system, and guide to selecting the right fly, American angling entomology had finally come of age.

Art Flick tying a Dun Variant, one of the patterns he designed and made famous with his book *Streamside Guide to Naturals and Their Imitations*. *Photo by the author.*

The Rodmakers

The modern bamboo fly rod was born in Easton, Pennsylvania, a small town on the Delaware River, passed through its developmental stages in Bangor, Maine, and was perfected and made famous in Central Valley and Highland Mills, New York, neighboring towns in the foothills of the Catskills.

Until about 1840, the best fly rods were made in England. Well-equipped anglers of the day swung ten-to-twelve-foot solid rods, exquisitely tapered from lancewood, greenheart, or other resilient woods. It was still the era of "sunk fly" downstream angling, and these twelve-ounce "saplings" were well designed for the task at hand.

Sometime around 1844, SAMUEL PHILLIPPE of Easton began building two- and three-strip fly-rod tip sections out of Calcutta cane to reduce the whippiness and fragility of the long, thin tapers. Phillippe had the right combination of talents and interests: he was an accomplished gunsmith and violin maker and an expert trout fisherman. Thaddeus Norris met Phillippe and got the idea for making what became his favorite rod: a white-ash butt section, a middle joint of ironwood, and a tip section of four-strip bamboo.

Samuel and his son Solon Phillippe kept experimenting on and improving their rods until, by the late 1850s, they were making a six-strip bamboo rod with twelve-strip handles of alternating hardwood and bamboo. This was the prototype of the American six-strip split-bamboo fly rod that revolutionized the sport of fly fishing.

HIRAM L. LEONARD built his first fly rod in 1871 in Bangor, Maine. It was of ash and lancewood and when a Boston sporting-goods house saw it they asked him if he thought he could make the four-strip bamboo rods then so much in demand. Examining the samples their agent had brought with him, Leonard answered, "Yes, and better than those." He started that same day, in his fortieth year, as a professional rodmaker.

Throughout his early years Leonard had proved himself a man of many skills. He had studied civil engineering and headed the mechanical department for a coal company in Honesdale, Pennsylvania. He had been a master gunsmith, his guns rivaling in beauty and workmanship those of the top gunmakers of the day. And he had learned from his father the craft of oarmaking; the Leonard racing sweeps were prized by rowers even in England. Outdoors, in addition to his fishing, he had been a market hunter of venison, and a commercial trapper and fur trader. On top of all that he was an accomplished taxidermist and violinist.

From 1871 on, Hiram Leonard dedicated himself solely and intensively to rodmaking and, over the ensuing thirty-six years until he died, distinguished himself as "the father of the modern split-bamboo fly rod." Having never heard of Samuel Phillippe, Leonard discovered by himself in 1873 the outstanding casting properties of six-strip bamboo construction. In fact, he thought he was the first ever to hit on this idea. What he *can* claim as innovations all took place in

A corner of Hiram Leonard's rod shop in Central Valley, in the late 1890s. Leonard is standing at the far right in background, Hiram Hawes is second from the left, and E. F. Payne is third from the left. *Courtesy The Museum of American Fly Fishing.*

his first and most creative ten years as a rodmaker. He invented the first beveling machine to cut rod strips of constant uniformity. This was such an astounding advance and so competitively beneficial that the machine was immediately placed in a locked room and remained off-limits except to the most trusted employees for more than seventy-five years!

Leonard was the first to make hexagonally shaped six-strip rods. He discovered by leaving the outside surfaces of the strips flat, instead of shaving them into round, that he retained more of the cane's primary fibers and could thus make a stronger rod. Also during this period, he invented the waterproof and serrated ferrules.

In 1881, three years after he began a partnership with New York tackle dealer William Mills & Son, Leonard moved his operation from Bangor to Central Valley, New York. He brought with him his highly talented employees Hiram and Loman Hawes, and recruited Fred E. Thomas, Eustis "Bill" Edwards, and George Varney. In 1885 he persuaded Edward F. Payne to come down and join the group. No more high-powered aggregation of rodbuilding talent has ever since been assembled under one roof. These men were so skilled individually that each except Varney eventually started a rod business of his own.

The H. L. Leonard Rod Company in its new location was just 50 miles north of Mills's store and only 25 miles east of the famed Catskill rivers that were to be the proving grounds for Leonard's emerging series of new rod designs. According to rod historian Martin Keane, the "first and foremost of the early super-Leonards was his Catskill series, which featured the lightest and daintiest rods available." The "Catskill" came out in 1883 at 9½ feet and 4⅝ ounces, followed by the "Petite Catskill" in 1890 at 9¼ feet and 3⅛ ounces, only to be topped in 1894 by the wispy "Fairy Catskill" at 8⅙ feet and an incredibly light two ounces. A number of these were shipped to England and the Catskill series in general was a major force in popularizing lightweight fly rods.

By the turn of the century, in response to the growing use of dry flies, Leonard designed a series of new rod tapers and came out with a battery of fast-recovery dry-fly rods which caught on quickly among his clientele. On the wings of William Mills's publicity and salesmanship, the Leonard name soared to fame among anglers. He bragged justifiably: "My rods took the first prize at Vienna, London, and at the world's fair, Philadelphia, and in all contests for fly, or bait casting, they lead the world."

Perhaps the highest praise he received was bestowed on Leonard by G.E.M. Skues, the noted English author and wet-fly authority. He became a faithful Leonard customer and was so fond of one particular nine-footer that he often referred to it in his angling books as "W.B.R."—the World's Best Rod.

For unknown reasons, most of Leonard's skilled employees left him in 1889 and 1890 to make rods on their own. Measured by years in business and rods produced, by far the most successful of these men was EDWARD F. PAYNE. After working with various combinations of partners and owners, Payne bought controlling interest in his business and moved it in 1898 to Highland Mills, New York, just two miles up the road from his old employer in Central Valley.

Ed Payne won acclaim for his precision craftsmanship and close attention to the finest details in a custom rod. His all-silver full-metal reel seats were so highly polished and elegantly formed that they ranked in a class with fine jewelry. The rods themselves were immaculately varnished, accented in silk by his hallmark jasper-and-red-tipped windings, with the glue lines so well concealed that the cane strips appeared to have grown together conveniently in their hexagonal, tapered sections.

Ed Payne made a special rod for Theodore Gordon around 1895—a 9½-footer, three pieces, with a wet-fly action. Gordon tied thirty-nine dozen trout flies to pay for it. In 1912, he gave it to Herman Christian, saying, "I don't know of anybody who would appreciate it as much as you would." Christian fished with it until the late 1940s and then sold it back to the E. F. Payne Rod Co. for its museum. Wendle Collins bought E. F. Payne shortly after that and eventually presented the rod to The Anglers' Club of New York, where it was destroyed in a display case along with several other historic rods by a terrorist's bomb in 1975.

JIM PAYNE began as an apprentice in his father's Highland Mills shop when he was ten years old. In 1914, when he was 21, his father died and Jim took over the family rodmaking business. Like his father, Jim Payne was a perfectionist, always looking for ways to improve his rods. Soon after he was on his own, young Payne invented a special tool, sort of a hot-iron clamp, with which he squeezed the leaf nodes down into line with the rest of the cane strip, thereby avoiding the filing away and weakening of the strip. Other rodmakers copied the idea for a while, but then gave it up as too time-consuming.

Over the next ten years, Payne developed a two-step process of flame tempering and oven curing the bamboo strips that made his rods considerably more resilient and powerful. The heat treatments also turned his rods a rich, deep brown, a characteristic that came to distinguish Payne rods from those of his competitors.

Other innovations by Jim Payne included, in 1925, a locking reelseat designed mainly by new employee and master metalsmith George Halstead; a new generation of "parabolic action" fly rods in the 1930s, based on the suggestions of French angler and rod designer Charles Ritz; a series of special-purpose rods for canoe casting and another series for streamer fishing. He even built a four-foot-four-inch "Banty Payne," presumably to suit a woman angler with designs on large steelhead.

Jim Payne was a well-known figure on Catskill streams. His fishing friends included Ed Hewitt, Roy Steenrod, and two up-and-coming rodmakers, Pinky Gillum and Everett Garrison. He also fished with and made rods for A. E. Hendrickson. In fact, Hendrickson was Jim Payne's biggest customer, especially during the Depression. There was most likely a feeling of compassion for a fellow angler whose orders were running thin, but Hendrickson was a perfectionist himself, and he once had Jim Payne build forty-eight ten-foot salmon rods before he was finally satisfied with No. 48.

Jim Payne walked out of his shop in May of 1968 saying that he didn't know when he would be back. He died a month later after sixty-four years of rodmaking. Together with his father, their joint careers in the E. F. Payne Rod Company spanned ninety-two years and resulted in some of the finest split-cane rods ever made.

H. S. "PINKY" GILLUM learned how to make rods pretty much on his own. After a brief indoctrination by expert rodmaker Bill Edwards—one of Hiram Leonard's original "Central Valley Six"—Gillum progressed steadily in his own self-reliant manner to become an extraordinarily talented rodbuilder. The way he became an instant flytier was typical of Gillum's independence and determination: two weeks after a single half-hour lesson from Harry Darbee, Gillum returned with flies of such exceptional quality that Harry tried to persuade him to be a flytying professional also.

From his rod shop in Ridgefield, Connecticut, Pinky Gillum turned out some two thousand rods from 1923 to 1966. Gillum was working on three rods the day he died; his wife Winnie finished and delivered them. He was not primarily an innovator, but he probably had no peer for consistent output of top-quality bamboo rods. With his wife as his only helper, he did everything himself except make his own ferrules; when he strung up a finished rod to try it on the lawn, if he didn't like it, he was known occasionally to take the rod apart, hold the sections together, and break them over his knee. Such persistence extended even to his feelings about how customers used his rods. "They are buying two weeks of my life," he would say, and if he could tell that a rod had been damaged through wanton neglect, Pinky simply refused to repair it. On one occasion he yanked a brand-new Gillum away from a startled angler who was jerking it to free a hung-up fly, gave him back his money, and stalked off the stream.

Pinky Gillum could best be understood as a professional's professional. He was truly at ease with only the most knowledgeable anglers who knew and could appreciate what he was trying to achieve. He would not give interviews to outdoor writers and did not believe in advertising. He felt that a good product would advertise itself and, in the case of Gillum fly rods, this was admirably true. After the first few years of rodbuilding, he always had more orders than he could fill. Harry Darbee's fly shop in Roscoe was Gillum's only "official" retail outlet.

The list of famous anglers who were loyal Gillum customers is long. Jack Atherton—angler, author, and artist—said, "If I could have only one rod, I would ask Pinky Gillum to make it for me." Harry Darbee fished with one Gillum rod that he would never consider selling. "This rod I'm taking in my coffin," he said. "They say there's fishing in the Styx."

Gillum was a loner and very secretive about his rodbuilding methods; he had no protégé. When he died, his widow sold Gillum's "book of tapers," equipment, and Tonkin cane to rodmaker Minert Hull.

For EVERETT GARRISON, rodmaking began as a hobby and became an all-consuming avocation. He had grown up in Yonkers, New York, and fished the Esopus as a boy. Throughout the 1920s, he made bamboo rods for his own use. Then Garrison had the good fortune to meet his neighbor, Dr. George Parker Holden, who made and collected rods and had written a definitive book on them, *The Idyl of the Split-Bamboo*. Holden's encouragement and knowledge from having studied the great master Hiram Leonard's techniques were invaluable to Garrison in his early rodmaking efforts.

The turning point came with the Depression when Garrison and his fishing friend Vernon Heyney both lost their jobs at the New York Central Railroad. Heyney went to the Beaverkill to live and fish; Garrison went down to his basement to make rods. His degree and professional background as a structural engineer then came into full play as he took on the ambitious task of scientifically redesigning the split-bamboo rod. Rodmakers before Garrison had worked out their rod actions and tapers by trial and error, but Garrison undertook nothing less than a full-scale analysis of the physical properties of bamboo, its capabilities and limitations under stress, and the resulting rod tapers for different kinds of fishing which could produce in each case the most efficient delivery of the fly.

Besides the tapers, which Garrison calculated in thousandths of an inch, there had to be a delicate balance between the cane and its moisture content, the glue, ferrules, guides, windings, and finish. Garrison called the rod action that resulted from all these components working in harmony a "progressive action." What this means is that at the moment the power stroke begins, the energy passing from the wrist into the lowest flexing point in the rod should travel at an absolutely even speed but with steadily diminishing force up the rod into the unfolding line until the leader has straightened out, the fly is over its target, and the force has diminished to zero.

By midsummer of 1932, Garrison had fashioned two eight-foot rods based on his new theories. One he gave to John Alden Knight, of Solunar Table renown, the other he sent to Vernon Heyney on the Beaverkill. Heyney had difficulty getting used to the new action, so accustomed was he to the conven-

Vernon Heyney holding the first rod designed and made by Everett Garrison, who sent it up to Heyney on the Beaverkill for testing in 1933. The rod was so successful that everyone Heyney showed it to wanted one also, resulting in forty orders for Garrison before the summer was over. *Courtesy Hoagy B. Carmichael.*

tional tapers of his favorite Payne rods, but he persisted and, with adjustments in his casting, he eventually laid aside his Paynes and became a permanent Garrison convert. By the end of the summer, Heyney had proselytized enough friends and acquaintances on the stream to send Garrison more than forty orders for identical rods.

Dan Brenan, from Syracuse, a fine rodmaker in his own right, was one of Heyney's converts. Brenan thought the new Garrison was "a sweetheart: trim, neat, superbly finished, and with a masculinity of action that belies the svelte femininity of appearance."

The Garrison rod was indeed more powerful than it looked. Its moderately tapered grip, light straw color, transparent windings, and visible glue lines between strips all conveyed an image of functional austerity. Nothing went into the rod that did not enhance its performance. It was what you would expect from an engineering genius bent on creating the ultimate casting instrument.

The Riverkeepers

Strictly speaking, a "riverkeeper" is an Englishman charged with the welfare of a stretch of some hallowed chalk stream or salmon river. In this country, we have stream watchers and caretakers. However, more broadly defined, anyone can be a riverkeeper who loves the river and the fishing enough to protect and improve them. In that sense, Catskill rivers have given rise to a long line of champion riverkeepers.

Collectively, the PRIVATE OWNERS of the upper Beaverkill, Willowemoc, and Neversink have protected their headwaters since the late 1800s. Because of these individuals and clubs, there has been less fishing, logging, and pollution, and the upper watersheds of these rivers have been sustained as prime spawning grounds for trout.

The same angling pressure that led to the forming of private preserves also brought on a decline in the trout population, all too often from abuses by greedy fishermen. The keeping of undersized fish got so bad that "a few choice angling spirits" got together in 1892 and formed "THE FISH AND GAME PROTECTIVE ASSOCIATION OF SULLIVAN COUNTY, N.Y."

The incorporators of this association included Abe Snedecor, Brooklyn, and James Rice, New York, both of whom three years later were founding members of the Fly Fishers Club of Brooklyn; William C. Harris, New York, editor and publisher of *The American Angler*; "Gum" Dodge, Rockland, local tavern keeper; Jay Davidson, Beaverkill, owner of Trout Valley Farm, a fishing hotel; and Theodore Gordon, Neversink.

The purpose of the Sullivan County association was to select six wardens who would be deputized as assistant state game protectors "with full power to arrest and prosecute any parties" who fished out of season or by illegal methods or took trout of less than six inches. There was no creel limit in those days. Two wardens each would be placed on the Beaverkill, Willowemoc, and Neversink

The last of the big rocks at Painter's Bend being dynamited to keep it from snagging wayward trees and diverting the river into the far roadside bank. Before World War I, a row of these rocks provided a crossing place for the panthers ("painters" to the old-timers) that still roamed the Catskills. *Photo by Francis W. Davis.*

rivers. The group also selected men who were permanent residents living near the rivers as members of its executive committee, and involved itself in promoting rearing ponds for trout fry provided by the state.

One man who needed no encouragement to build rearing ponds was ED HEWITT, riverkeeper par excellence. The story of his fisheries management ingenuity and Neversink preserve is told in two other chapters. A poignant episode involving Hewitt's fish occurred in 1944, illustrating the difficulties often faced by private owners of ponds and streams. In a letter to Elsie Darbee while Harry was away during the war, Hewitt poured out his heart:

> Since you were here poachers got into my place and stole most of my trout from my ponds and pools. They must have taken 4,000 in all. We know who stole the fish but did not catch them.
>
> It is plain that I can't raise fish here anymore to stock the stream as I can't afford such losses, and I can't afford a night watchman even if I could get one. I am going to dismantle all my ponds now and cease raising fish. If the local population want it this way they can have it. I may buy a few fish to put in the stream if I get enough Rods but this is doubtful. The thing I mind most is that they took all my Norwegian salmon which cost so much to bring over and raise. I have only two or three left. This loss alone amounts to over $500.
>
> I hate to stop raising trout and improving the fishing but there is nothing else to do. I can get what fishing I want anyway without

any stocking. I have certainly improved the Neversink fishing in the last dozen years quite a lot and this is a poor reward for what I have done for the River.

Actually, Hewitt bounced back in typical fashion and maintained his Neversink water even after New York City had condemned two-thirds of it for a reservoir.

As a Catskill riverkeeper, ELLIS NEWMAN was without question unique. He took care of the Marks's water on the upper Beaverkill, both for Arthur Marks, president of the Skinner Organ Company, and for Mrs. Marks after her husband died. Newman was so dedicated to the family and the river that he had his own cottage and fishing-guest privileges.

In the winters, Newman taught hunting and marksmanship in Florida. He was an expert wing shot, and owned a fine collection of shotguns. But when it came to a fly rod, said *The New York Times* columnist John Randolph, "Newman can do anything except conjugate verbs, and he hasn't tried that. He winds up casting without even the rod." And that's not all, folks. Listen to Red Smith describe this feat:

Wetting the fingertips of one hand so the line would run between them as through the guides on a rod, he laid out incredible lengths of line, right-handed, left-handed, side arm, overhand, throwing curves and screwballs and drops and upshoots and pitches that halted in midair and doubled back.

A woodchuck came out from under the barn, watched for a while in disbelief, shook his head, and waddled with great dignity back under the barn.

Newman was under the impression that he would inherit the Marks property. He had plans to take in a few paying guests each season and teach

Ellis Newman could cast an entire fly line using only his hands. Said Red Smith of Newman's casting, "He laid out incredible lengths of line, right-handed, left-handed, side arm, overhand, throwing curves and screwballs and drops and upshoots and pitches that halted in midair and doubled back." *Courtesy Harry Darbee.*

shooting and casting. Shortly after Mrs. Marks passed away and the entire property went to a non-fishing relative, Newman was killed by the blast from one of his shotguns. No one ever determined for sure whether or not it was an accident.

ART FLICK more or less got forced into being a riverkeeper. When he arrived in the Schoharie valley in 1934, it was with the intent of taking over his parents' inn and running it especially for fly fishermen and grouse hunters. First he found the river so full of bass that the trout were being crowded out. For the next five years, Flick lobbied and cajoled the state into building a barrier dam to confine the bass to the lower river and the Schoharie reservoir. He persuaded landowners to donate land for the dam abutments. Then he kept after the state to pass a special no-limit regulation applying to Schoharie bass only. In the end, he beat back the bass enough to restore the trout fishing to acceptable levels.

Savoring these encounters on behalf of the river, Flick pushed on to become an adept fishing politician. His influence grew steadily, first as president of the Catskill Mountain Fish and Game Club, then as president of the Greene County Federation of Sportsmen's Clubs, until he became vice president of the New York State Conservation Council. In this capacity, and working on his own, he helped start on Schoharie Creek one of the state's earliest public-fishing-rights acquisition programs. In 1962, largely through his efforts, New York's first no-kill fishing section was established on the Schoharie.

On a more personal basis, Flick and his two sons began a riverkeeping venture in the 1940s by planting willow seedlings to protect the banks of the West Kill, a ritual that he has continued each spring to the present day.

When HARRY DARBEE passed through his teens and started caring for the rivers and his native Catskills as much as he cared for fishing, he did so under the tutelage of Richard "Pop" Robbins. Once a wealthy club fisherman before his health and finances declined, Robbins retired to Roscoe as a fishing guide. He saw in Darbee a reflection of his own love of rivers and independent spirit. These traits moved Darbee, in later years, to become a determined conservation fighter.

To protect their hunting and fishing from a mounting series of threats, Darbee and his friends founded the Beaverkill-Willowemoc Rod and Gun Club of Roscoe, a small but feisty organization that lasted until the early 1960s. Its mascot was the Beamoc, a two-headed brown trout that lives in Junction Pool.

Rallied behind this fabulous creature, Elsie and Harry Darbee and their friends fought with the dam builders, the DDT sprayers, the streambed gravel-mongers, and the highway engineers. They won the dam fight. Of all the prime Catskill trout streams—Schoharie, Esopus, Mongaup, Rondout, Neversink, East and West branches of the Delaware, Beaverkill, and Willowemoc—only the last two have not been dammed.

They won the DDT fight by enlisting the aid of their scientist friends from Cornell. On the day the Neversink was sprayed, their troops were deployed up and down the river. Specimens of trout killed by eating the contaminated insects were gathered and presented as evidence in a movement

Editorial cartoon by Francis W. Davis that appeared in newspapers when the Catskill angling community realized there was no hope of preventing a superhighway from running alongside and criss-crossing more than twenty miles of prime trout water on the Willowemoc and Beaverkill. *Courtesy Harry Darbee.*

that quickly curtailed further spraying. And they won against the bulldozing of the stream for gravel to build roads and supply other local public-works projects. They influenced the drafting of a much stronger Stream Protection Law, which has nearly eliminated these streambed ravagings.

But the Darbees and the Beamoc lost their bitterest fight, an effort to stop a superhighway from running more or less down the riverbed, disrupting and defacing twenty-two miles of lovely pools and runs on the lower Willowemoc and Beaverkill. Sparse Grey Hackle saw it happen:

> It was a savage fight, from which both the State and the Darbees bear scars. The Darbees lost, but they delayed the actual construction of that stretch for seven long years, and a lot of politicians, tame engineers, contractors and Highway Department placemen knew they had been in a fight.

The Publicists

There are many streams in America more densely populated with trout and productive of more trophy catches than the Beaverkill. But none are more famous.

Promoting Catskill trout fishing has come a long way if this photograph, taken on the Schoharie for state fisheries publicity purposes, is any indication. Examine it carefully. How many bogus ingredients can *you* discover? *Photographer unknown.*

From THAD NORRIS and JOHN BURROUGHS in the 1860s down to modern times, the Beaverkill and other Catskill streams have cast a continuing spell on American angling writers. All the ingredients were there—natural beauty, pure waters, restive trout, top professionals—and the publicists rounded it out by giving them a coherent image, by documenting the birth of fly fishing in America.

The first sporting periodical in this country devoted entirely to fishing was *The American Angler.* It was published in New York City by William C. Harris from 1881 to 1900. Austin S. Hogan, director emeritus of The Museum of American Fly Fishing, called it "the most important to fishermen of all our 19th century periodicals."

Once a week, subscribers to *The American Angler* could read about their favorite streams. BEN BENT, ROBIN RUFF, AND S. K. PUTNAM reported regularly on the Catskills in such articles as "The Best of the Beaverkill," "How to Fish the Lower Beaverkill," "The Beaverkill Last Season," "Trouting Near New York—The Neversink and Streams of the Catskills," and "The Delaware and How to Fish It."

A generation of early American anglers was sustained between outings by settling down with the likes of Robin Ruff: "I well remember the first time I fished this part of the Beaverkill. It was early morning, and having started in at the upper edge of Weaver's farm, I had come down to the bend pool without having raised a fish. While standing there and changing my cast of flies . . ." Another report might indicate that "the fish of the Beaverkill are not rising well to the feathers"; or to entice the reader, an article might open, "Fishermen who fancy they must worry a few trout on Opening Day may gratify their desires . . ."

The quality and credibility of angling correspondents varied tremendously in the early days of American fly fishing. Many of the articles were

Title-page illustration for an article in *The American Angler*, "the most important to fishermen of all our nineteenth-century periodicals." Given the size of the angler and the implied scale of the East Branch of the Neversink—a small and intimate stream—artists were as prone to exaggeration as were the fishermen themselves. *Artist's name illegible*.

unpaid contributions sent in by fishermen who wanted to see their names in print. Or, if they were being paid to promote a certain river, as was KIT CLARKE by the Erie Railroad, it could result in overstated if colorful reporting:

> Some day some one will learn how to reduce gold to flow like ink, and dipping his pen in this glowing liquid he will exhaust the English language in an effort to justly describe the beauty of the glorious upper Delaware, for of a truth to do it justice would bankrupt our mother tongue.

Clarke more often wrote newspaper fishing columns than railroad pamphlets; in the former he was more rational. Interestingly, Kit Clarke lived very near Louis Rhead in Brooklyn, and the two men, besides their shared commercial interest in fly fishing, enjoyed weakfishing together in Flatlands Bay.

As an angling publicist, THEODORE GORDON was at the other end of the spectrum from Kit Clarke. In his many articles for America's *Forest and Stream* and England's *Fishing Gazette*, Gordon wrote in the simplest language of his daily experiences on the stream. He believed that "experience is the greatest teacher," and hoped that his "random notes and recollections" would remind other fishermen of their interesting experiences and induce them to write also.

Gordon never pretended to be an authority on fly fishing and considered his "jottings" to be merely "chronicles of small events." In a 1909 letter to G.E.M. Skues, he seemed unaware that he had built up such a large following of readers in twenty years of reporting from his favorite Catskill streams:

> "Little Talks about Fly Fishing" were only a series of articles written mostly on the stream and published in *Forest and Stream*. It is funny that I should have had inquiries for them in book form and that publishers should have wished me to write a book. The things are just simple little gabbles or talks.

ED HEWITT's considerable achievements on the Neversink in fish culture and stream improvement were rivaled by his ability to publicize them, as he readily acknowledged:

> My book, *Better Trout Streams*, was the first book on improving trout waters and was instrumental in starting the movement to make better conditions for trout life which has spread so widely over this country. I feel that in focussing public attention on the environment of trout in streams, I performed a real service to my fellow fishermen.

Coming from SPARSE GREY HACKLE, full-time professional publicist, the following generous admiration of Hewitt's talent with words rose to lofty heights of its own:

> I always maintained that, if he had been born poor, Ed Hewitt would have made the greatest feature writer in the world. As a speaker and writer of the King's English he had a genius—nothing less—for structure and summary, and a keen sense of the right word. He was a master at making scientific things comprehensible to the layman, and he had a gift for the unqualified statement, flat as a board and just as unvarnished. He could make the truth sound like a lie, which always makes for better reading and arouses controversy, and this was part of his talent for getting publicity.

Sparse was a steady contributor for more than forty-five years to The Anglers' Club *Bulletin*, an astounding record. Only recently retired and now ninety, he served as its editor, either with or without title, for most of that period. He wrote angling articles for *Sports Illustrated, Outdoor Life, Harper's,* and numerous other publications. He was guest columnist for Red Smith when Red was in a bind. And

The redoubtable Sparse Grey Hackle, chronicler of the golden era of Catskill angling, and occasional stand-in for his friend, columnist Red Smith, who once said, "Sparse Grey Hackle? Oh, yes—courtly, portly, deeply evil." *Photo by Hermann Kessler.*

he preserved beautifully many of the events and personalities from a seminal era of Catskill angling in *Fishless Days, Angling Nights*. Here from the endpiece of that book is the essence of his genius as a chronicler of the times:

> Golden to me was the decade on the Neversink that ended with 1940. Edward Ringwood Hewitt had some five miles of the river between Neversink Village and Hall's Mills, and his fishing "camp" was an old farmhouse on high ground overlooking the largest flat along that part of the valley. Here the "rods" who rented annual fishing privileges used to assemble at the end of the day for unforgettable nights of fun and companionship and fishing conversation.

> And what a goodly company was there, the choicest spirits of the angling age, the finest sportsmen, the best fishermen, the liveliest wits, the best-stored minds; the kindest and most helpful, too, as we novices quickly learned, and of course the best of teachers. Here was no stupid competition for big baskets, no vulgar boasting and lying, none of the boozing and gambling that are traditional in some camps. These were the spiritual descendants of Walton, Norris, Hills, Prime, and Marston, and the atmosphere was the sublimated atmosphere of The Anglers' or the Flyfishers'.

The Catskills have had many champions in print. RAY CAMP, former outdoor columnist for *The New York Times*, loved the Schoharie. He considered it a fragile stream and disguised it as the "West Kill," one of its tributaries, when he wrote of his outings there. RAY BERGMAN, columnist for *Outdoor Life* and author of the original *Trout*—the all-time best seller of American angling books—lived in Nyack, New York, *and* in the trout streams of the Catskills. One of his favorites was the North Branch of Callicoon Creek, a tributary of the Delaware River. Many of the experiences and anecdotes in *Trout* are taken from Bergman's Catskill fishing trips.

ARNOLD GINGRICH, founding editor of *Esquire*, could be located on many of his days off fishing below Five Arch Bridge on the Esopus. He was a member for two years of Ed Hewitt's Big Bend Club on the Neversink. And he was "more or less the constant guest" over five fishing seasons of Al McClane on the upper Beaverkill. His reminiscences of these Catskill experiences, including a humbling encounter with Preston Jennings on the Esopus, are part of his book *The Well-Tempered Angler*. Besides his own writings on fishing, Gingrich encouraged many others to make lasting contributions to the literature of the sport.

In the May 1946 issue of *Fortune* magazine, a most unlikely place, there appeared a long, deeply researched, engagingly written article on the development of American angling and flytying. The author was the magazine's associate editor JOHN McDONALD, who had persuaded *Fortune*'s editor-in-chief that many corporate executives were also fly fishermen and would enjoy such an article. The payoff was the rediscovery of Theodore Gordon, whose articles and letters had lain forgotten for thirty years, and the realization that Gordon should henceforth be recognized as "the father of modern American fly fishing."

Full documentation came the following year when Scribner's published McDonald's sensitively edited collection of Gordon's notes and letters under the title *The Complete Fly Fisherman*, restoring Theodore Gordon permanently to public view.

RED SMITH is probably the greatest sports columnist of all time. Although he usually wrote on the major sports, as demanded by the average reader of *The New York Times*, where he last appeared, Smith occasionally slipped in a column on fishing. When he did, there was something special about the way he presented his subject that distinguished these columns from all the rest. The reason was that Red Smith was a dedicated fly fisherman. It was his favorite

A gathering of publicists, riverkeepers and flytiers—fishermen all—on the Marks water of the upper Beaverkill. Harry Darbee and Ellis Newman are talking in the background, as Elsie Darbee reaches to tie on a fly for Red Smith. Looking on are Red's brother Art, back to camera, and Lawton Carver. *Photo by Joan Sydlow.*

sport. He also had a favorite river. Should anyone doubt which river this was, or who was the paragon of angling publicists, let him reflect on these words:

> One stormy April night three men rode out of the darkness into the streets of the Catskills village of Roscoe. "Gentlemen," said Sparse Grey Hackle, "remove your hats. This is it."
>
> "This is where the trout was invented?" the driver asked.
>
> "Oh," Mr. Hackle said, "he existed in a crude, primitive form in Walton's England—"
>
> "But this," said Meade Schaeffer, artist and angler, "is where they painted spots on him and taught him to swim."
>
> It was the eve of Opening Day of the New York trout season. It can be said without irreverence that to celebrate Opening Day on the Beaverkill is a little like observing Christmas in Bethlehem. For the Beaverkill is the shrine, the fountainhead, the most beloved and best-known trout stream in America, the river of George LaBranche, Theodore Gordon, Guy Jenkins and the Flyfishers Club of Brooklyn.

FIVE

Women Anglers of the Catskills

The best chum I ever had in fishing was a girl, and she tramped just as hard and fished quite as patiently as any man I ever knew.

—THEODORE GORDON

She wore a tam-ó-shanter, sweater, short jacket, and skirts, with stout shoes and leggings, and waded, as did Gordon, without waterproofs. As she fished, her long skirts caressed the ripples, creating the illusion that she moved along on the surface of the stream. We never learned her name; only that she was a visitor around 1895 in the Catskills. By the time Gordon met other fishing friends on the Neversink, she had already left him—"very much disappointed in love," said Herman Christian. Gordon remained a bachelor for the rest of his life.

Ahead of his time as he was in many other aspects of angling, Gordon looked beyond his loss and welcomed the entry of women into an almost exclusively male sport. He was surprised that more women did not go fishing, noting that they were usually great enthusiasts when they did. He greatly admired the modern sporting woman:

> The ideal heroine nowadays is far removed from the wasp-waisted, die-away creature of the early portion of the last century. The girl of the twentieth century is a fine upstanding woman, with a flat back, large frame, and the limbs of a Juno.

Women were rarely seen on American trout streams until after World War I. When the more courageous female anglers ventured forth, they did so at

Here are the only two fishing photographs known to exist of Theodore Gordon, both taken around 1895 with the unnamed woman who left him "very much disappointed in love." The setting is believed to be in front of Chandler's boardinghouse a few hundred feet above the old Neversink bridge. *Courtesy Louise and Alfred W. Miller, John McDonald, and Roy Steenrod.*

their peril, not knowing if they would be ridiculed, ignored, or treated as invaders of a male domain.

Fred White, who began fishing at Jay Davidson's Trout Valley Farm on the upper Beaverkill at about the same time Gordon was escorting his "best chum" around the Neversink, witnessed the emergence of women anglers. In 1923, he looked back on twenty-five years of Beaverkill fishing with a certain amount of ambivalence regarding women anglers:

> I remember distinctly the first woman at Beaverkill to put on boots and, even with a knee length skirt, dare to brave the disapproval of the porch sitters at Davidson's. It simply wasn't done and she came pretty near being regarded as fast as the water that rippled about her knees. Now the river is full of 'em and they don't bother with skirts either. And they catch fish—some of them—and big ones, too.
>
> Whether you like it or not the women are here to stay in trout fishing as on the golf course and at the ballot box, and when all is said and done, I believe it to be an excellent thing—for the women. They can wear my second best waders any time.

From these hesitant beginnings and lukewarm acceptances, women anglers advanced gradually but were always outnumbered on Catskill trout streams. In the early days, a pioneering woman could never be sure what she would encounter in an angling environment. There is an anecdote that appeared in the history of one of the Catskill trout clubs about an incident involving their sole woman member. It took place in the days when the lighting was furnished by large oil lamps and there was no illumination on the porches.

> One night the only woman who had ever been a member walked out of the rod room and in the darkness stepped off the porch, falling three or four feet to the lawn below. George with his lantern rushed to her aid. He picked up her glasses, her plates, and a false front. Then innocently, perhaps curiously, he asked her, "Anything else?" Fortunately this was before the era when women thought that a bustle added to the symmetry and charm of the female figure.
>
> Thereafter twisted ropes were run from post to post, not to provide clotheslines for wet socks and waders, but to protect lovely, but possibly synthetic, ladies from similar mishaps.

Presumably true, this anecdote was written around 1940 and illustrates both the exasperation a fly-fishing woman sometimes faced as well as the prevailing view of femininity in the fishing camp. It is probably also true that this particular woman was no longer a member when the account was published.

Louise Miller so impressed her husband Sparse Grey Hackle with her

This pioneering woman angler is the one who waded into the Beaverkill and dared to brave the disapproval of the porch sitters at Davidson's Trout Valley Farm. According to Frederick White, "she came pretty near being regarded as fast as the water that rippled about her knees." *Courtesy The Anglers' Club* Bulletin.

mastery of fly fishing and devotion to the sport that he named her "Lady Beaverkill." It was very natural therefore that Sparse should become a keen observer of women as anglers.

Sparse credits the dry fly with luring women onto the stream, noting that the coming of the dry fly into general popularity coincides approximately with the coming of the woman angler. Indeed, he advances the argument that "dry-fly fishing is more a woman's than a man's game."

What are the requirements? Dexterity and good coordination, fast and well-controlled reflexes, a light and sensitive touch, keen eyesight, and close concentration. Any industrial personnel man will assure you that women are greatly superior to men in these respects.

Joan Wulff is exceptionally well qualified to judge the abilities of women anglers; for sixteen years she was women's national fly-casting champion, and today she and her husband Lee run a fly-fishing school on the Beaverkill. There each season they teach casting and the essentials of angling to about forty women and one hundred and sixty men. Observing her male and female students over the years, Joan has noticed these differences:

"Ah, it is spring, the river is full and troutsome; what better way to celebrate modern womanhood than by joining the anglers down on the Beaverkill!" *Photo at Junction Pool around 1920, courtesy Ray Pomeroy, Winnie and Walt Dette.*

Physical strength. Men can wade in rougher water and cast a longer line than women. This is a factor on big rivers and under windy conditions. Perhaps this is why the smaller, more sheltered rivers of the Catskills have a special appeal for women anglers.

Coordination. Joan agrees with Sparse that women are more natural fly casters because they have a better sense of rhythm and timing. "It's like dancing," she says. "When you get that rod loaded behind you, it is a perfect feeling of balance, weight, and the force you've exerted—a beautiful flow of line that you feel right down to your toes."

Concentration. "I don't see this as a male or female trait. I've seen lots of men who can't fish much longer than an hour without a break, and women who can fish all day without knowing where the time went, and vice versa. You either have it, or you don't."

Capacity to learn. "Women who have reasonable strength in their hands learn to cast much more easily than men because they listen to what you say. They are not handicapped by ego the way most men are."

Outdoor confidence. "This is something boys usually acquire growing up, the feeling of being at home with the forces of water and wind, all the discomforts of nature. When wading in strong currents, a man seems instinctively to understand the river's hydraulics while a woman feels the river is bigger than she is and that she has to fight for control."

Joan has noticed an increasing number of women taking up fly fishing. As they become more independent financially, they are seeking the same leisure sports that were once considered male preserves. Also, more married couples are coming to the Wulff School because they want to do things together rather than have the wife stuck at home not knowing how to cast or tie on a fly.

"I have always felt that fishing is a very good testing ground for marriage," said Joan. "If you fish well with someone, you can live with them."

"When did you develop that?" asked one of her students.

"Years ago; and it's been consistently true. Because when you are fishing, whatever you are shows."

"What sort of things do you mean?"

"Like who catches the most fish, how you handle that. How you handle who's going to fish the best area first. Whether you get joy out of the other person's catching fish. Whether you can handle difficulty without complaining. All of these things show up quickly in fishing, and if they show up there, they are going to show up in many of the other areas of life."

*   *   *

Jane Smith was sitting in the Icelandic Airlines lounge at the Reykjavik airport waiting for her husband and their flight back to New York. It was the summer of 1975 and they had been fishing salmon on the Leirasveit. Another fisherman came along and, noticing her rod case, engaged in the usual where-and-what-luck conversation. He further noticed that she was wearing a gold pin with a fly on it.

"What kind of a fly is that?" he asked.

"A Rat-faced McDougall," she answered.

"Is that a club emblem?"

"Yes, the Woman Flyfishers Club."

"What is this club anyway, a woman's lib organization?"

Mrs. Smith pulled herself erect in her seat, and in measured tones, replied, "We are a club incorporated in 1932. Our members are all dedicated women fly fishers. We have our own clubhouse and water and we fish all over the world."

The Woman Flyfishers Club was conceived by Julia Freeman Fairchild, Frank Hovey-Roof Connell, and Mary Ashley Hewitt as a way of extending the enjoyment they got from fishing with their husbands, two of whom were members of The Anglers' Club of New York. As recalled by Mrs. Fairchild, one day in 1931 all six of them were seated on the porch at "Wintoon," the fishing preserve assembled by Clarence Roof in the early 1880s on the West Branch of the Neversink. "We started talking about how much fun the men had in their club," said Mrs. Fairchild, "and we said, 'Let's form a club of our own!' So, a small group of us got together at the Hewitts' downstream on the main Neversink and made up a list of women we knew who enjoyed fishing. Later that year we had the details worked out and on January 28, 1932, we were officially incorporated with thirty-three founding members."

The Woman Flyfishers Club gathered for their 1955 Outing at the Campfire Club. Kneeling: Talia Manser, Connie Terry, Martha Bulkley, Ann Ordway. Standing: Julia Fairchild, Vega Juhring, Jane Smith, Gladys Straus, Betty Jennings, Margaret Walbridge, Martha Averett, Mary Geyer, Candace Stevenson. *Courtesy The Woman Flyfishers Club.*

The Woman Flyfishers Club, with Julia Fairchild as its first president, was an instant success. The following year they raised their dues and took in twenty-two more members. Quite a few of the members had husbands or fathers who fished and who owned private water or belonged to fishing clubs; so even though they had no headquarters of their own at first, they received invitations right away to fish many of the choicest streams of the Northeast. Ironically, the husbands rarely got to fish each other's water, which led one of them, Dr. Whittington Gorham, to nickname his wife and her clubmates "The Lady Wanglers."

Mrs. Fairchild and her directors had been searching from the outset for a "home pool" for their fellow members, and in 1936 they found it on the upper Willowemoc, above its junction with Fir Brook. As she remembers it:

> The property belonged to Mrs. Walter Bolling of Alabama and was about to be sold for taxes. She was very ill at the time and the negotiations were tedious and prolonged but we finally got

possession. Along with the lease we inherited a caretaker who could talk more and do less than any one I ever knew.

The Bolling place contained 265 acres and one mile of stream. Three more miles of private water were made available through the courtesy of the Willowemoc Fishing Club. By 1937 the women had hired a new caretaker, fixed up the house, stocked the stream, and they were in business. Until 1946, the Willowemoc was the home of the Woman Flyfishers Club. Then Mrs. Bolling came back, terminated their lease, and reclaimed her house. Said Mrs. Fairchild, "We had a lot of fun there and left it with regret, especially as we had no home to go to and the future looked dim."

To the rescue came Ed Hewitt, who had a soft spot for women anglers. He had heard of some water in the valley next to the Neversink, and quickly arranged a merger for the homeless anglers with new landlords in a "little red house" on Sundown Creek, a tributary of the Rondout. Unfortunately, the fishing turned out to be disappointing, especially as the stream had not been posted until the Flyfishers took over, and they would often arrive "just in time to see a poacher sneaking away with a heavy string of trout trailing a large hook festooned with worms."

Discomfort on the Sundown led to restlessness, to continued searching, and finally to the West Branch of the Neversink, less than two miles upstream from where the club was born. In 1950, Frank Connell graciously offered the upper end of her Neversink water complete with clubhouse to her fellow members, and the women anglers came home to their native stream. They are there still, over eighty members strong, having recently observed their fiftieth anniversary.

Ed Hewitt—shown here with Grace Vanderbilt Davis on his Neversink water—loved teaching women to fish. He also taught his daughter Candace and the daughter of Mabel Ingalls, to whom he said, "You know, Mabel, it will be a great resource for her later on." *Photo by Henry G. Davis.*

Catskill Rivers

A member of the Woman Flyfishers Club excites a great deal of curiosity when it is revealed that she belongs to the only organization of female fly fishers in the world. She is often asked, for example, how she got started fishing.

"Most women fishermen come from sporting families," said Jane Smith, current president of the Flyfishers. "It's a rare woman who goes out and becomes a fisherman by herself. I fished with my father as a child."

"What started me fishing?" pondered another woman angler. "Love wielding a fly rod; four years later I cast well enough to marry."

Mabel Ingalls did her first fishing around 1915 at summer camp in the Adirondacks. She remembers catching two small fish, on dropper flies, on a backcast. "I really started fishing seriously through boyfriends," she said. "Only 'boyfriend' didn't mean the same thing then as it does today. These were just nice boys who were friends; sex was not involved, certainly not. But all kinds of fun things were—like camping, hunting, and fishing.

"We fished with a group of young men who had gotten out of Harvard, been in the war, and were back in New York in business. Two of them would ask two of us, or maybe there would be three boys and three girls. We took the West Shore Railroad at noon on Saturday, because they all had to work Saturday mornings, and we got off some place near Bear Mountain, fishing various places the boys had been going to alone. They knew the streams."

Inevitably, a woman is more attractive and intriguing to a fisherman if she too fishes. Pure love of fishing is the strongest of bonds. Mabel Ingalls married one of the young Harvard men and they hied away to a Catskill stream. Julia Fairchild pondered the motives of these suitors and husbands:

> Why do they waste their precious, hard-won weekends teaching us the secrets of the trout? Is it because they like to show how good they are (and aren't they), or is it because, underneath their condescending, lovable, patronizing ways, they really like to have us with them?
>
> I often wonder what I might have become had I not chanced to marry a member of the Anglers' Club. By now I would have degenerated into a fat, bridge-loving piazza person, content to eat tomato sandwiches, cakes, and tea, instead of which, as a fisherman's wife, the earth is mine.

Once it is in the family, the angling tradition tends to perpetuate itself. Fishermen are notorious for raising fishermen. Mabel Ingalls recalled when her daughter was a little girl, that Ed Hewitt "took a lot of trouble trying to teach her to fish. He said to me one day, 'You know, Mabel, it will be a great resource for her later on.'" Hewitt's own daughter Candace was an accomplished angler.

The instinct for tradition that exists between father and son can be just as strong between mother and daughter when it comes to fishing. On their first outing in 1932 at Henryville House on the Brodhead, the correspondent for the Woman Flyfishers reported:

> There were a number of male guests at the inn who cast appreciative eyes at our two young members Jane Erdmann and Talia Fairchild, who not only could fish well but looked well while they fished.

This same Talia also captured the eye and imagination of Ray Bergman, who rhapsodized on women anglers in the closing words of *Just Fishing:*

> Just recently I visited Tappen Fairchild at his summer cottage on the Neversink. All his family are enthusiastic anglers and the memory of his daughter Talia fishing Le Roy's Pool will always haunt me. Tappen and I sat on the cliff overlooking the pool when she came up the stream casting. Just below the pool she took a trout. It was a picture to be painted. The rose pink of sunset caught the edges of the dense foliage bordering the stream and the trout started rising in the pool. I could not help thinking how wonderful it would be if all anglers' wives loved fishing. Certainly it would create a bond between them which none other could equal.

Of even greater interest than how she started fishing, a woman angler is sometimes asked how she differs from men anglers. And the answer is—if she is a true angler—there is *no* difference. "Lady Beaverkill" once firmly declared to her husband Sparse Grey Hackle, "I am *not* a lady fly fisher; I am a fly fisherman!"

Reflecting on their outings and relationships with male anglers, Julia Fairchild said, "I think there is an equality of sexes in fishing that is entirely different from any other sport. We never had the slightest feeling with any of our fishing men that we weren't just as good as they were. In fact, it never occurred to any of us that we were men or women; we were fishermen."

In spite of this equality there are certain personality traits commonly associated with men and outdoor sports which a woman must possess if she hopes to be a successful angler. She must be self-reliant. "One of the things Julia was very firm on," said Jane Smith, "was that we were women who were not dependent on anybody but ourselves. We were expected to take care of our own equipment, to know what flies we had, to clean our own fish in places where they didn't have somebody to do it for us. This made quite an impression on me; we didn't come up and forget our wading sneakers."

Joe Knapp, whose wife Margaret was a Flyfisher, was very fond of hosting her fellow members at annual outings on his Beaverkill water. "They are the most remarkable women," he said. "They come; they bring everything they

ATTENTION LADIES

PLEASE OBSERVE THESE RULES OF THE CLUB

NO FISH OVER 3 LBS TO BE CREELED

LIMIT.   100 FISH PER FLYFISHER WOMAN
500 FISH PER LADY ANGLER

ROCKS   MUST NOT BE THROWN AT SLEEPING FISH

UNSNARLING STATION at head of STRETCH #5
OIL may be obtained but no worms or wet flies.

ABSORBINEJR. at STRETCH #6

OSTEOPATHIST at STRETCH #7

HARD LICKER only at the KNAPPSES

"DAMN" is O.K anywhere
BUT REALLY ARTISTIC CUSSIN'
only permitted to those who sign below.

Caro Ely
Julia Fairchild   Margaret Wright
Jerry Guildine (x her mark)

"Rules of the Club" for the Knapp Outing on the Beaverkill, a perennial favorite with the members of The Woman Flyfishers Club. Joe Knapp, whose wife Margaret was a Flyfisher, had devilish fun with her clubmates at these outings, as evidenced by his list of particulars. *Courtesy The Woman Flyfishers Club.*

own; they never borrow anything; they keep very few fish; and when they go away they take everything they own. I wish my men friends were like that; the men come in here with those hobnail boots and ruin Margaret's floors and then take all the damn fish home with them."

A Flyfisher is also expected to cope with the physical stress and discomforts of an outdoor sport. She should have an appetite for hiking, wading, and long sessions of casting. She knows how to have fun in spite of rainstorms, biting insects, cuts, and bruises. In short, she is a good sport, a rugged individual.

If women anglers are so little different from men anglers, and so at ease in their company, why should there be any reason for them to start their own club? What is the rationale for a women-only fishing club? "I think it is the same for women as for men," said Jane Smith. "There is a certain kind of fellowship that seems to be present if there is only one sex. Once you get rid of the men, there's a kind of letting down of effort to appear anything but what you are."

Angling by its nature is a sport for escapists. "It's my secret life," said Tappen Fairchild, and he introduced his wife Julia to a world of privacy and solitude. She and her fishing friends embraced this world and intensified its pleasures by forming their own club. In it, they enjoyed the freedom to be themselves, to abandon care and recapture the joy and innocence of their youth.

The pressures of your city existence which have built up all winter long—

attending important dinners with your husband and other social obligations—fall away as you head up to the Beaverkill for the Knapp Outing, the year's favorite get-together. After a full day's fishing and a sumptuous dinner at the Knapps', you and your fellow Flyfishers retire just downstream to a nineteenth-century Catskill three-story fishing hotel, which the Knapps have commandeered for the weekend. It is a very magical evening.

> At bedtime we felt like girls at boarding school as we flitted about the halls in pajamas, gossiped in each other's rooms, and on a few occasions, had an athletic contest. Mary King and Jane Smith outdid us all in pushups and standing on the head!

There is as well a female camaraderie of open supportiveness and free emotion that male anglers in their competitiveness find impossible to understand. Can you imagine the following report coming from a man?

> *Ten* fighting, silvery pounds leading me up and down stream for one mortal hour. My 4½ oz. rod bent without snapping, everything held, due mostly to fervent prayers cried aloud to heaven, and I scooped his 30-inch length ashore and lay down beside him! I really was afraid of him, for in my wildest dreams I have never hoped to land such a trout.

or the following event taking place among male anglers?

> On Saturday, Doris caught a very large rainbow in the Flyfishers' pond. Debbie played it, Beverly netted it, we all admired it, patted it, and put it back.

There are things important to a woman angler of course which are entirely irrelevant to a man. She describes her fishing as "an unparalleled opportunity for fun, friendship, intellectual stimulus, and slimming sport." She sees her clubhouse as "a sweet place, the neatest little two-story affair with every comfort and the crispiest curtains and fluffiest blankets." She arrives at her host club's "gorgeously homely and flat-chested clubhouse around 9:20 P.M." She appreciates it, in spite of her ruggedness, when on an outing the host "watched over the Lady Flyfishers with tender care, escorted each to her place on the stream, whispering an encouraging word about a large trout stocked that morning." And she occasionally fantasizes about her other life as she fishes:

> While tying on a fly under a tree a wild mink walked right past me over a log forming a natural bridge. It gave me a thrill to see part of a mink coat wandering within reach of my hand.

Bookplate designed in 1939 for her clubmates by Marguerite Kirmse Cole. *Courtesy The Woman Flyfishers Club.*

She sprinkles her bulletin liberally with recipes for "Queen's sauce, for smoked salmon," "Baked trout, a good recipe for larger trout," "Trout with herbs," "Foiled trout, a charcoal recipe," "Poached salmon," and "Hollandaise sauce, for big trout."

And she sets herself apart from the male angler in the ultimate gesture of female angling bravado:

> On Friday we visited Gioia Gould Larkin, and fished Dry Brook. We finally persuaded her that her baby should not be born in a trout stream. So we all climbed into the car in fishing attire and at five o'clock headed for the Margaretville Hospital. Gioia's son was born at six; we suggested Brown or Brook as an appropriate name.

One of the reasons there is only one woman's fly-fishing club in the world is that there is only one Julia Fairchild. Mention her name to any Flyfisher and she will undoubtedly exclaim, "Julia is the most extraordinary person!" and then proceed to tell you why.

"Dame Juliana" as she is sometimes called—after the legendary nun who wrote the first account on angling in 1496—conceived the idea for a women's club, mapped out the details, formed a cadre, delegated tasks, and served as president for *forty-two* years. She recruited members who liked to fish and enjoyed each other's company. She made sure that enough of them owned water or had husbands whose clubs owned water to give them a variety of places to fish. She taught her charges how to behave as visiting anglers so they would always be welcome back.

The secret of Julia Fairchild's success is her love for people. She was always looking after the needs of her fellow Flyfishers. Jane Smith recalls a recent outing when the two of them were passing out beats to the various members. "After she had suggested easier stretches for several women in their seventies, Julia suddenly turned to me and said, 'Jane, you know, I think we'd better go way up to the top two beats. It's pretty rough fishing up there. I think you and I should go up there.' Now this was when she was already past ninety!"

Julia Fairchild is now ninety-six. Her co-founder Frank Connell is ninety-eight. These hardy Catskill anglers appear just as enduring as they are enthusiastic about their sport. In a bulletin note to her clubmates that transcends fishing, Frank Connell is filled with love for the stream:

My greatest joy and many peaceful hours have been spent in the far past, loafing along the river bank watching a "big one" wag his tail from under a shadowing rock, knowing full well I wouldn't get him if I tried, sending him a howdy as it were and thinking of those lovely lines of Rupert Brooke about "Fish, fly-repleat in depth of June," or this poem written and sent to me last summer by my friend Adin Ballou:

> Here I become a part
> Of river rock and tree,
> Something of nature's heart
> Has pulse in me.
> All that has fed the wood
> Or warmed the stone—
> This has place in my blood
> Is of my bone.

SIX

Managing the Fishing

S eth Green, a contemporary of the great fisherman and author Thaddeus Norris, made just as important a contribution to American angling as did "Uncle Thad." While Norris was having his "noonday roasts" on the Beaverkill, Green was pioneering in fish culture a short distance up the road in Caledonia, New York.

Green began in 1835, at the age of eighteen, as a commercial fisherman. He fished the lakes and streams around his home and sold his catch in Rochester. His inventiveness and motivation soon led to the propagation of brook trout in order to meet the demand for more of "the diner's delight." In later years, when he was employed by New York State to raise fish for its lakes and streams, Green became a skilled fly fisherman. Describing his technique, an associate said, "He gazes far off over the rippled water looking after the falling of his fly, as time after time he lifts the long line with a powerful yet elegant motion and, winging it far behind him, casts it forward with the perfection of easy force. This is his forte and few may dare to enter the lists against him."

In 1864, Green built the rearing ponds on Caledonia Creek which, through several evolutionary stages, still operate today as America's first and oldest trout hatchery. He could not have chosen a better location. Rising out of the limestone strata around Caledonia, the creek bursts full-blown out of several springs, some the diameter of a barrel. Its crystal-clear water flows continuously

Seth Green, "father of American fish culture," who built the hatching troughs and rearing ponds in Caledonia, New York, that still operate today as America's first and oldest trout hatchery. The general principles of modern fish culture are the same as those developed by Green over a hundred years ago. *A. N. Cheney Collection, courtesy Dr. Charles H. Townsend.*

Seth Green's rearing ponds at Caledonia depicted as a gathering place for fashionable folk and leisurely anglers. *Frank Leslie's* Illustrated Newspaper, *September 1, 1866.*

and evenly at temperatures between 43° and 55° all year round. The creek's lime-and-sulphur tincture supports an abundance of water cresses and mosses laden with myriads of shrimp, caddis worms, mayfly nymphs, miller's-thumbs, snails, and other trout food.

Green's first "brook shanty" was a crude affair that simply screened off and sheltered a section of the brook as it flowed through a protective enclosure. Then New York State entered the picture in 1868, and the science of fish culture accelerated rapidly. In that year, the state legislators established the New York Fisheries Commission—three years before the U.S. Fish Commission was founded—and Seth Green was appointed one of the three commissioners. His first accomplishment was to persuade the state to appropriate ten thousand dollars for a propagation program to revitalize the streams of New York. The money was used to lease Green's hatchery and to hire him away from his short-lived commissioner's job to become the state's first superintendent of fish culture.

By 1875, the Caledonia facility, now called a "hatching house," had been bought outright by the state and improved with buildings and rearing ponds to such an extent that it was described as "the most economical and largest fish-breeding establishment in the world." Under Seth Green's aggressive management, Caledonia became a widely known center for the exchange of fish and fish-raising techniques.

In 1869, the first international exchange occurred when Caledonia sent a can of brook-trout eggs to England. That same year 15 million shad fry were planted by Caledonia in the Hudson River. In 1870, Green survived a roaring gale seventeen miles off the Canadian shore of Lake Ontario, netted thirteen lake trout, stripped them of eighty thousand eggs and raced back to put them into the Caledonia troughs. When they hatched he swapped four thousand of the fry with Canada for four thousand Atlantic salmon eggs. A month later he went to Detroit, netted white fish in the St. Clair River, and returned with several boxes of eggs.

In 1871, Seth and his brother Monroe personally accompanied four eight-gallon milk cans of just-hatched shad fry all the way to California. The surviving fry were stocked in the Sacramento River and have multiplied to give the western shad fisherman better fishing than his eastern counterpart. California reciprocated in 1875 with a batch of "mountain-trout" (rainbow) eggs, 260 of which lived to become the breeders that supplied not only New York but much of the East. The strain was mingled three years later with 113 so-called McCloud River rainbows that two Caledonia hatcherymen brought back alive from California, having traded 99 mature smallmouth bass, which went into Lake Temescal near Oakland.

The year 1882 typified Seth Green's enterprising nature. Cut off by the state from his annual appropriation, and laden with millions of impregnated California rainbow eggs he could not hatch, Green blanketed the nation with an offer of up to five hundred eggs to "any responsible party for a small packing fee." The response was so great that rainbow eggs were shipped to every state in the country, including California.

In 1883, a year famous in American trouting history, the German brown trout arrived at the Caledonia hatchery via the Cold Spring Harbor hatchery. The story of the event and its effect on American fly fishing is told in Chapter 3.

Fred Mather, superintendent in the late 1800s of the state's Cold Spring Harbor hatchery on Long Island, was responsible for bringing the European brown trout to American waters. He sent some of the 80,000 eggs he received from Germany in 1883 to Seth Green who hatched and stocked them in Catskill and other Northeastern streams. *A. N. Cheney Collection, courtesy Dr. Charles H. Townsend.*

Seth Green was also an innovator in fish culture. He discovered that the dry process of mixing ova and milt together in a pan without adding water produced a higher yield of fertile eggs and with less effort. He made fixed troughs obsolete by creating "hatching boxes," perforated containers which could be placed at such an angle in flowing water that the resulting "rotary ebullition" of the eggs was exactly akin to the motion the eggs received when deposited naturally in a streambed. His most significant innovation was the first cross-breeding of trout in history. Starting in 1877, he failed several times and then, after repeated back-breeding, produced an offspring of the male brook trout and female lake trout that could reproduce itself. Eventually named the "splake," this hybrid combined the larger size of the lake trout with the fighting and table qualities of the brook trout and became a highly popular game fish in the Northeast.

After Seth died in 1888, his brother Monroe carried on as supervisor of the Caledonia hatchery. In true family tradition, he helped establish a shad hatchery in Germany on the Rhine and introduced black bass to English waters for the Duke of Newcastle. However, in spite of the far-flung influence of the Green brothers, their most consistent contribution was made right in their own backyard through the annual stockings of Catskill rivers with "all the salmon tribes of fish." Throughout the years of stream recovery from hemlock deforestation and tannery pollution, Caledonia was the official Catskill hatchery. Testimony to the Green brothers' success is evident in Kit Clarke's 1893 comment: "The Beaverkill and Neversink have yielded more and larger trout than at any time in the past 20 years." Even after 1894, when a hatchery was built on the Beaverkill, Caledonia continued to supply most of the Catskill stocking needs.

How the Beaverkill hatchery site got approved in the first place is something of a mystery. The site selection committee of fish commissioners visited several Sullivan County locations in August of 1893. All were in accord that "this section of the State is in the greatest need of a hatchery and liberal planting of trout, as there are endless numbers of splendid trout streams. More summer visitors of the middle classes visit Sullivan County than any other county in the State."

The commissioners came to Roscoe on August 22. They examined Darbee Brook, which runs through the Rockland flats, and found it of insufficient volume. Then one of them asked that they go farther up the flats and test the temperature of the Beaverkill, which had been "spoken of as an elegant trout stream ever since he was a boy."

To the great surprise of the whole party, the water of the Beaverkill registered 59° while the Willowemoc that same day stood at 71°. "The test being highly satisfactory," according to an eyewitness report, "the Commissioners stayed over night at Rockland, and on the 23rd they located their probable site for the hatchery. Secretary Doyle, who was engineer of the Commissioners, made the remark that they could build a hatchery at Rockland with Beaverkill water which he thought would be superior in every way to their Caledonia hatchery."

Either political influence or the magic name of the Beaverkill, or both, certainly weighed heavily in this decision, for in 1895, the very first year of operations, the new hatchery started running into problems. It was flooded on April 1 with "one of the worst freshets that had visited that section in twenty-five or thirty years." In succeeding annual reports from the fish commissioner himself there were these bits of news:

1895   This type of freshet is liable to occur at any time. It is simply impracticable to build any breeding ponds at this hatchery. During the summer the temperature remains for weeks above the limit that would sustain trout. It is very unfortunate that this hatchery was ever located where it is.

1896   Operations were entirely suspended during about three months last summer. This was necessary on account of the water supply not being of the required quality to carry trout during the warm weather, and until a change for the better is made, I would recommend the closing of this hatchery for at least five months of the year.

1897   Little can be expected from this hatchery more than to hatch and turn out a few hundred thousand fry annually.

1900   An estimate has been made of the cost of moving the Beaverkill hatchery.

1901   I would recommend that the hatchery at Rockland, Sullivan County, be abandoned and disposed of.

1902   A new hatchery has been built on Whortleberry Creek in Cold Spring Valley (Margaretville, Delaware County). It is located in a part of the Catskills where there are numerous trout streams, making it an admirable location for distribution.

Following its six-year abortive effort on the Beaverkill, the state became more conservative in its hatchery location practice. In his 1906 report, the commissioner noted that good hatchery sites were scarce and difficult to find, ending with this revelation: "The difficulty is too often increased by the importunities of persons who have some private interests to advance in the selection of a site, and who bring to bear influences which are entirely foreign to a proper fish cultural policy."

The Delaware hatchery was much more productive than its Beaverkill predecessor. It provided millions of trout for Catskill streams well into the 1930s. However, in 1935, during its biological survey of the Delaware and Susquehanna watersheds, the state discovered Toad Basin Spring on Mongaup Creek and decided that it offered even greater potential and a more central location for the Catskill hatchery. The only problem was that Bob Ward, whose brother Charles owned the DeBruce Club Inn, had discovered it earlier and built a private hatchery there. He refused the state's offer to buy him out. When the war came and forced him to shut down, the offer was renewed and Ward eventually sold Toad Basin Spring, all the hatchery facilities, and 335 surrounding acres. The sale was closed on August 30, 1946. Over the next few years, the state moved the hatchery closer to the spring source and built what was described at its opening in 1949 as "the most modern fish culture facility in the world." The DeBruce hatchery continues its operations today as the official Catskill trout farm and one of the finest of the state's twenty-odd fish hatcheries.

*   *   *

Because so much of its success depends on nature—and certainly no less on fickle fishermen—the fisheries management profession has been typified through the years by continuing experiments and policy changes. A great deal has been learned since the days of Seth Green, but the ability to satisfy anglers is still something of an art.

For its first twenty-eight years, the New York Fisheries Commission and successor organizations (today it is the Department of Environmental Conservation) stocked only fry in Catskill and other New York streams. It was inconvenient and in some cases impossible to raise larger fish and more difficult to distribute them when hatcheries were few and far apart. Beginning in 1896, more than 140,000 eight-month brown and lake trout fingerlings were stocked in New York waters, and ever since then the choice of fish size has depended less on hatchery limitations and more on survival and growth potential.

Hatchery experiments over the years have attempted to make captive fish look, fight, and taste as much like wild fish as possible. In one set of experiments conducted at DeBruce and several other locations, "wild" colorations were achieved by feeding the fish various diet additives of either paprika, alfalfa meal, or ground shrimp heads.

To get a natural-looking brown trout, with a yellow and orange cast to its body and fins, highlighted with orange spots, alfalfa meal or paprika worked well. Shrimp heads produced browns with a more reddish coloration. For brook trout, both paprika and shrimp heads produced reddish fins and body colors.

To condition the trout and toughen them up for a stream environment, they were given more room in the raceways and the water current was trebled for four hours a day for several months before they were released.

One of the most rewarding changes was the gradual shift from a passive to an active stocking policy. From the earliest days of Caledonia, individuals or groups initiated fish-stocking by submitting applications directly to the state fisheries officials, who routinely filled them on a first-come, first-served basis until the fish ran out. There were many problems with this system: bass got stocked in trout habitats and vice versa; certain rivers got overstocked or left out because of duplicate applications; hatchery production was based on the desires and whims of thousands of individuals, some not even fishermen.

Slowly at first, in the 1920s, serious attention began to be given to uniformity of species in given waters and to stocking quotas according to the size and quality of water. The breakthrough came in the 1930s with the biological surveys of state watersheds for the purpose of formulating a stocking policy for each lake or stream studied. By the early 1940s these individual policies were defined and, except for refinements, they are the same ones that are in effect today.

Transportation of fish was always a major consideration in stocking the streams. In the beginning, the only transportation was by boat, buckboard, or baggage car. The Ontario & Western Railway, among others, issued passes for fish cans and their chaperones and even provided free wagons to meet and carry shipments to streams along their right of way. The hatchery messengers were paid $1.50 per day and they often had to board the trains at midnight, keeping scores of fish cans aerated with a tin dipper and cooled with ice whenever they could beg some for free. Today, a fleet of hatchery trucks carries automatically oxygenated tanks holding up to 1,600 pounds of fish per load.

Fisheries management of necessity has been paid for by taxpayers and conducted by public employees. It is true that there were any number of private hatcheries and rearing ponds throughout the Catskills, but the total preoccupation with all the disciplines required to oversee, maintain, and improve

In 1925, the annual report of New York State's Conservation Commission contained a detailed explanation of trout-stocking methods with a photo sequence of the entire procedure. The photo above, taken from this report, is entitled "Aeration of Water En Route." *New York Public Library*.

Members of the Beaverkill-Willowemoc Rod and Gun Club receive hatchery trout to float-stock the river from Livingston Manor to East Branch. Better fish distribution to places unreachable from the road could be achieved by pulling the fish box from the bank or behind a boat. Harry Darbee (right) said, "We did this in the spring and if the river was heavy, which it often was, it was dangerous work. You could say we got a few thrills on the job." *Courtesy Harry Darbee.*

the fishing belonged to the state. The notable exception to this was Edward R. Hewitt.

Instead of pursuing a family tradition of investments and corporate directorships, Ed Hewitt dedicated his inheritance and considerable talent to a lifetime of "making better trout fishing." He bought twenty-seven hundred acres and four miles of the Neversink in 1918 and made it his trout laboratory. For his hatchery he ran a sluiceway from a spring on the hillside into hatching troughs and on into screen-protected rearing and storage ponds. He tapped the same spring and ran it onto the back porch of his fishing camp and through pipe coils he installed in an antique ice box. This was where the day's catch was kept. Mabel Ingalls recalls that he also kept in his ice box the breasts of great blue herons that visited his rearing ponds once too often: "We brought some friends down from Albany one time, and we warned them, 'If he likes you, he'll give you the breast of blue heron, but the trouble is, it's the *blue* breast of blue heron.' It was always really awfully far gone; of course, he had been brought up in the old English grouse tradition where they shoot the grouse and let them hang until they drop off."

In the river, to improve its hospitality to trout, he built current deflectors, winter holes, and plank dams. Hewitt's dams were engineering marvels, intricate

Ed Hewitt working in his trout hatchery on the Neversink. He ran a sluiceway from a spring on the hillside into hatching troughs and rearing ponds that were screened to keep out predators. Commenting on the success of his Neversink operation, Hewitt said, "I can get more big fish in a week than are taken in the whole Catskill country in a whole season." *Photo by Henry G. Davis.*

yet stable, designed to withstand the destructive force of Catskill ice and floods. He built a half dozen or more of them, each creating a large pool of great trout-holding capacity—Dugway, Camp, Molly's, Shop, Flat, Home, and Big Bend. Hewitt stocked these pools with hundreds of big fish—trout of two to six pounds—and at the end of the season it was his custom to catch out as many as he could and winter them in his rearing ponds, safe from the destructive Neversink floods. Said Sparse Grey Hackle, "We whom he used to invite to help him used heavy rods, strong leaders, and bait; and we horsed our fish out and into carrying cans as quickly as possible so as not to exhaust them with long play."

Hewitt's fishing, experimenting, and reporting from his Neversink laboratory established him as the country's leading authority on stream improvement. He wrote countless articles and three books on the subject: *Better Trout Streams* (1931), *Handbook of Stream Improvement* (1934), and *Hewitt's Trout Raising and Stocking* (1935). He advised private stream owners and fishing clubs on where to build dams, how to get rid of predators, and what to do to increase the food supply in their streams. His fee in the 1930s was $100 a day. His own stretch of the Neversink was considered a model of trout water and was inspected and photographed by the fish commissions of New York and several other states.

A good example of the often-changing policies among fisheries managers is Hewitt's theory on the best size of trout to stock in a stream. In 1928, he wrote in The Anglers' Club *Bulletin:* "The State has been putting in hundreds of thousands of fry every year in the Neversink, but I firmly believe that I have accomplished more with my few well-grown fingerlings, usually about five inches long, than the State has with its enormous amount of fry." By 1936, Hewitt had reversed himself, a habit that never bothered him:

> When you plant fingerlings, you are pouring money down a bottomless well. They easily fall prey to predators and probably not more than 5 per cent grow to catchable size. The answer is—plant fry. They sink into hiding places in the gravel and feed on plankton and algae. They will grow faster than hatchery-raised fish, they will be wiser and stronger, and their education in a natural environment better fits them for the struggle of existence.

Among the many theories and findings growing out of Hewitt's Neversink experiments were these:

Natural raising conditions. "I do not believe we can grow hatchery fish which will make good long-lived stream fish unless we give them plenty of room in the water and feed them largely on their own natural diets. Trout must be fed on the minute organisms in early life which are natural for them, or they never learn to feed on these foods and do not grow well in wild streams."

Attracting insects. "A small electric light hung low over the water will attract vast numbers of insects and be surrounded by slashing fish all night. This is a very easy and cheap way of feeding trout."

What makes a trout. "Few fishermen realize that it takes four or five pounds of insects to make one pound of trout. Trout are fat fish. Where bass and perch are only 1 or 2 percent fat, the normal trout is 10 to 11 percent fat. Insects average about 15 percent fat which trout can digest with a range of 8 to 30 percent. Minnows are not suitable trout food because they contain only 1 or 2 percent fat."

Stream insects. "Ascellus bugs, one of the few insects I have successfully been able to transplant into the Neversink, average 21,000 to a quart. These are pretty good-sized bugs, which were brought from Scotland. Other common bugs run as high as 50,000 to a quart."

Winter holes. "All streams ought to have winter holes for trout made at points not more than a mile apart. They are of far greater value than dams or other improvements. It is the cheapest thing which can be done to increase trout in the streams."

Rearing ponds. "It is absolutely essential that the pond be drained dry every season and exposed to the light to oxidize organic acids. Sprinkle the mud with ground limestone rock to neutralize any free acid. Insect life will be far more abundant in an alkaline medium. And make certain all fish are removed before new fish are put in. One or two remaining fingerlings will eat the fry and destroy the results of a whole year's trout raising."

Vermin. "A constant war has to be waged against them. A kingfisher will consume two or three thousand fry in a season. They are very easily gotten rid of by putting one or two posts in shallow water in the pond and setting a steel trap on top. They light on these traps and are readily caught. I asked my man what he had caught while I was away one year. He reported seventeen kingfishers, three owls, three herons, and one crane."

Limiting your kill. "There is only one answer to making better trout fishing for everyone and that is to reduce the number of fish each fisherman takes per day and season. I believe four fish a day for a fisherman to take home is enough. With our present New York State limit of ten fish this would give potentially two and a half times as good fishing as we now have with no additional work."

Ed Hewitt had a singularly effective way of making sure that not too many of his own fish got taken out of the Neversink. He usually kept a close eye on his guests and when a good-sized fish was reeled in, he waded right out and released it, with the chagrined angler working his mouth in silent protest. Johnny Woodruff had another technique on his stretch of the Willowemoc: he instructed his female servants to sow the stream with double rations of trout chow before his guests arrived.

*   *   *

It used to be that fishing on Sunday was a misdemeanor under the old Blue Law of the New York Penal Code. The restriction died in the late 1800s from widespread disregard, but the law was not repealed until 1919. A closed season on trout did not exist in New York until about 1910, when increased fishing pressure made the seasonal restriction necessary. At first the second Saturday in April was always Opening Day, then in 1960 it got moved to April 1. Today, on the no-kill stretches where pressure doesn't matter, anglers may fish all year long.

The state laws of 1879 were very explicit in prohibiting abuses to trout streams: "No person, association, company or corporation shall throw or deposit any dye stuff, coal tar, refuse from gas houses, saw dust, lime or other deleterious substance into any of the rivers, lakes, streams within the limits of this State." Violations were misdemeanors with a penalty of fifty dollars for each offense.

The laws of New York allow private parties to own and control access to trout streams, but the state controls what can be done to the stream by these owners. In 1965, the Stream Protection Law was revised to simplify the state's surveillance of streambed disturbances, dredging or filling in navigable waters, and the repair or construction of dams and docks. All these intrusions require permits before work can be done.

A continuing priority of state fisheries management has been public access to the trout streams. In the early days of American trout fishing, access was never a problem. There was very little fishing pressure and the farmers were friendly. Then the picture began to change with the growth of angling popularity and the advent of individual and club ownership of stream mileage. Probably the worst period for public access in the Catskills was from 1915 to 1930 when dry-fly angling had become the rage and fishing clubs were at their peak.

The Depression brought on a change and presented an opportunity to farsighted Conservation Commissioner Lithgow Osborne. During his ten-year tenure in the 1930s, New York State began its public-fishing-rights acquisitions. Streams were surveyed and selected on the basis of fishing quality as desirable for public use, and state representatives visited with the owners to offer a lump-sum amount per foot of stream bank. The owner who sold granted a permanent easement to the state to allow public fishing on his section of the stream. No other rights were conveyed, and the owner continued to hold full title to his property.

The bulk of the state's fishing rights—approximately 740 miles including both banks—were acquired in the thirties and forties for an average of $475 a mile. Some of those easements had been donated to the state. The first Catskill rivers on which this program succeeded were the Beaverkill, Willowemoc, and Schoharie. By 1950, 13 miles, 9 miles, and 12 miles of fishing rights respectively had been purchased on each of these rivers.

The typical sale of fishing rights was made by a local resident who owned a rather small amount of stream footage and was not posting his water anyway. Because he was letting people fish there already, why not get paid for it? The larger owners tended to be nonresidents who were operating clubs or private preserves, and they were not interested in selling their fishing rights.

After a slow period in the 1950s, the acquisition program picked up momentum and today the major Catskill rivers and their tributaries offer a total of 119 miles of public fishing access. The areas are marked by yellow signs with green wording and usually have parking areas with access paths leading to the rivers.

In addition to the fishing rights owned by the state, it also owns outright in the Catskill Forest Preserve several hundred more miles of stream. Most of these are small, higher elevation feeders full of small brook trout and many can only be reached by hiking fishermen. A map of the Catskill Forest Preserve shows these areas.

Anglers new to the Catskills should know that there are four kinds of stream ownership: private and posted, that is, forbidden water; private and not posted, which usually means the owner will let you fish if you ask; public fishing rights; and state-owned water. All four are governed by state fishing regulations, and in some cases special regulations are posted to govern a particular stretch of water.

One special regulation tried and abandoned was that of "fly-fishing-only." In April 1952, sections of five New York streams including a one-mile stretch on the Willowemoc were restricted to the use of unweighted artificial flies. The theory advanced by the state, with evident apprehension, was that the fishing on these sections would improve because fly fishermen release more of their fish than other classes of fishermen, and because bait and spin fishermen had several other species of game fish besides trout which responded to their tactics. Therefore, it was reasoned, the fly fisherman deserves a break.

The experiment failed and the fly-fishing-only sections were returned to normal status in 1954. It was never clear that more and bigger fish were caught in these areas; in fact, some of the sections were both less productive and less popular than adjacent unrestricted water. Comparisons of the Willowemoc restricted area with sections above and below were totally inconclusive. The public reaction to the experiment was more telling than the fishing results. It was seen as an elitist regulation by bait and spin fishermen, and, rather than continue to anger such a large part of its angling constituency, the state abandoned the idea. In other parts of the country with less fishing pressure and longer trial periods, fly-fishing-only has succeeded as a permanent part of the public-fishing management policy.

New York State had much better success when it introduced no-kill fishing. By placing the emphasis on fishing for *fun*, the restriction was accepted as less discriminatory even though bait fishermen were excluded from the no-kill sections of the stream. It was common knowledge that trout swallowed bait too deeply to be released with much hope of surviving.

The first no-kill section in New York was established in 1962 on Schoharie Creek near the Little West Kill. The U.S. Fish and Wildlife Service had pioneered the concept in 1954 on Bradley Fork and the West Prong of Little Pigeon River in Great Smoky Mountains National Park. Pennsylvania was next in 1958 on the left branch of Young Woman's Creek.

Schoharie Creek was selected for the no-kill experiment perhaps because it was one of the most lightly fished of Catskill streams and the state wanted to go easy after its fly-fishing-only embarrassment. Politically this was sound but, unfortunately, the stream conditions did not justify the special status.

After just two years, it was clear that the trout were not surviving in spite of the no-kill regulation. The Schoharie gets too hot in the summer to sustain a protected population of stocked fish. The Schoharie no-kill was terminated following the 1964 season.

Then came the Beaverkill no-kill in 1965, and finally everything worked: public acceptance, stream conditions, and trout staying power. The no-kill area became so popular that it was extended to 2.5 miles, and another 1.6 miles were added farther downstream after that. The Willowemoc got its no-kill section in 1969, with a later extension to 2.4 miles. The regulations state: "artificial lures only, no fish in possession," and in the opinion of many anglers, the Catskill no-kill sections offer some of the finest fly fishing for trout in the world.

Perhaps the most confusing regulation, whether you are setting it or following it, is the size limit. It has fluctuated through the years, each time with a new logic and strong convictions to support the change. The end goal has always been to encourage the growth and survival of the resident fish. A six-inch limit on trout was one of the earliest New York fishing regulations. You could keep hundreds of fish as long as they were at least six inches long. In 1937, the state upped the limit to seven inches on the theory that more trout would grow large enough to spawn at least once and thus increase natural reproduction.

By 1954, it had been determined that the seven-inch limit had "locked up" a valuable resource since a large percentage of brook trout in Catskill and other streams had grown up, matured and died without ever becoming legally available to the angler. So, the limit was eliminated altogether. Then, in 1976 the limit was raised to nine inches for browns and rainbows only, to respond to increased fishing pressure. After five years it was decided that the nine-inch limit did not work in most streams. This was a bitter pill because New York fisheries managers had to admit that the average freestone stream in the Adirondacks and Catskills was not a good enough habitat to justify conservative regulations.

The final conclusion was that only a small percentage of New York streams deserve a size regulation, so on October 1, 1981, after more than one hundred years of experimenting, the statewide size limit on trout was eliminated altogether. Now, only on those streams where a size limit contributes to survival and growth is there a specified size limit. The current philosophy, as expressed by Wayne Elliot, manager of fisheries for most of the Catskills, is that "we have a whole range of trout streams in New York State, some of them unusually good, but most of them are better managed with a more liberal regulation."

PART TWO

Portraits of the Rivers

SEVEN

Catskill Rivers

In the beginning water covered everything that is now the Catskills. There were no mountains or rivers, just a flat-bottomed, shallow sea extending past the present Atlantic coastline across the Chesapeake and Delaware channels on up over Pennsylvania and New York into Canada.

Sediments—fine grains and fragments of rocks from older mountains—washed in and settled on the sea bottom, compressing into layers of stratified rock. The constitution of this rock was mostly red, gray, and green sandstones, red and gray shales, quartz conglomerates. There were very few lime rocks; no granites, obsidians, basalts, or pumices from cooled earth core, and no gneisses, schists, slates, or marbles transformed from other rocks by extreme heat and pressure.

These rock strata were well embedded when, about 10 million years ago, a series of bucklings in the earth's crust formed the Appalachians. Instead of taking the peak-and-valley shape of its neighboring strata, the Catskills upheaved from the sea as a level plateau.

Even as the land rose, deep channels were being worn into the rocky strata by subsurface currents and, later, by giant watercourses occupying the position and flowing in a direction that corresponded to our present streams. Thus began the valleys, in whose centers the principal rivers were to carve their beds.

The erosion continued, fed by rains, creating tributaries, smaller brooks, creeks, and then tiny rills etching their way branchlike up onto the peaks of the adolescent mountains. In the two million years since, a number of influences have produced today's well-worn mountain range: sideways movements of the earth's crust tilted the strata and gave character here and there to the otherwise flat-layered plateau; four or five glaciers, the last about thirty-five thousand years

Photo by the author.

ago, left their baggage of gougings, mineral salts, and imported rocks; plant and animal decay, combined with fine bits of worn-off rocks, made the sandy, gravelly soils in which the native hemlocks and pines were to thrive.

The Catskill Mountains occupy about four thousand square miles west of the Hudson River, a little over one hundred miles upstream from the Atlantic. From the Hudson, which is at sea level, the land rises gently to the base of the mountains, about four hundred feet above sea level. From this elevation the mountains climb sharply to more than three thousand feet in less than a mile.

Dozens of rounded Catskill summits rise to over three thousand feet, and a few giants of the interior range exceed four thousand feet. Compared with Adirondack peaks, which are taller but whose bases lie well above sea level, the Catskills possess a greater vertical relief. Their sharp rise above the Hudson Valley and nearness to the paths of coastal storms are the principal reasons that the Catskills is one of the most water-rich regions in the country.

Catskill peaks stand in the path of southeast winds blowing inland from the ocean. Their heights force the humid air upward, cool it, and draw out its moisture as rain or snow. The Catskills are also periodically inundated by cyclonic storms moving up the east coast; winds in advance of these storms blow from the east and dump huge amounts of water when they collide with the eastern slopes of the Catskills. When added to the more widespread precipitation caused by low pressure systems, fronts, thunderstorms, and snowstorms, it is easy to understand why the Catskills get so much water.

Water is the Catskill's most valuable resource. It grows the trees that have sustained local industries for centuries. It is exported to New York City by the hundreds of millions of gallons each day. And it provides a home for one of the finest freshwater fish populations in the world.

The Catskills overall get at least forty inches of precipitation annually, against a national average of twenty-nine inches. Spreading out from Slide and Hunter mountains are two even wetter zones of about two hundred square miles each that get from fifty to well over sixty inches a year. These two wet zones are centered over the headwaters of six major Catskill trout streams: Esopus, Schoharie, Rondout, Neversink, Willowemoc, and Beaverkill.

Although there is no pronounced wet or dry season in the Catskills, it is the big thunderstorms and hurricanes that create stories and are remembered for years after they have hit a valley, leaving its residents and the rivers in turmoil. A Catskill thunderstorm that probably still holds the record for the most rain in thirty minutes occurred in 1819: "A powerful rain commenced . . . the air became so obscure that trees, buildings and other large objects could not be discerned at the distance of a few yards . . . the descent of rain was most copious between a quarter before 6 o'clock and a quarter after 6. In this half hour the descent of water exceeded 12 inches upon a level."

Such storms, when they are highly localized or when the ground is dry, do not always produce floods. The rain is soaked up in the rocky streambeds as it heads for the larger drainageways. However, when the rains persist over a general area and each yard downstream adds a new swollen rivulet, the effect can be devastating. The great flood that hit the Esopus valley and eastern Catskills in November 1950 is probably the most intense and destructive on record:

On November 23 and 24, the days before the storm, Catskill Creek had a flow of about 35 cubic feet per second at the Oak Hill gauging station. Its stage was 3.3 feet. By 8 A.M. on the 25th the flow had increased to 55 cfs and by noon to 103 cfs, although the stage was only 3.76 feet, a rise of about six inches. By 4 P.M. the flow was 1,250 cfs and by 7 P.M., 4,000 cfs—the stage having risen more than five feet to 8.99. At 10 P.M. the flow had increased to 6,000 cfs and at 11 P.M. it reached a peak of 12,500 cfs with a stage of 14.08 feet, an increase in flow of nearly 4,000 times its normal value with a total increase in depth of about 11 feet. By the following midnight the flow was down to 1,000 cfs and a few days later, on December 1, 100 cfs.

Because the Schoharie's headwaters are farther east than other Catskill rivers, it often gets hit harder by the coastal hurricanes. Tropical storms Connie and Dianne dumped six and four inches of rain there one week apart in August 1955, producing severe floods all over the Catskills, especially on the Schoharie. Already soaked by Connie, its flow was raised by Dianne to a record 55,200 cubic feet per second! This created a force over 1,000 times more powerful than a wading fisherman experiences under normal conditions.

The fury of a Catskill river in flood, according to one of the old-timers who ran log rafts down the lower Beaverkill, "is as merciless as the savage catamount attacking a defenseless deer on one of the timbered mountains." Water roars down the steep-walled, V-shaped valleys with incredible force, capable of pushing large boulders around, creating or obliterating pools, straightening bends, and depositing bankside trees in twisted masses miles below their point of departure. There was one flood of record height that washed out a cemetery at Shin Creek. It took several days after the water receded to find all the coffins strewn along the banks down the Beaverkill.

A persistent belief among Catskill anglers, especially old-timers, holds that the rivers are gradually drying up. Actually, flow data from one of the U.S. Geological Survey's oldest Catskill gauging stations show that the amount of water flowing down the Beaverkill has been surprisingly uniform over the years. In the 40-year period from 1913 to 1953, the Cooks Falls gauging station recorded extremes of 23 cfs and 31,600 cfs, whereas annual average flows fluctuated narrowly between 551 cfs and 578 cfs. The annual average in 1928 and 1952 was exactly the same, 567 cfs, and the slowest flow of 23 cfs established in 1913, has never since been equaled or approximated. Since 1953, annual average flows at Cooks Falls have fluctuated more widely from a low of 350 cfs in 1966 to a high of 764 cfs in 1974, reflecting a five-year dry period from 1963 to 1967 and a six-year wet period from 1973 to 1978. In 1980, the 66-year cumulative average flow at Cooks Falls was 561 cfs. Steady flows the Beaverkill.

Catskill rivers are perfect examples of mountain freestone trout streams. As a class, freestone streams contrast with spring, limestone, and chalk streams, all of which share common characteristics and are coming to be called as a group "spring creeks." The typical spring creek rises full force from a large underground source and flows with steady volume year-round, seldom flooding and rarely experiencing drought; it stays cool in summer and resists freezing in winter; its waters are rich in lime salts, plant life, and insects; and its bed is of uniform depth, with very few pools and a low gradient of as little as one foot per mile. Add lots of meadows, grassy undercut banks, and silty weed-trailing bottoms and you have the portrait of a spring creek.

Catskill freestone streams are the opposite of spring creeks in almost every respect. Far from being constant and placid, they are decidedly changeable and temperamental. Their most noticeable feature besides water is rocks. The very name "freestone" accurately conjures the image of riverbeds strewn with loose, well-traveled stones. Indeed, Catskill rivers are true partnerships of water and stone.

To John Burroughs, these streams were "cradled in the rocks, detained lovingly by them, held and fondled in a rocky lap or tossed in rocky arms . . . Now it comes silently along the top of the rock . . . then drawn into a narrow canal only four or five feet wide, through which it shoots, black and rigid, to be presently caught in a deep basin with shelving, overhanging rocks . . . then into a black, well-like pool, ten or fifteen feet deep, with a smooth circular wall of rock on one side worn by the water through long ages, or else into a deep oblong pocket, into which and out of which the water glides without a ripple."

About fifty years earlier than Burroughs, Washington Irving had come back from learning to angle in England and created his own vivid image of these streams:

> Our first essay was along a mountain brook among the highlands of the Hudson, a most unfortunate place for the execution of those piscatory tactics which had been invented along the velvet margins of quiet English rivulets. It was one of those wild streams that lavish among our romantic solitudes unheeded beauties enough to fill the sketch-book of a hunter of the picturesque. Sometimes it would leap down rocky shelves, making small cascades over which the trees threw their broad balancing sprays, and long nameless weeds hung in fringes from the impending banks, dripping with diamond drops. Sometimes it would brawl and fret along a ravine in the matted shade of a forest, filling it with murmurs, and after this termagant career would steal forth into open day with the most placid demure face imaginable; as I have seen some pestilent shrew of a housewife, after filling her home with uproar and ill-humor, come

dimpling out of doors, swimming and courtseying and smiling upon all the world.

Even without the benefit of large underground springs, the entire Catskill region is a lacework of rivers. T. Morris Longstreth, while hiking the Esopus valley in 1915, remarked, "Instead of the Mountains of the Sky, the Indians might have called this country the Land of the Little Rivers, for down each glen springs some brook to join the bright Esopus . . . It is for its streams that the Catskills has a right to be ranked with the great family of American parks." Out of each hollow flows a brook, and fifteen smaller brooks unite to lend it volume before it has run three miles. Water runs everywhere and one wonders how it keeps flowing from the ridges without daily replenishment.

It flows from highly absorbent layers of water-bearing sand, gravel, and rock, from countless seeps and smaller springs, from the blotting-pad forest of leaf-mold, mosses, ferns, and trees, themselves living reservoirs. There are also spring holes in the streambeds helping keep them cooler in summer, warmer and moving in winter, sustaining their flow through the year. The greater amount of overhead canopy and steeper gradient typical of these freestone streams also contributes to keeping them cooler in summer and flowing in winter.

Just as these rivers were created by erosion, they lead precariously erosive lives, changing slightly each day with the shifting of their stones and gravel. After every big storm, with its attendant filling of old holes and digging of new ones, the Catskill angler has something new to learn about his stream.

A Catskill freestone stream is a delicate balance of its volume, width, depth, bottom roughness, suspended solids, and velocity. Change one of these variables and the others adjust to bring the stream back into dynamic equilibrium. All of the variables are continually changing, but the critical one is velocity. The faster velocity on the outside of bends gouges out pools; on the inside of bends, where velocity is reduced, gravel is deposited. This is part of the natural process that causes the formation of pools and riffle areas, each important to the fish—deep pools provide shelter, and riffles produce food and the fine gravel beds for spawning.

Besides its shallows and deeps, a Catskill stream is naturally crooked. Should it be artificially straightened or "channelized," its velocity increases and it immediately begins trying to slow down; it "wants" to meander and bend. Catskill streams are seldom straight for longer than ten times their width; even where they seem straight the line of greatest depth wanders back and forth between banks.

Of all the irregularities essential to the making of a proper freestone stream—riffle, run, pool, eddy, glide—the one that most clearly defines the character of these streams is the *pocket*. Flowing toward a pocket, the water strikes a barely sunk boulder, rises on its rounded shoulders, slides both over and around, angles off twin rocks just below on one side, hits a slanting ledge and recourses sharply to the other side into a final obstacle before gathering itself singly and flowing on through other pockets and infinitely diverse configurations of water and stone to the lowlands and on out to sea.

The pocket is a contorted fluidity whose swirls, whorls, and compressions are an exquisite combination of convenience to the fish and challenge to the fisherman. The water slows *and* quickens as it moves through a pocket, giving the fish a choice of easier holding lies that nonetheless are right on the edge of food lanes, those concentrations of flow wherein the bugs are served up in richer profusion. For the angler, pockets are what chess is to the gamesman; successfully reading and fishing the pocket water is the highest achievement of streamcraft.

In winter, Catskill streams freeze. After a few back-to-back zero days, particularly if snow cover is sparse on the banks, anchor ice—pale celadon blotches—forms among the rocks on the bottom. Near the banks, in the eddies, and on other slow-moving stretches, the surface begins to gel. Soon, these isolated patches join and the stream flows sluggishly, sandwiched between its anchor and surface ice jackets, reappearing here and there as an interrupted stream within a stream. Occasionally, the water flows up on top of its frozen self creating ice sculptures, terraced layers in shades of muted amber. Snow comes again, sticking now to the stilled stream, softening the outline of its banks, flattening its boulders, and finally making it over as a silent roadway of white winding up the valley.

In good years the melting occurs slowly, brought on by the first rains and warming days. The rivers rise, snow water turns them a murky green, ice goes out in smaller chunks, and the spring freshets herald another angling season.

In not-so-good years, after a hard freeze, when it's too warm and too rainy too early, the surface ice breaks into large slabs, some weighing several tons. They head downriver until a few of them come onto a fallen tree, large boulder or other hard place where they pile up. Others follow and soon a dam forms of all shapes and sizes of ice parts and continues to build as more pieces arrive, the water rising ever higher behind it even while digging out the streambed beneath it.

When it finally breaks up, the entire jam moves down the river like a ten-foot-high plow, and there's hell to pay downstream. Nothing escapes. Insects, trees, and the fish are all swept headlong, tumbling and twisting into eternity. Theodore Gordon reported a mid-February 1908 ice jam:

> I am sorry to say that my worst fears in regard to the trout have been realized. We had very cold weather in January with temperatures down in part of the county (Sullivan) as low as 28 below zero and the ice was very heavy. Several days of mild weather followed by rain on Saturday of last week resulted in a sudden breaking up of the ice and there is no doubt that large numbers of fish were destroyed. The ice was twenty inches to two feet thick and there was much snow upon the ground. A large portion of the latter ran off in a few hours, and this, with rain and high temperature

forced the ice to go out. Jams are said to have formed in many places, only to go out with a rush, and many large trout were killed. A brown trout was picked up with its head crushed that weighed about six pounds. The Neversink, Willowemoc, and Beaverkill have been affected and doubtless all the streams within a large area.

In July and August, the Catskill streams are usually less wild. Those without an upstream reservoir to maintain flows can in fact get quite dry. This does not happen every summer, but when it does, their stony beds and token trickles bring groans to the breasts of passing anglers, who head for other waters until the streams rise again. It is not uncommon for the volume of flow in a Catskill stream to range in a single year from highs of 12 to 15 thousand cfs to lows approaching 10 cfs.

These times—of ice jams, drought, and damaging floods—are interruptions in a more sustained rhythm of the rivers. Said Louis Rhead of the upper Beaverkill, "Excepting in those rare years when all nature languishes in drought, the stream is broad, deep, and copious. To the fly-caster it is the ideal stream, as he can—after the spring "fresh" is over—wade the entire stream, excepting at two or three very deep pools and at the falls."

Catskill streams have the virtue of appearing full most of the year. They have no clearly defined high-water mark, so that a few inches more or less of water are not perceived as high or low. Stones always line the banks regardless of water level unless a full freshet is in progress. Let the water go down six inches, a few more stones join the bankside array, the grasses advance, and the stream still seems full. Or, the water glides against a rock face whose only memory of an earlier stage is a thin band of wetness from the night before. Siltier rivers leave lines of earlier heights along their course; not so the cold, clear, pristine streams of the Catskills.

The pureness of Catskill streams contributes to a smaller average fish than in most spring creeks. Starting at the bottom of the food chain, a Catskill stream's lower concentration of lime salts leads to less plant life to fewer insects and other freshwater fauna on which trout feed. There is also a shorter growing season because of colder winters and the attendant slowing of the trout's metabolism.

However, Catskill trout are far from disadvantaged. Even though they do not live in the spring creek potpourri of watercress, elodea, shrimp, grasshoppers, and jassids, they have plenty of mayflies, stoneflies, and caddises, on which some of them—with the help of a little cannibalism—have achieved weights exceeding ten pounds. Writing to Englishman G.E.M Skues in 1912, Theodore Gordon said:

I fooled the old potted trout at last and he smashed me after a terrific fight. He had a deep hole among rocks under bank and had to be stopped. Extraordinary strength, but he had lived in cold water and won through many fierce floods. No limestone or chalk stream trout leads such a strenuous life.

Seventy years later, Len Wright fishes the same stretch of the same river and echoes Gordon's feelings:

> A one-pounder on the Neversink will jump higher, pull harder and fight longer than a trout three times that weight from a pampering chalk stream. And in both form and color, the fresh-water fish stands head, shoulders and ventral fins above its soft-living relatives.

Catskill rivers provide an ideal home for trout. In their upper reaches, they are narrow, shaded, fed by cold, clear springs, with beds of clean gravel and sand. A more perfect trout-spawning grounds does not exist. In terms of fishing, Ed Van Put thinks the best parts of these rivers are their middle sections: "The lower parts are always the best for food production, organic enrichment, minnows, but the problem is temperature; the middle has acceptable food and temperatures; the upper is lacking in food."

Distribution by species, in terms of wild trout only, can also be reckoned by dividing the rivers into thirds from their source down to an elevation of one thousand feet. The upper third is brook-trout water, the middle third a mixture of brooks and browns, and the lower third almost all browns. There are of course exceptions to this guideline, principally in the Delaware and its branches—low-elevation rivers whose water temperatures have been lowered by releases from the Cannonsville and Pepacton reservoirs.

Only two major rivers in the Catskills have established populations of wild rainbows—the Esopus and the Delaware. The rainbow's heritage is that of a sea-run fish; it must have big water to grow up in. On the Esopus, this is the Ashokan Reservoir. On the Delaware, the river itself serves this purpose.

Except for landlocked salmon in the Neversink reservoir, New York State stocks almost exclusively brown trout in Catskill waters. Some private owners and clubs stock rainbows and brook trout out of individual preference, but the state has found after many years of experimenting that brown trout grow faster and are much hardier, while both rainbows and brook trout cannot be sustained outside of those areas where they already thrive without man's interference.

*   *   *

There are more than fifteen hundred miles of trout streams one mile or longer in the Catskills. Most of this trout water is accessible to the public through state ownership or fishing easements or because it is not posted by the owner. However, posting is on the rise. In a state survey covering the years 1963 to 1973, posting increased 67 percent, the reasons most often cited by owners being the prevention of trespass by hunters and snowmobilers. In 1975, an estimated 42 percent of private land in the Catskills was posted.

In 1982, Catskill rivers supported over half a million days of angling, generating over $8.5 million in local revenues. These figures are based on the DEC's estimates of Catskill fishing trips in 1974, holding that number constant, and the U.S. Department of the Interior's 1970 survey of nationwide fishermen's spending habits, adjusted for inflation.

Before describing each of the major Catskill rivers in subsequent chapters, I wish to give a brief profile of each as an overview of the general character of Catskill angling:

Beaverkill River. This is the river that made the Catskills famous. It is divided into two distinct sections by its junction with the Willowemoc in Roscoe. The upper river in the late 1800s was lined with friendly farmers who boarded itinerant fishermen; today it is almost entirely posted by private owners and fishing clubs. The lower river is all public and easily accessible. Beginning with Junction Pool in Roscoe, it is a succession of historic pools including Barnhart's, Hendrickson's, Cairns's, Horse Brook Run, Mountain, and Cemetery. Two no-kill sections, the most-fished river stretches in the Catskills, abound in twelve- to fifteen-inch browns.

Willowemoc Creek. The headwaters and uppermost tributary of this river produce more wild brook trout than any other area of the Catskills. Its lower tributaries are well developed little rivers themselves, offering excellent spawning grounds for brown trout. Above Livingston Manor, about five of the twenty river miles are posted; from the Manor down to Roscoe it is all public. The no-kill section on the Willowemoc is equal in quality to those on the Beaverkill; releases of browns twelve to fifteen inches are common, with a few in the twenty-inch class.

Neversink River. The two branches of this river "went private" beginning with Clarence Roof's four-thousand-acre "Wintoon" in 1882. Theodore Gordon held forth on the main stem from shortly after 1890 until his death in 1915, then it too went private when Edward R. Hewitt bought twenty-seven hundred acres and four miles of river. Today, public trout water begins with the Neversink Reservoir and extends below the dam for six miles to Woodbourne. Because the Neversink is colder than other Catskill rivers, a very high 60 percent of its fish are trout and its hatches are about two weeks later than those on the other rivers. Of its wild fish, brook trout dominate the branches, browns prevail in the main river.

Esopus Creek. Some twenty thousand anglers fish this river each year, making it the most popular river in the Catskills. Only the Beaverkill and Willowemoc no-kills get more pressure. The Esopus is one of the East's most productive wild trout streams; at any given time there are over one hundred thousand wild rainbows from Big Indian to the Ashokan Reservoir. Except for its headwater section above Big Indian, the Esopus is almost entirely open water

Courtesy Harry Darbee.

and easily accessible. Cold-water releases from "the portal" at Allaben have a major effect on fish life, fly hatches, and angling conditions in the remaining twelve miles down to the reservoir.

Schoharie Creek. Because it is the most scenic of Catskill rivers, the Schoharie won its earliest renown as a tourist mecca. Only by the late 1930s did it achieve popularity among fly fishermen. The Schoharie is an early-season trout river. Dark shale in its bed and a broad, sunny valley drive its temperatures consistently into the middle eighties after June 1. Then it becomes a dawn-and-dusk or a bass river; in its lower reaches smallmouth bass range up to twenty inches. Access by owner consent is excellent along the main river, with posting prevalent only on the tributaries. The Schoharie is liberally stocked with brown trout.

Delaware River. From Halcottsville to Callicoon, the Delaware and its East Branch behave as four distinct trout rivers. Almost no posting exists along these sixty-eight river miles, but owner permission may be necessary for access, especially to the main Delaware. Above Pepacton Reservoir, the East Branch offers lots of twelve-inch wild and stocked browns with an occasional twenty-incher up from the reservoir. This eight-mile section has moderate gradient, good hatches, sand-and-gravel bottom, and easy wading. Below the reservoir, sixteen miles of river to the junction with the Beaverkill are like a spring creek because of the moderated, colder releases from Pepacton dam; pools are long, flat, and slow with easier fishing in the riffle areas for browns of fifteen inches and larger. In its final seventeen miles to Hancock, the East Branch resumes a freestone character, its flows influenced mainly by those out of the Beaverkill. Fewer but larger browns prevail, and wild rainbows begin showing up around Read Creek. The twenty-seven-mile "trout zone" of the main Delaware from Hancock to Callicoon is like a giant spring creek when the cold-water releases are flowing from the Cannonsville dam. Riffles between long eddies are the best fishing for rainbows and browns of fifteen to twenty-two inches and larger. Nearly all fish in the main river are wild, including trout, bass, shad, walleyes, and eels.

EIGHT

Beaverkill River

The Sun Trail ran with the sun up the valleys, across the mountains, connecting the village of the Esopus Indians on the lower Rondout with their hunting grounds on the upper Beaverkill. It passed through Grahamsville, crossed the Neversink at Hall's Mills, and continued westward through Willowemoc and Brown's Settlement to join the Beaverkill just below Shin Creek. Of course, none of these communities existed then. Another trail ran up the Beaverkill to its head, crossed between Graham and Doubletop mountains to the tip of Dry Brook, then over Big Indian mountain into Oliverea and down Esopus Creek.

These two foot trails were the earliest human penetration of the Catskills, passing through what is still today a wild and remote region. It was rugged territory even for the Indians, who only hunted there; for living and farming they preferred the gentler valleys of the Hudson, Esopus, and Delaware rivers.

The first white settler of the Beaverkill valley, Jehial Stewart, came in on the Sun Trail in 1789 and went downriver to settle in Big Flats, now Roscoe. In 1815, John Hunter converted the Sun Trail into a pole road which is now paved and bears his name. As late as 1873, the year the first fishing club appeared on the river, access to the upper Beaverkill was still primitive; a wagon road came up from Roscoe, joined Hunter Road and went a short way beyond where it stopped at a Shin Creek sawmill. From there to the headwaters was still only a footpath; members of the club found it quicker to come in over the top from the next valley to the east.

Some idea of the remoteness of the Beaverkill in the mid-1800s can be gained from a story involving P. T. Barnum, the New York showman, and Bill Hardie, a native of Shin Creek. It seems that in 1856 Barnum ran an ad offering five hundred dollars for a live brook trout weighing five pounds or more, delivered to him in New York, so he could display it in his museum aquarium on the corner of Broadway and Ann streets.

Hardie, a great fisherman and hunter, heard of Barnum's offer and laid his plans to earn the money. The Beaverkill and its tributaries were the home in those days of unusually large trout, and Hardie knew the hiding place of one old mossback that had to be the father of them all.

After trying for two days, Hardie succeeded in netting the trout. It was too smart to be caught any other way. He weighed it and found that it beat the five-pound requirement by almost a full pound. Hardie put the trout in a washboiler of water and began wondering how he was going to get it to New York and Barnum. Shin Creek was between forty and fifty miles away from the Erie Railroad at Cochecton on the Delaware, and the roads over the mountains between the two points were not built for either speed or comfort; but Hardie loaded the washboiler on his buckboard, started early in the morning, and by changes of water along the way, arrived with his prize intact in Cochecton in time for the night train to New York.

The train conductor took a liking to Hardie and kept his trainmen busy livening up the trout with fresh water all the way to Jersey City. Hardie crossed the Hudson and landed in New York at Duane Street with his five-and-a-half-pound trout still alive but in rather weak and travel-worn condition. He lost no time in getting to a hotel near the museum, housing his trout, and hunting up Barnum to inform him of what he had brought down from the wilds of Sullivan County. Then, as Hardie told it:

> Barnum said he hadn't never made such an offer for a trout, and I says to the wily old showman, right on the spot, that I'd bet him a hundred dollars that he had made the offer, and produced the money, but he wouldn't take me up, but said all right, he'd go 'round to the hotel and take a look at the trout.
>
> He went along. He sized up the big fish's state o' health and told me that if the trout was alive next morning he'd pay me $150 for it and my expenses of getting it to New York.
>
> I sort o' had an idee that I'd be goin' back home with the carcass of that trout next day, minus the $150 and out all the expenses, but I calc'lated to make an effort to keep the critter alive if the thing could be did. I sat up all night with the fish, nussin' it along, but los' hope as time went on. The prospec's took to lookin' so dark 'long to'rds daylight that I concluded to try herb treatment on the old feller, and freshenin' up his water nice an' cool, I put a good ol' raftsman's hooter of Sullivan County redeye in along with it.
>
> Say, that trout seemed to recognize the smell o' home in that hooter o' rum to wunst, an' he begun to brace right up and git lively.
>
> 'The poor feller's homesick,' said I, 'that's all that ails him!'

An' I turned in another three or four fingers. The consequence was that when Barnum came around next mornin' that trout was sportin' in the washb'iler as chipper an' sassy as he ever did up in his native brook.

Barnum forked over the $150, and $40 more that I calc'lated my time and trouble and expenses was worth, and had the trout carted down to the museum in my ol' woman's washb'iler an' all. But I hadn't give him the secret o' that trout's good health an' the keep of it, and next mornin' he was deader'n the bottom mackrel in a kit.

As it turned out, Barnum had the trout mounted, and for years it was one of the most admired attractions of the museum until the building burned with the trout and all its contents about nine years after Bill Hardie's arduous journey.

*   *   *

In Bill Hardie's time, Catskill fly fishing was in its infancy. "Uncle Thad" Norris was wet-fly fishing the Beaverkill with his small band of "Houseless Anglers" in the 1850s. John Burroughs made trips in 1860 and 1869 from Big Indian over the mountains to the upper Beaverkill. He fished the streams with the anal fin of a brook trout to represent a minnow. He did use flies but mostly on Balsam Lake and other ponds.

The residents of the Beaverkill valley in the mid-1800s farmed for subsistence and when they fished it was for the same reason. Worms were leisurely; nets or spears were quicker. And there were plenty of trout to go around; that is, until the railroads opened up the land to the crowds of "Yorkers."

In 1872, the Ontario & Western railroad was completed, opening up the Beaverkill to visiting fishermen. Among its stops on the Beaverkill were Rockland Station (Roscoe), Cooks Falls, and East Branch. In that same year, it is interesting to note that Roscoe consisted of two tanneries, a grist mill, two sawmills, one church, three blacksmith shops, a wagon shop, two hotels, four stores, a carpenter shop, two schools, 45 dwellings and about 225 inhabitants. It was a typical village of the time.

Although most trout fishermen today are more familiar with the Beaverkill from Roscoe down to East Branch, the upper Beaverkill was where the trout were in the late 1800s. The earliest sport fishing at that time on the lower Beaverkill was mainly for black bass. The European brown trout, with its tolerance for the warmer water in the lower rivers, first came to America in 1883 and did not get established and win over Catskill anglers until after 1900.

Another railroad, the Ulster & Delaware, gave access to the upper Beaverkill in the days when it had no wagon road up its full length. Fishermen got off at the Arkville station on the East Branch of the Delaware. From there they took a mountain buckboard up Dry Brook to Seager's and then hiked in over Graham Mountain. For the more courageous, there was the "Cat's Ladder," a rough wagon road from Seager's that skirted the other side of the mountain. One of the travelers over this road had this to say: "Its heathenish and unconscionable construction is very destructive, yea even fatal to piety, and therefore it is not only productive of physical and mental torture in this world, but liable to compromise our comfort in the next."

To be an angler in this remote territory in those days required both vigor and determination, evidenced by this May 6, 1897, logbook entry of the Balsam Lake Club:

> While going over the top of the mountain, passing the Lover's Leap, the wagon turned completely over twice. We were precipitated over a precipice of some 2685½ feet alighting on the tops of tall trees which we carefully climbed down. Then ascending the mountain we turned the wagon over twice so it would be where it was before our aerial flight, and once more resumed our trip. On arriving at the clubhouse and finding no other members here, we inspected all of the rooms and finally chose the best. We have slept under four blankets. Ice formed on the lake at nights, but the days have been pleasantly warm.

Let us go then, you and I, on an old-time trouting trip to the Beaverkill! The year is 1891 and our guide is H. D. Forsyth, noted angler, author, and stream familiar.

The day is nearly done, the sun being within half an hour of the treetops, when our driver pulls the horses up before Ransom Weaver's door. It has been twenty miles since we left Livingston Manor, and though we are tired out with the long drive, we postpone Weaver's offer of supper.

"Not yet, old man; fish comes before meat, you know!" Hastening to our rooms, we change to our fishing togs and head for the stream. There is something very peaceful-looking about this bit of the river, no falls, rapids, or pools, as it winds its way through level land, closely shut in by trees and bushes. We fish down through the meadow taking half a dozen trout of from six to seven inches long on a brown hen with a ginger hackle dropper, and then go back up for supper.

Generous slices of fried country ham, plentifully flanked by newly fried and really fresh eggs, with griddle cakes swimming in new butter and sure-enough maple syrup, and these well supported by such trifles as cottage cheese, apple pie, marmalade, cakes, cookies, tea, and simon-pure milk, constitute a meal that no angler can afford to pass up. Weaver sets a bountiful table.

We arrange to have our traps forwarded the next day to Beaverkill, and after sundry pipes and talk of fish, retire to our couches.

Rap! Rap! Rap!

"Four o'clock, gentlemen," and we bounce out of bed. After a hearty meal and a goodbye to Weaver, we start for the river and fish it down until we strike private water, the preserve of the Salmo Fontinalis Club. Here we reel up, intending to walk by, but upon meeting a member who pressingly invites us to try our luck, we succumb and creel several fine half-pounders.

And so on down the river: Jones Mill, where a grand fall thirty feet high and a splendid pool below offer up a few speckled beauties. From the mill down begins the best of the Beaverkill. Grand riffs, one after another, and pool after pool. Two and a half miles to Alder Creek, another mile and a half to the outlet of Murdock's Pond. On the shore of this pond there is a boardinghouse kept by John Slater, who sets a tip-top table. One mile more and we reach Jim Murdock's, five miles from the mill, and as it is nearly dark, we put up for the night. Murdock is one of the old-timers in that section, a landmark so to speak. There are very few of the old Beaverkill fishermen who do not know him; his house is pleasantly located and well kept.

From Murdock's we start early and fish down to Shin Creek where there is a small settlement. Here we run against a snag in the person of Bill Hardie, who is dead sure to order anyone off the stream, and it is go or fight, for Hardie is a man of brawn and muscle. Fortunately, he does not cover much water, so one can easily walk around him.

From Shin Creek to S. A. Voorhess's place is one and a half miles. We pass Sprague's on the way. Both of these parties keep excellent houses, and the river is good fishing. In the next mile we fish four or five pools in a bunch, a very fishy place, and pull in at Jersey's. Since morning we have creeled over eighty trout, one of our baskets weighing nearly ten pounds. Many fish are eight to ten inches long, several more than twelve inches.

About this time we begin to think of Mrs. Jersey, with her hot dinner and her cookies and cream, and we reel up and start for the house. For strangers she has the pitcher and bowl from her spare room placed on the front porch, all ready to wash before eating, but regulars go through the shed where the creamer is standing, and thence around back by the great water wheel that does the churning, to a water spout where they wash.

The river flows on in this style clear to Rockland, with many fine boardinghouses along the way. After dinner we fish on down to Hank Ellsworth's at Beaverkill, where our traps are waiting. Ellsworth used to run the tannery, which is a thing of the past. Now he runs the post office and his farm and takes boarders. Tomorrow morning he will take you, me, and Forsyth to the Rockland station.

*   *   *

The boardinghouses of the Beaverkill were institutions in themselves, combining the services of hotels, chambers of commerce, and fishing outfitters. They ranged from small farms with a spare room to well-organized manor houses that printed illustrated booklets and took in up to fifty guests. Prices at the time of our "fishing trip" with H. D. Forsyth were $4 to $7 per week, about $1.25 for overnight, and $.25 for a fisherman's lunch. One-way train fare from New York City ran about $2.50 and the welcoming horse and wagon was on the house.

River View Inn, one of the well-known Beaverkill boardinghouses, was located a mile or so downriver from Roscoe. After many years as a farmer and river raftsman, John Ferdon added wings to his farmhouse in the 1890s and opened it up as a boardinghouse called Hillside Summer Home, in keeping with the Catskill trend from an agricultural to a recreational economy. His son Edwin eventually became manager and changed the name to River View Inn to reflect the growing popularity of the lower Beaverkill among trout fishermen. By the 1920s, River View Inn had attracted a following of angling notables the likes of A. E. Hendrickson, Gene Connett, Louis Rhead, Charles Ritz, and George LaBranche, and it buzzed with excitement at the height of each fishing season. In the thirties, Edwin Ferdon's daughter Winnie ran the inn with her new husband Walt Dette, but along with many similar Catskill establishments it succumbed to the Depression and ceased operations as a boardinghouse in 1933. Having already tied and sold flies from the cigar case at the inn, the Dettes became full-time flytiers.

THE HILLSIDE SUMMER HOME
ROSCOE, N.Y.

Altitude 1500 ft.

Centerfold from a brochure for John Ferdon's Hillside Summer Home in Roscoe, near Junction Pool. Ferdon switched from farming to innkeeping when tourism flourished at the turn of the century. Appealing to a health-conscious clientele in a time of widespread lung ailments, the brochure proclaimed: "That the existence and accessibility of this remarkable region are a matter of profound concern in these days, when the battle of life involves so terrible a waste of vital force, it is needless to urge." *Courtesy Winnie and Walt Dette.*

A. E. Hendrickson, after whom Roy Steenrod named the Hendrickson fly, and his fishing pals Dr. J. S. Chaffee and George Stevenson, display their catch from a day on the lower Beaverkill. This photo was taken in 1920 on the porch of River View Inn (formerly Hillside Summer Home), Hendrickson's base of operations, from which he and his friends often fished a circuit of several Catskill streams, or as they called it, "fishing around the world." *Courtesy Winnie and Walt Dette.*

Trout Valley Farm, situated seven miles upriver from Roscoe in the community of Beaverkill, was another of the celebrated Beaverkill boarding-houses. Theodore Gordon stayed there for weeks at a time over several summers; he also stayed at River View Inn when he had his mother with him and wanted her to be closer to the conveniences of a larger village. Trout Valley Farm was operated for seventy-six continuous years as a fishing hotel, from 1887 to 1922 by Jay Davidson, and by the Frederic Banks family from 1922 to 1963 when it was sold to the state, which torched it to clear the land. As a note from bygone days, even with its capacity of fifty guests, the rooms of Trout Valley Farm never had locks on the doors.

Frederick White fished at Trout Valley Farm for over twenty-five years, beginning in the 1890s, and witnessed there many of the changes taking place during an era of ferment in American angling. He saw bait fishing fall into disrepute even among local residents; he watched as the first women showed the courage to don boots under their knee-length skirts and wade out into the river; and in 1909 he experienced with some poignance the coming of the dry fly to Beaverkill village:

Trout Valley Farm, in the village of Beaverkill, was run as a fishing hotel by the Davidsons and then the Banks from 1887 to 1963—seventy-six years of angling hospitality. Beaverkill was once a community of several dozen families with a tannery, sawmill, its own post office and school. *Courtesy Frederic Banks IV.*

Fred Banks III, proprietor of Trout Valley Farm, holding the kind of trout that brought anglers back year after year to his establishment on the upper Beaverkill. *Courtesy Frederic Banks IV.*

Dr. R. E. Brown arrived one day with an assortment of #14 and #16 midges fresh from England. I happened to be fishing the Bridge pool with a wet fly while the trout were feeding where the current turns into the quieter water of the pool, but they would not take. Dr. Brown stood beside me and in fifteen minutes pulled out five fish from 12 inches to 14 inches with his little floaters much to his gratification and my own chagrin.

Other inns favored by turn-of-the-century Beaverkill anglers included the Roscoe House, torn down when the four-lane highway went through in the early sixties. Its owner, William Keener, was an insatiable fly fisherman; his 8½-pound brook trout caught in 1908 once held the state record. There were also the Campbell Inn, an imposing white manor house with long veranda across the front, nestled on the hill overlooking Roscoe; Bonnie View, a large Victorian house set almost at the river's edge on the upper Beaverkill above Lew Beach; and the Antrim Lodge, formerly Central House, in Roscoe, whose downstairs bar and common room are famous in angling literature.

Religious segregation was practiced widely in the Catskills during the early days of the old fishing hotels. Vacationers from the city sought out communities of their own faith; Liberty was almost totally Jewish, and fifteen miles up the road Roscoe was as dominantly Christian. Beaverkill fishing hotels bore this out with lawn signs and pamphlets including such phrases as "A Country Inn for Christian Clientele," and "No Hebrews Taken." Such overt discrimination began to disappear shortly after 1900, and gradually the hotels swung with the growing popularity of fly fishing and opened their doors to all.

By 1900, the upper Beaverkill had been transformed into a largely posted, private river. A combination of fly-fishing clubs and individual owners bought or leased almost all the fishing rights from the headwaters down to the village of Beaverkill. There, Trout Valley Farm still catered to the public, but below Beaverkill private ownership extended the rest of the way down to Rockland, leaving only a couple of miles of unposted water before the river joined the Willowemoc at Junction Pool.

Unless a fisherman knew one of the new owners or was a member or guest of one of the half-dozen clubs, there was no longer any legal way to fish the upper Beaverkill. Thus, Catskill anglers of the twentieth century necessarily turned their attention to the lower Beaverkill, or the "Big River," as many of them began calling it, and today, with more than eighty years of added tradition and publicity, it is this part of the river that writers have in mind when they speak of "the most celebrated trout river in the world."

To achieve its preeminence, the lower Beaverkill of course had to remain open to all fishermen. And for this the angling public owes its gratitude to one man, Lithgow Osborne. As recalled by Sparse Grey Hackle, "when Osborne was the State's Conservation Commissioner back in the thirties, each year he took a little of the Catskill anglers' license fees and devoted it to a most sagacious and forward-looking use—he bought up fishing rights of private landowners along the north bank of the river; the south bank was already owned by the railroad, which had never prevented fishermen from clambering down over its tracks to the river. I doubt if he ever paid as much as $100 to any one landowner. It would be worth a million or more today, I'm sure."

Including the fishing rights Osborne bought on the Willowemoc between Livingston Manor and Roscoe, this twenty-three-mile stretch of river is the only uninterrupted public fishing water of appreciable size in the whole Catskills.

With all the right ingredients—easy access to a big, beautiful river full of large brown trout surrounded by friendly innkeepers—the lower Beaverkill began accumulating its store of characters and legends that have made it unique in angling history.

"Opening Day" of trout season authenticates each year the Beaverkill's hallowed position among trout rivers. In spite of the usually raw weather and turbid waters, hordes of anglers make the annual pilgrimage, ignoring the odds against catching anything but pneumonia. Indeed, they return more to observe a ritual and renew tradition than they do to catch trout. More than thirty years ago, Dana Lamb described the scene that has changed very little since:

> All night long, the night before, fishermen's cars have been rolling into Roscoe and until long after midnight the lights have burned brightly in the bar of the Antrim Lodge. Cramped, chilled and weary after the long drive from New York or Newark or Binghamton, the occupants gather over drinks; hail one another over drinks; treat one another to more drinks; glow with memories of former years, and plan great things for the morrow. . . . The great day has come. "Good morning." "What's good about it?" "Tight lines." "Boy, do I feel lousy." Forget how you feel, it's OPENING DAY and the Beaverkill is waiting. . . . Down at the Junction Pool, where the Willowemoc joins the larger river, there are already a score of sweatered but shivering fishermen. . . . The cavalcade of anglers' cars sweeps on down stream, spilling out its occupants at Barnhart's, Cairns', the Wagon Tracks, the School House, the Mountain, Painter's Bend, the Red Barn, Cook's Falls, the Acid Factory, at every over-crowded pool on the river. Back and forth, upstream and down the mob surges, but wherever the angler goes there are dozens ahead of him. Spinning lures whistle through the air, gobs of worms plop, bucktails dart across the stream and wet flies jerk or drift in the icy waters. . . . Long before noon the cars are parked in rows outside Seven Gables and Hicks' Bar and Grill, and the whiskey sour is king for a day. Discouraged by the competition or congealed by the frigid water and the biting wind, the less rugged or persistent repair to the shops of Harry Darbee and Walt Dette where they order dozens of flies, talk endlessly and get in each other's way.

Wherever they gather the talk invariably turns to memorable days on the river, unforgettable characters, and, always, big fish.

Someone remembers Roscoe "Dizzy" Disbrow, said to be the most intimidating man on the Beaverkill back in the 1920s and 1930s. The unlucky angler who happened to be on the pool Dizzy wanted to fish would get a pickerel spinner past his nose and as much verbal abuse as it took to drive him off the pool. Then Dizzy took the spinner off, tied on a fly, and settled down to fishing. His appearance alone was enough of a threat; he was a tall, raw-boned man with a hook nose crowding narrow-set, smoldering eyes. With his battered black felt hat, a belt tightly cinched around his wader tops, and a cigar always jutting out of his unshaven face, Dizzy cut a wide swathe in his determination to prove that the best fishing belongs to the strongest fisherman.

Then there was Irma Shein, "The Widow of Mountain Pool." Irma and her husband Julie both loved to fish. When Julie died, Irma doubled up on her fishing. Some said she did it in memory of Julie, others to get over her loss. Whichever, she became a constant sight up and down the Beaverkill, always talking about "Old Fighter," a fish out of the cartoons. Her outgoing nature—she often called fishermen in off Mountain Pool for a cup of coffee—and her ability to outfish most of the men on the river made her one of the best-liked women anglers on the Beaverkill.

Ernie Maltz ranks high among the colorful characters of the Beaverkill. After years of constant fishing on the first few miles downriver from Roscoe, Ernie got to know the river and its regulars so well that he could instantly spot newcomers, especially those who seemed a bit uncertain about their fishing. One day he waded out uninvited and began instructing a stranger on the stream about the correct flies, where it was dangerous to wade, where the fish were, and so on. He came to enjoy kibitzing on Barnhart's and nearby pools as much as he did fishing, moving methodically from one angler to the next along the river. Ernie was an expert at matching and presenting the caddis fly, and though his pupils may not have asked for it, they were always getting the highest quality advice.

Johnny Woodruff was famous for his all-night drinking and fishing escapades on the Beaverkill. He was a member of one of the clubs on the upper river, but he spent a lot of his time on the Big River. One night he and Harry Darbee were down around Cooks Falls, and as it began to get light they ran out of gin. They had been catching a lot of fish and didn't want to quit. "Goddam it, I'd fish 'til noon if we had another bottle of gin," said Woodruff.

"All right, let's go to town and get one," said Darbee. So they went to the annex of the Antrim where Frank Keener, the owner, was sleeping and began pounding on the door. Finally, they heard a muffled yell, "Go away!"

"No, we've got to have a bottle of gin!" bellowed Darbee.

"Who's out there with you, that damned Woodruff?"

"Yes, Frank, and we're both dry, and we're going to stand right here and keep pounding on your door until you get the gin."

Realizing his hopeless position, Keener surrendered a bottle and Darbee and Woodruff returned to the river.

In the cookhouse of the club where Johnny Woodruff was a member, there hangs a watercolor likeness of the man, with his big ears, Oriental squint, and the little white skullcap he always fished in. His nose is painted one color, his ears another, around his eyes and cheeks yet a third. Beneath the likeness is a color key: red for scotch, purple for rye, and green for gin.

George Gordon of Arlington, Virginia, fished the public waters of the Beaverkill and Willowemoc steadily from the early twenties to the late forties. In 1947 he said, "After fishing in some 20 states, I really believe there is no accessible fishing anywhere in this country as good as the Beaverkill."

Although the lower Beaverkill attracts even more anglers than it did in either George *or* Theodore Gordon's day, old-timers will tell you that the fishing will never be as good as it was back in the golden era. Certainly a lot has changed, and—regardless of the state of current fishing—one naturally grows nostalgic when talking about the good old days of Catskill angling.

There was a time when, arriving in Roscoe, you could buy the right fly at every store on Main Street except the undertaker's. A diligent salesman from William Mills & Son in New York had made the rounds of the jeweler, the dry-goods man, the druggist, everybody, and impressed on each merchant his role in supporting the proud reputation of the Beaverkill.

And that reputation has become timeless, because then or now, if asked to choose their river, legions of fishermen would line up behind Sparse Grey Hackle: "Hell, give me Greenwell's Glory and Campbell's Fancy and Beaverkill, all wet and about No. 12, and May on the Big River, and anyone else can have whatever else he wants."

*   *   *

The Beaverkill River rises in a narrow, rocky hollow nestled between Graham and Doubletop mountains. The stream there is small enough for beavers to build dams from time to time; their ponds give added cover to the wild brook trout thriving in these upper reaches. Spring floods usually tear out the dams and purge the ponds, but some of them fill in, become meadows, and grow back as soft-padded, level forest land. All these stages are evident in the first few miles of the upper Beaverkill, demonstrating vividly an ecological process that has been going on for centuries.

The Beaverkill flows in a westerly direction for 43½ miles until it joins the East Branch of the Delaware. Over this distance the river falls from an elevation of 3,080 to 995 feet, beginning precipitously and leveling as it flows downstream. Analyzing its rate of fall is instructive, for often a single gradient is assigned to a mountain river from its source to its mouth—48 feet per mile in the case of the Beaverkill—and this can be very deceptive. Because steepness is one of the main determinants of water speed, which in turn influences the style of angling, a river's *effective* rate of fall is important to fishermen.

In its first half mile, the Beaverkill plunges 690 feet per mile until it joins its first unnamed fork. From there to the outlet of Balsam Lake, a distance of about four miles, it falls at 100 feet per mile; the next 12.3 miles to Shin Creek it falls 50 feet per mile; then 10.8 miles to Junction Pool at 31½ feet per mile; and finally, 15½ miles to East Branch at 17½ feet per mile.

The 27½ miles of the upper Beaverkill remain today a largely private, posted, and patrolled trout stream, except for its uppermost two miles, another 1½ miles at the state campsite at the Beaverkill covered bridge, and its last 2½ miles from Morton Hill bridge down to Junction Pool.

In its upper reaches the Beaverkill is a wild, remote, thinly settled river. Many of the farms that once dominated the valley are now large private estates, fishing clubs, or religious retreats, all enjoying the contemplative and restorative virtues of the valley.

The view up Beaverkill valley from Morton Hill around 1955. Beyond the iron bridge and the mouth of Spring Brook on the left are the private estates and fishing clubs of the upper river. Sparse Grey Hackle described this as the "loveliest trout water in America . . . what the oldtimers referred to when they wrote about the Beaverkill, the classic water of the Golden Age." *Courtesy Department of Environmental Conservation.*

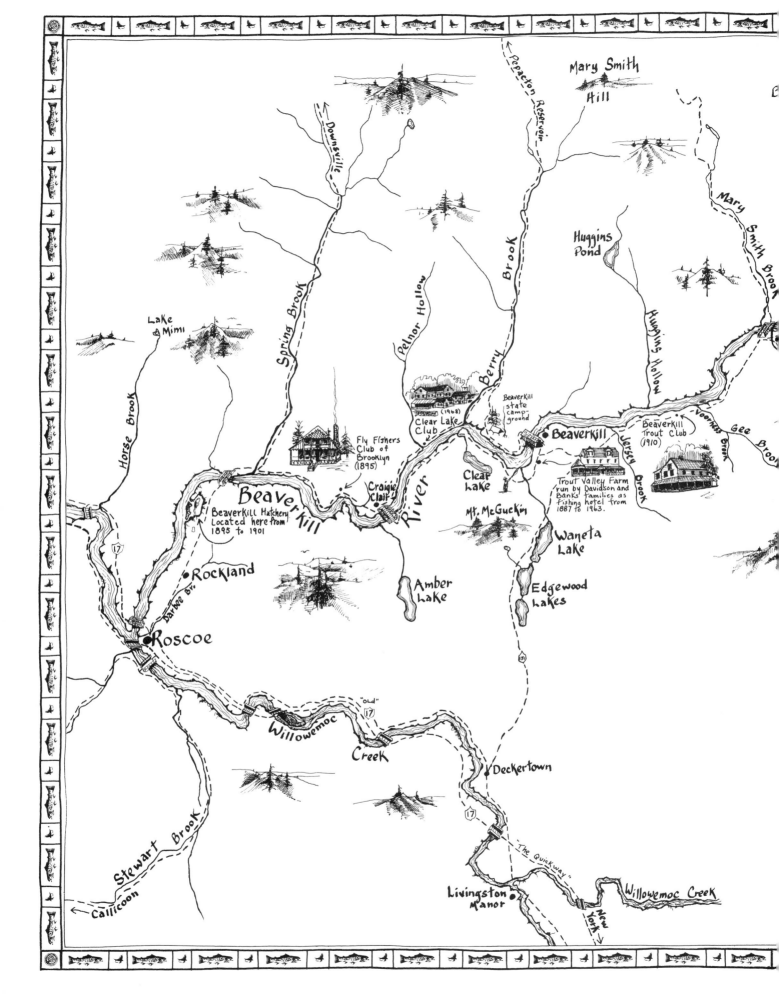

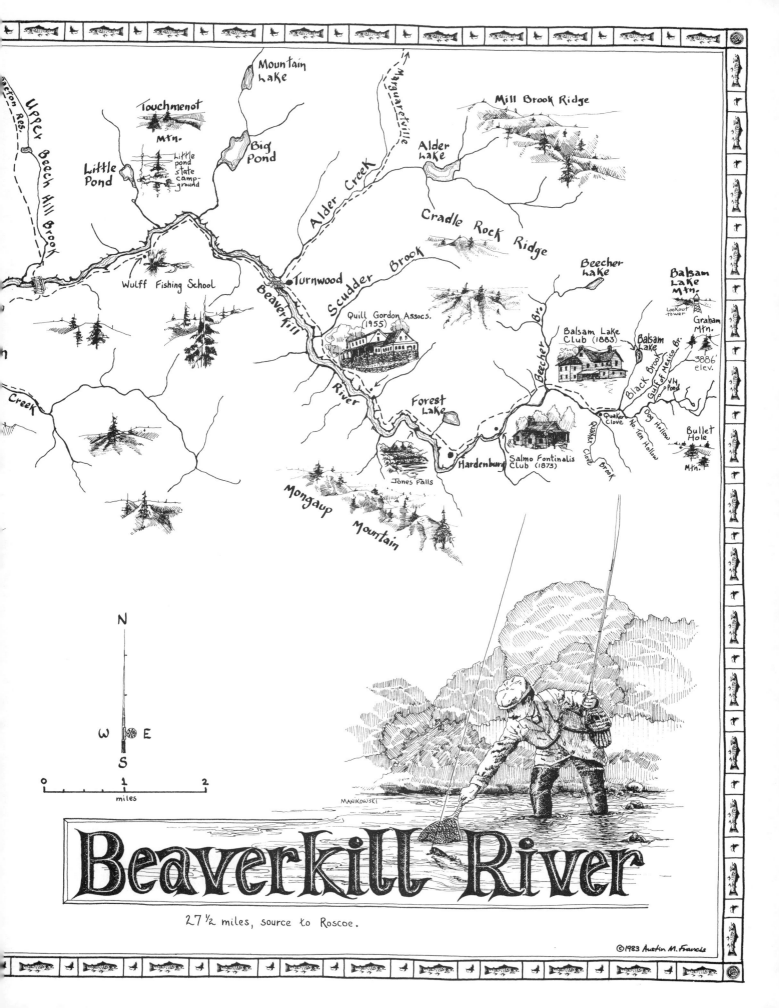

Beaverkill River

27 ½ miles, source to Roscoe.

©1983 Austin M. Francis

In its physical character, the upper river begins as a steep, narrow, rocky little stream, varying from five to twenty-five feet wide in its first five miles. The bottom is of sand and gravel, large, crowded, angular rocks, and interspersed pocket-sized pools of one to two feet deep. The stream is arched over with a dense growth of beech, birch, and maple, with scattered cherry, ash, and hemlock.

Occasionally, an exposed section of bedrock forms the bank or stream-bottom. At these places are the larger pools of the upper river, where solid rock surfaces direct the water's cutting force over, down, and around, continually sweeping out the sand and gravel, maintaining pools that are as deep and permanent as a pool can be in the continually shifting bed of a freestone stream.

Bedrock pools of the upper river are nature's green parlors: ledges covered with emerald mosses, dripping jeweled drops, ferns rising from the moss all around, and hemlocks with their shallow roots clinging to the rock surfaces where other trees cannot, their branches reaching over the stream, deepening the blue-green color of the pools.

Because much of the upper Beaverkill is protected by these cool glens and long archways of hardwoods, and is fed also by many cool springs, its waters rarely rise above 70°, a principal reason for its abundance of trout.

The next 12 miles from the Balsam Lake outlet to Shin Creek at Lew Beach range in width from 20 to 60 feet. The large boulders are more spread out, shallow riffle sections are more pronounced, and there are a few medium-sized pools.

The most prominent feature in this section of the Beaverkill is Jones Falls. Located about two miles above the community of Turnwood, the falls are formed where the river cuts through a large section of bedrock and plunges 30 to 40 feet into a deep, frothing pool.

Less than a mile below Jones Falls is a big hole formed by several big rocks, or at least there was in August of 1926, when Fred Shaver pulled out of it a 28-inch, 9¾ lb. brown trout on a brown fly. "You take them great big flies along late in the season," he said, "drag 'em on top of the water and they'll make a wave—boom!—when they hit it, they hit it!" He entered his trout in the *Field & Stream* contest that year, and it won a national prize.

From Lew Beach to Junction Pool, about 11 miles, the Beaverkill grows in all its dimensions. It is wider, from 50 to 75 feet; the riffle sections are longer; and there are more pronounced pools, ranging in depth from two to four feet. Several pools are even deeper, the largest of which is the Covered Bridge pool at the state campsites. Here the river enters a broad, full run, hits a rock wall about twenty feet high, and digs out—next to the stepped, underwater ledge beneath the bridge—a long, left-curving pool up to eight feet deep. Each year a couple of very large trout are taken from this pool, often during the first week of the fishing season.

The last comprehensive survey of the upper Beaverkill's fish population was conducted by the state in 1953. From the samplings taken at twenty-nine sections of the stream, there emerged two distinctly different distributions of trout: from Junction Pool to the thirty-foot barrier of Jones Falls, there were 78 percent brown trout, 19 percent brook trout, and 3 percent rainbows (commenting on these figures, Ed Van Put said, "My current angling experience is more like 57 percent browns and 40 percent brook trout"); above the falls up to the last sample point at the outlet of Balsam Lake, the three species were distributed almost evenly in thirds. The explanation for so many rainbows appears to have been the stocking preferences of several of the fishing clubs and individual owners. No samples were taken in the uppermost five miles, but presumably there would have been almost all brook trout. Chubs were not found above Junction Pool and smallmouth bass disappeared from the samplings one mile farther upstream. Suckers existed up to Jones Falls, beyond which there were only trout and sculpin.

At Junction Pool the Beaverkill is joined by the Willowemoc, doubling in size and fully earning the distinction of its lower mileage as the "Big River." The sharply angled convergence of two streams of equal force creates a pool of complex currents and eddies, on which anglers sometimes watch hatching insects riding upstream. The story is that Junction Pool's confusing currents cause migrating trout to linger for days trying to decide which stream to enter and this is why so many large trout are taken from this pool. The mythical leader of these indecisive trout is the Beamoc, a brown trout with a beaver's tail and two antlered heads, one of which gazes longingly up the Beaverkill, while the other hankers for the Willowemoc. Unable to make up its minds, the Beamoc lives out its life in Junction Pool. One of the reasons for Junction Pool's fame and popularity is the longstanding competition to land the Beamoc.

Junction Pool is also famous because it unites two of the country's best-known trout streams, with the result that it has become the symbolic center of Catskill angling—the official site for the observance of Opening Day of trout season. Readers of the sports pages on April 2 have come to expect the opening-day photograph in *The New York Times* and other northeastern newspapers showing several dozen fishermen jammed together in Junction Pool casting everything from the tiniest nymphs to the fattest night crawlers for their first trout of the year.

The first five miles downstream from Junction Pool contain a series of pools and riffles that are possibly the most historic in the lore of American angling. Ferdon's, Barnhart's, Hendrickson's, Wagon Tracks, Mountain Pool, are but a few of the names familiar to fly fishermen. These pools are classic dry-fly water and are heavily fished today, as they have been ever since the brown trout established itself in Catskill rivers.

This section of the Beaverkill is upwards of one hundred feet wide, with plenty of room for a backcast. Hardwoods, hemlocks, and small groves of willows and alders line the banks. The pools are long and range in depth from two to six feet with a few that have deep holes of eight to ten feet. The riffles are also long and there are extended stretches of pocket water. The bottom is mostly

The upper Beaverkill, left, and Willowemoc meet at Junction Pool, forming the lower Beaverkill, bottom right, with the village of Roscoe in the background. Except for a four-lane highway and its concrete bridge in place of the O&W railroad and its trestle, everything today looks much the same as it did in this 1947 photograph. *Courtesy Harry Darbee.*

sand, gravel, large boulders, and in areas of quieter flow, a mixture of silt and organic debris, offering an excellent home for all types of crawling, swimming, and burrowing larvae and nymphs. As a result, the hatches are heavy and varied and the trout usually quite fat.

The Beaverkill no-kill section, considered by some to be the best stretch of trout water anywhere in the country, begins where the Delaware County line crosses the river at the upper end of Barnhart's Pool and continues for 2½ miles to the old railroad trestle downstream from the Red Rose restaurant and motel.

The no-kill regulation, put into effect on this stretch in 1965, has kept a lot of one- and two-pound fish in the river. Anglers are always fishing over fish, those who know the river well often catching twenty to thirty fish a day.

More than fifteen hundred anglers per mile are estimated to fish the no-kill section every year. "This river has never been more popular than it is today," said Ed Van Put. "You always want to remember one thing about the good old days—they never fished down here after the Fourth of July. By that time all the fish had been caught out. That was it. Now, because the fish can be caught over and over again, they fish here all year long." Several years ago the open season for trout was extended to the full year on the no-kill sections of the Beaverkill and Willowemoc, and there are now very few weekends even in mid-winter when a few stout-hearted (foolhardy?) anglers can't be found casting in the pools and pockets of the no-kill.

No-kill fishing has worked extremely well for the Beaverkill and Willowemoc. In fact, the catches per angler went up so dramatically right after the new regulations took effect that the state tried not stocking for a year or two, but they found that natural reproduction in these sections of the river was not good enough to maintain the stream at its carrying capacity. In October and November the bigger fish would move upriver to spawn, but not enough of them, or their young, returned to the lower river. There is plenty of food, and growth rates are excellent, but annual stockings are required to get the best return from these sections. Thus, no-kill fish are probably 90 percent from the hatchery; however, the large majority are holdovers whose muscles are now firm. As bait fishermen (not allowed in the no-kill) have been heard to remark when they creel wild or holdover trout along with soft, recently stocked fish, "I got three fish, two 'hard ones.' "

Horse Brook Run and Cairns's Pool are typical no-kill water. Flowing between Hendrickson's and Cairns's pools, Horse Brook Run is a quarter-mile of fast, broken water littered with huge boulders that create perhaps the finest stretch of pocket water on the whole river. These boulders give respite to thousands of brown trout from the twisting currents in which they have grown to be vigorous, hard-fighting fish. When Horse Brook Run is running high it is treacherous wading. Fifty years ago, Vern Heyney used to wade through its rifts in high water and the banks would be lined with fishermen gaping in disbelief. No one else would dare go out there, but Heyney, who was built like a moose, could wade like one too.

On almost any day during the trout season, Cairns's Pool will have more fish *and* more fishermen in it than any other pool on the river. Adding to its popularity as part of the no-kill section is a magnificently deep, boulder-lined run that is just right for big trout. The far bank of this run plus the remainder of Cairns's thousand-foot length is reinforced by huge rock riprap of the abandoned O & W railroad bed, a legacy from the old days that has helped preserve the pool in times of flood.

Cairns's is a very noisy, social pool—literally and figuratively a crossroads of angling. The four-lane highway crosses the river at its head, and beneath it and parallel to the river runs two-lane "Old 17," now used only by fishermen and local traffic. All the heavy traffic roaring overhead is in part a blessing for it used

© 1983 Austin M. Francis

MANIKOWSKI

BeaverKill R

15 ½ miles, Roscoe to East Branch.

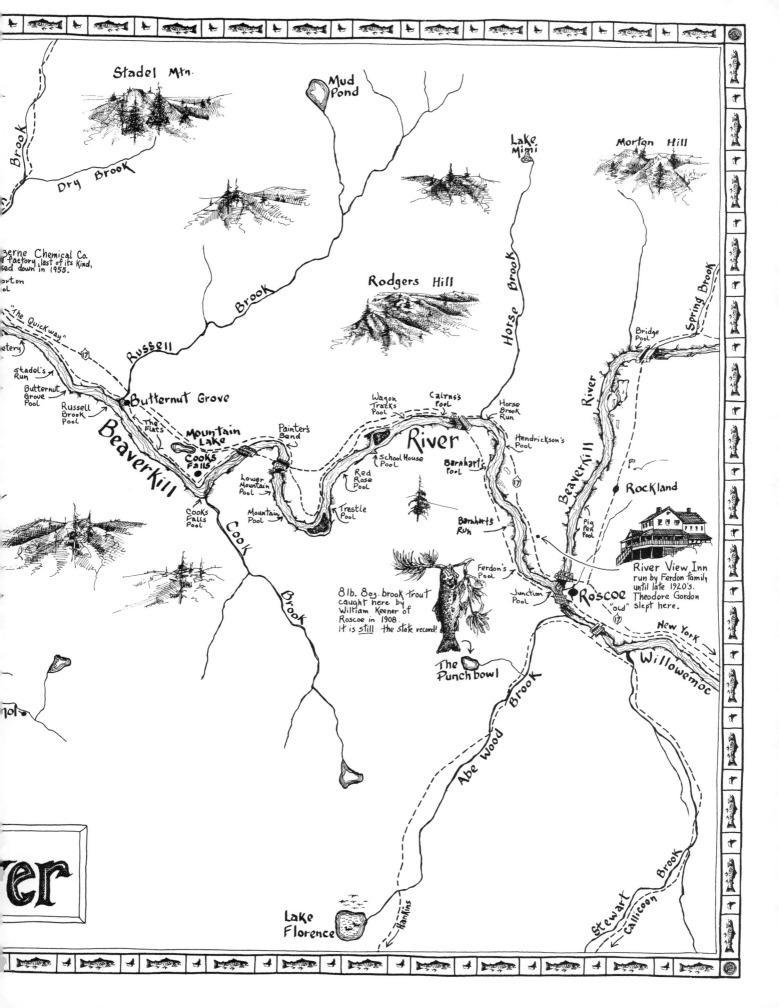

Stadel Mtn.

Mud Pond

Lake Mimi

Morton Hill

Brook

Dry Brook

Zerne Chemical Co.
factory, last of its kind,
sed down in 1955.
orton
ol

Rodgers Hill

Horse Brook

Spring Brook

Russell Brook

"The Quickway"

etery

17

Stadol's Run

Butternut Grove Pool

Russell Brook Pool

Beaverkill

The Flats

Butternut Grove

Mountain Lake

Cooks Falls

Painter's Bend

Wagon Tracks Pool

Cairns's Pool

River

School House Pool

Red Rose Pool

Lower Mountain Pool

Mountain Pool

Trestle Pool

Horse Brook Run

Hendrickson's Pool

Barnhart's Pool

Bridge Pool

Beaverkill River

Rockland

Pig Pen Pool

River View Inn
run by Ferdon family
until late 1920's. Theodore Gordon
"old" slept here.

Barnhart's Run

Cooks Falls Pool

Cook Brook

8 lb. 8 oz. brook trout
caught here by
William Keener of
Roscoe in 1908.
It is still the state record!

Ferdon's Pool

Junction Pool

Roscoe

17

New York

The Punchbowl

Willowemoc

Abe Wood Brook

Hankins

Stewart Brook

Callicoon Brook

Lake Florence

to be on the old road, to cross which was to take your life in your hands. Hard-bitten no-killers tune out the din because they know that if trout are rising anywhere on the Beaverkill they will be rising at Cairns's.

During a good hatch there are over two-dozen fishermen crowded waist-deep into Cairns's, little more than a rod's length apart, all casting to rising fish. Lined up on the bank another group sits watching, giving gratuitous advice, almost all of it supportive, with perhaps an occasional gibe for an inept cast or a lost fish. And back up at the road is yet a third group standing around their cars, debating tactics, showing off flies, exchanging tackle, and making plans for next week's fishing.

Below Cairns's is the favorite pool of Sparse Grey Hackle, one in fact that he named, the Wagon Tracks. At its head is the ford where Chester Cairns used to cross the river to his cornfield. It was in the Wagon Tracks that Sparse developed his keen appreciation for night fishing, which he considered the essence of angling.

> It is a gorgeous gambling game in which one stakes the certainty of long hours of faceless fumbling, nerve-racking starts, frights, falls, and fishless baskets against the off-chance of hooking into—not landing necessarily or even probably, but hooking into—a fish as long and heavy as a railroad tie and as unmanageable as a runaway submarine.

"Old 17" follows closely down the right bank of the river, providing easy access in turn to School House, Red Rose, Trestle, and Mountain pools. A series of horse-watering troughs used to line the road along most of the lower Beaverkill into the late 1920s, tapping the cold springs that flowed from the mountainside into the river. The troughs are gone but the springs remain and are vitally important to both fish and fishermen when the temperature of the river gets into the mid-eighties, as it does occasionally each summer. In its last 10 miles, the lower Beaverkill flows through long, shallow riffles between pools, with numerous exposed gravel bars, and ranges in width from 150 to 200 or more feet, so that even the largest trees provide only a fringe of shade along the banks.

When the river heats up the trout seek out the cold spots next to tributary mouths, bankside springs, and spring holes in the riverbed. Knowing where these are can produce good fishing even in the warmest weather. The best way to locate springs is to walk along the river, keeping out of sight of the fish, and see where the fish gather when the river is warm; the fish themselves will tell you where the springs are. Another way is by wading wet. The water from a spring hole comes in at around 45° to 50° and if you step right into one when the river is warm, it's like stepping into a bucket of ice water.

Harry Darbee had yet another way to locate springs when he was learning the river: "If you see bright green algae, that's what they call 'frog spawn,' a slimy algae, no leaves, no stems, no nothin'—wherever you see that you got cold water. It won't grow in warm water. There are species of it that grow in warm water, but they would be brownish green."

"Why is it called 'frog spawn'?" a fisherman asked.

"Because that's what they thought it was, the old-timers. They didn't know their ass from third base; they thought milk snakes would milk a cow, too!"

The two sharpest bends in the lower Beaverkill come one right after the other, forming a giant, backward "S"—Mountain Pool and Painter's Bend. Each is formed where the river runs head-on into the steep side of a mountain and is forced almost entirely back on itself. Painter's Bend used to be a far more interesting place to fish before all its big, block-shaped boulders got blown out. Back when panthers roamed the Catskills, they used to leap across the river on those boulders. The old-timers called them "painters," and that is how the bend got its name. During World War I, when they wanted to float four-foot wood down the river to the acid factory at Horton, most of the big boulders were dynamited to clear the way. One of them survived into the 1950s when it too was blasted out because a tree had hung up on it and was diverting the river against a roadside retaining wall.

Painter's Bend and the half-mile straightaway just below it are beautiful pocket water. Like Horse Brook Run upstream, the shallow sections of these pocket stretches can be very productive during the *Isonychia* hatch. The fish come up into the shallows to get the *Isonychia* nymphs before they crawl onto the bankside stones to hatch. "If you ever get in here and the Isonychia is hatching," says Harry Darbee, "cast the Isonychia nymph across in the shallow riffs and pull it along in little jerks, but pull it *fast*, because the Isonychia nymph swims like a minnow, and he can move and stand the current, and that swimming across the current will get you a fish!"

Next downriver is Cooks Falls Pool, a deep hole beneath a bridge that has held some very large trout over the years. Farther down from that is a full mile of excellent pocket and riffle water, known as The Flats, that used to have a deep run in front of a restaurant and bar then known as the Swiss American. It was in this run that Sparse Grey Hackle cast his own invention, a bead-chain nymph painted poison-green with Duco airplane enamel:

I cast as far as I could upstream with a big 9-foot rod (it was a terribly bitching thing to cast, that nymph), let it come down on a loose line and straighten out below me.

I got a strike that nearly straightened out my arm, and brought in the biggest chub I ever saw in the Beaverkill. I kept getting these big chubs and then I got a hell of a strike that took off the nymph. That weekend and the following I lost all of these nymphs that I had—either three or four—the same way. I never could figure whether it was an extra big chub or a big trout that did it.

Anatomy of an ice jam: looking downstream, lower Beaverkill above Cooks Falls, winter of 1947/48 . . . river froze on top . . . thaw and rain broke up ice . . . chunks and slabs moved slowly down to narrows in background and began backing up . . . increasing weight of jam and pressure of dammed water built to irresistible force . . . entire mass tore loose and swept downstream . . . large numbers of insects, trees, and trout were killed. *Courtesy Harry Darbee.*

Another mile downstream is the beginning of the Horton no-kill section, 1¾ miles of water including Stadel's Run, Cemetery Pool, Freeman's Flat, Horton Pool, Acid Factory and Railroad runs. This section was established by the state following the success of the no-kills upstream on the Beaverkill and Willowemoc. Only its newness and location farther downstream have kept the Horton no-kill from being as popular as the ones upstream, for it contains some excellent trout water.

Below the Horton no-kill, there is only one more pronounced bend, at Baxter's Pool, over the remaining 6½ miles to the end of the Beaverkill. The river widens, to more than 200 feet, running straighter, shallower, and slower than in its previous mileage. Pools are fewer, not as deep, and gravel bars meander down the center of the broadened riverbed. A single major exception to these conditions occurs at Peakville where the lower Beaverkill is joined by its largest tributary, Trout Brook. At the point where the brook enters, the river also narrows and runs against a high rock cliff on the right, veers to the left, and conforms into a deep ledge pool that continues downstream in several generously deep runs.

The Beaverkill ends, figuratively, at Keener's Pool, for that is where many Beaverkill anglers go to continue their fishing when they come off the river. Keener's Pool, also known as the Antrim Bar, got its name back when Frank Keener ran the Antrim Lodge. It is common knowledge that the biggest trout taken out of the Beaverkill have been landed at Keener's Pool.

R.A. Cunningham

NINE

Willowemoc Creek

In the 1870s, when railroads opened up the Catskills to visiting fishermen, Willowemoc Creek became a tender bit of accessible remoteness. It beckoned and the anglers followed.

New Yorkers rose early, bundled their gear and lunch, and jumped the ferry to Weehawken, New Jersey. There they took a 7:35 A.M. Ontario & Western train at the foot of Jay Street. It ran up the Hudson River to Cornwall, then turned westward through Middletown, Monticello, and Liberty, arriving at Livingston Manor on the Willowemoc at 12:48 P.M.

Pushing on to the upper river, they took a 1:30 mail stage from the Manor which deposited them in the village of Willowemoc around 4:00, where they were met by Mr. Horatio Smith in his buckboard. From there Smith drove them to his boardinghouse on Lake Willowemoc, arriving in time for his guests to wash up and have a short fish before supper. The cost of such outings, in 1890, was $14.81, which included both the train and stage round-trip fares plus board for one week at Mr. Smith's.

J. D. Benham and his friend George Hand stayed at Horatio Smith's in August 1890 and fished the upper Willowemoc. George had never caught a trout before, and he wasn't much of an outdoorsman, but he "caught on" to twelve nice trout, as well as about all the old roots and logs he could find. The last day of their visit, J.D. and George caught thirteen in about twenty minutes, all good-sized fish. George was champion with a twelve-incher. "We could have taken a hundred and thirteen if we had wanted them," said J.D. A lot of small fish was the rule. Earlier that year, Mr. Smith and a companion caught two hundred trout in three hours, eighty of them from one bend in the stream.

The next community downstream, DeBruce, is rich in fly-fishing history.

It was there at the mouth of Mongaup Creek around 1899 that George La-Branche cast his first dry fly, "due more to the exigency of the occasion than to any predevised plan for attempting the feat." From his house next to the junction of these two streams, he began working out the theories that he articulated in 1914 in *The Dry Fly and Fast Water*. LaBranche was also a member of the Beaverkill Trout Club.

Charles B. Ward's DeBruce Club Inn, a carriage-trade fishing hotel, offered golf, tennis, and several miles of the choicest water on the upper Willowemoc. George LaBranche cast his first dry fly a short distance from this porch. Home of the Pink Lady cocktail *and* the Pink Lady fly, the DeBruce Club Inn was a favorite of the Anglers' Club for its outings throughout the 1930s and 1940s. For Gene Connett, it was a place "where the angler is accorded that patient consideration of meals at almost any hour, served by maids who can actually smile." *Courtesy Department of Environmental Conservation and Ed Van Put.*

George LaBranche and Ed Hewitt used to own a stretch of the Willo-wemoc above DeBruce. In an interesting switch on the then current habit of farmers' selling their fishing rights and keeping their land, Hewitt and La-Branche sold their entire Willowemoc property but retained personal fishing rights for the rest of their lives.

During the early 1900s, in the heyday of Catskill resort hotels, there were two recipes for Pink Ladies around DeBruce. One called for pale pink floss ribbed with gold tinsel, duck wings, ginger hackle and tail, all on a #12 hook. It was one of George LaBranche's favorite dry flies. The other recipe called for gin, apple brandy, lemon juice, grenadine, and egg white, shaken strenuously with cracked ice and strained into a tall-stemmed glass. It was a favorite drink of the sporting clientele at Ward's DeBruce Club Inn.

One wants very much to believe the story of a voluptuous blonde guest at Ward's back in the Roaring Twenties who, on her first attempt at angling, anointed her Pink Lady in her Pink Lady and caught a monstrous, bibulous trout. Apocryphal, no doubt.

Mr. Ward ran a carriage-trade fishing establishment. The DeBruce Club Inn had tennis courts and a nine-hole golf course, but it was set up mainly for fishing. Gene Connett, proprietor of the Derrydale Press, known for its deluxe limited editions of sporting books, stayed at Ward's regularly. "The Willowemoc is one of the most charming trout streams," he said. "Its variety of water is almost unlimited, and there is a really comfortable inn at DeBruce where the angler is accorded that patient consideration of meals at almost any hour, served by maids who can actually smile."

In the early years of the inn, servants met you at the door, took care of your horses, and carried your luggage up to enormous rooms with big brass beds. Or you might have been escorted to one of the brown-shingled guest cottages dappled about the inn. The meals were fresh country food, deliciously prepared, and generously heaped. The next morning, by fishing time, your rod would have been taken out of its case, assembled, and hung on a peg next to your own locker in the tackle room. There were no beats. With several miles of water, and genteel angling companions, there was plenty of fishing to go around. At sundown, it sometimes got crowded in the tackle room as fishermen vied for benches to unlace boots, get out of waders, and gather in front of the big open fire in the common room.

Ward sold the DeBruce Club Inn in the late 1940s and the new owner continued to operate it in the old tradition. However, along with many other Catskill hotels in the 1950s, it suffered a continuing loss of business and had to close in 1960. The year before, a group of its regulars including the new owner formed the DeBruce Fly Fishing Club. They lease the stream rights from their fellow member and have fitted out as a clubhouse one of Ward's old brown-shingled guest cottages. The inn itself was torn down and sold for timber in 1970.

The DeBruce Fly Fishing Club seen across one of its ponds in February. This club was formed by regulars of Ward's DeBruce Club Inn who bought Ward's water and property in the late 1940s and set up their clubhouse in one of the inn's guest cabins. *Photo by Robert A. Cunningham.*

*   *   *

If rivers could emote, the Willowemoc would surely envy the Beaverkill. Where they join, the Willowemoc gives up its name to its nobler twin. But why should *it* be the tributary when, before they were settled, the Willowemoc was every mile as good a trout river? Look at the evidence.

Above their celebrated Junction Pool, the Willowemoc is only 4 percent shorter than the Beaverkill. Its tributaries, almost equal in number, are more extensively developed and definitely superior as trout spawning grounds. Its headwaters produce more wild brook trout than any other Catskill river. And, where they join, it continues flowing in the same direction while the Beaverkill almost doubles back on itself to accommodate the "lesser" river. And, based on calculations by Ed Van Put, it puts more water into Junction Pool: the Willowemoc drainage area measures approximately 130 square miles while the upper Beaverkill drains 100 square miles. So what happened that it should not be the main river or, more logically, the "South Branch of the Beaverkill"?

The Willowemoc came in second because the Beaverkill was destined for greater fame and protection. Already by 1869, none other than John Burroughs stepped out onto its bank and proclaimed:

> Hail to the Beaverkill!
> How shall I describe that wild, beautiful stream, with features so like those of all other mountain streams? And yet, as I saw it in the deep twilight of those woods on that June afternoon, with its steady, even flow, and its tranquil, many-voiced murmur, it made an impression upon my mind distinct and peculiar, fraught in an eminent degree with the charm of seclusion and remoteness.

What began as a trickle grew to a torrent as outdoor writers followed each other in embellishing the reputation of an already famous river. "Uncle Thad" Norris, Robin Ruff, Ben Bent, Frank Forester, Louis Rhead, William A. Bradley, Frederick White, Arnold Gingrich, Red Smith, Sparse Grey Hackle. Can you imagine Sparse naming his wife "Lady Willowemoc"?

The name itself evolved painfully over the years: Weelewaughwemack, Weelewaughmack, Wilenawemack, Williwernock, Willerwhemack, Williwemauk, Williwemock, Willowemock, Willowemoc. Even that is too cumbersome for stylish anglers; they come and go, speaking of the "Willow." But you will not hear them confuse or shorten the other one. It has always been either Beaver Kill, Beaver-kill, or Beaverkill.

As for protection, the upper Beaverkill was never a thoroughfare, even in the late 1800s when a wagon trail came into the head of its valley over Graham Mountain from Seager on Dry Brook. Soon after the turn of the century, a rough

Sand Pond, formerly Willowemoc Lake, setting of the earliest private fishing club in the Catskills. Formed in 1870 by the Van Cleef, Van Brunt, and Van Norden families, the Willowemoc Club owned this lake plus—over in the Beaverkill valley—Balsam Lake, Thomas Pond (now Beecher Lake), and several miles of the stream. Members walked back and forth over the far mountain separating the two rivers and their lakes. *Photo by the author*.

motor road was completed from the lower river up to the headwaters. The wagon trail grew over from disuse and the upper Beaverkill remained a secluded angling paradise of large land holdings, fly-fishing clubs, and privately owned river mileage.

By contrast, the Willowemoc has always been very accessible by rail or road along its lower seven miles between Livingston Manor and Roscoe. The next fifteen miles upriver have from the earliest sportfishing days been paralleled by a rough road through DeBruce, Willowemoc, and up Fir Brook into the Neversink valley.

As a result, the Willowemoc got chopped up into smaller parcels, and except for the Ward estate and a few other longer stretches higher up, it sprouted into a patchwork of hotels, boardinghouses, bungalow colonies, summer camps, sanitariums, and campsites. In the 1950s, the hotels and inns declined and gave way to even smaller lots, vacation cabins, and trailer homes.

It is unfair to suggest that the Willowemoc is a steady procession of unsightly development. There are beautiful, unspoiled sections of the river, both public and private, which run away from the road and through more sparsely populated parts of the valley. Conversely, the Beaverkill valley has eyesores of its own. Moreover, the differences between these two rivers cannot be proven to have influenced the selection of their names. To a fisherman, the notoriety of his stream is secondary to its productivity. He can even tolerate a trailer or two if he is catching fish. And in this regard, the Willowemoc has no reason to be envious at all.

*　　　*　　　*

From its source to its mouth, Willowemoc Creek is 26.7 miles long. It rises on the south flank of Beaverkill Range at an elevation of 2,900 feet, turns, and flows almost due west, falling over 200 feet per mile in its first few miles. It levels out quickly to one of the gentler headwater grades to be found in the Catskills. In fact, Fir Brook, the first major tributary, is like an Adirondack bog stream. Silent and slow, ten to 15 feet wide, it meanders among grassy hummocks, grown up on the silt from centuries of beaver dams. For nearly five miles it flows through a hemlock-lined meadow, its series of still pools like little ponds, with sandy silted bottoms up to four and five feet deep. Deep for a small stream. And productive.

You walk along the bank, throw a nymph in, let it sit for a while, twitch it a couple of times, and catch a brook trout. Then go to the next pool. It's almost like worm fishing; you don't have to do much casting. It's better one-man fishing. You can't fish side-by-side, as on the lower river; you've got to cover the water, jump from pool to pool, maybe leapfrogging with one other fisherman.

On the Willowemoc itself, north of and parallel to Fir Brook, the same approach works very well. "You could easily have a fifty-fish day up here catching little eight- to ten-inch brook trout," says Ed Van Put.

The entire upper Willowemoc basin is perfectly suited for raising brook trout. Plenty of springs seep in from all sides, keeping the streams full and cool most of the year. A rich broth of plant decay, microorganisms, and stream insects is there to support an abundance of wild fish. And there is excellent bank cover with more than the usual number of hemlock and spruce lining the banks.

Public fishing rights were bought by the state along much of Fir Brook in the 1950s. Since then, other sections on the main stream have been acquired, either outright or for fishing only, so that the upper Willowemoc is open in many places to public fishing. The middle section of the river, from the village of Willowemoc down to Livingston Manor is largely unposted or open via public fishing rights; posting is intermittent on about six of the 20½ miles. Below Livingston Manor, the remainder of the Willowemoc down to Roscoe is open to the public.

Brown trout appear in greater numbers below the mouth of Fir Brook. The state stocks only browns in the Willowemoc. Brook trout thrive without help in the upper reaches and rainbows have never done well in this river—except when they're getting handouts, as did the fish that used to live at Hazel Bridge below Harry Darbee's.

A woman living in a trailer next to the bridge stopped Ed Van Put one day and said, "You want to see something?" She took him out onto the bridge and threw bread off the bridge. A huge rainbow, about twenty-one inches, zoomed up from beneath an old railroad abutment almost two hundred feet below the bridge. He ate every piece she threw out there, wolfing them down.

"I was down there one day standing on the abutment," said Ed, "and saw her walk out on the bridge, and saw that fish *leave* just as she came onto the bridge. It was amazing! Elsie Darbee and I later identified him with binoculars as a big rainbow. He must have come from one of the clubs."

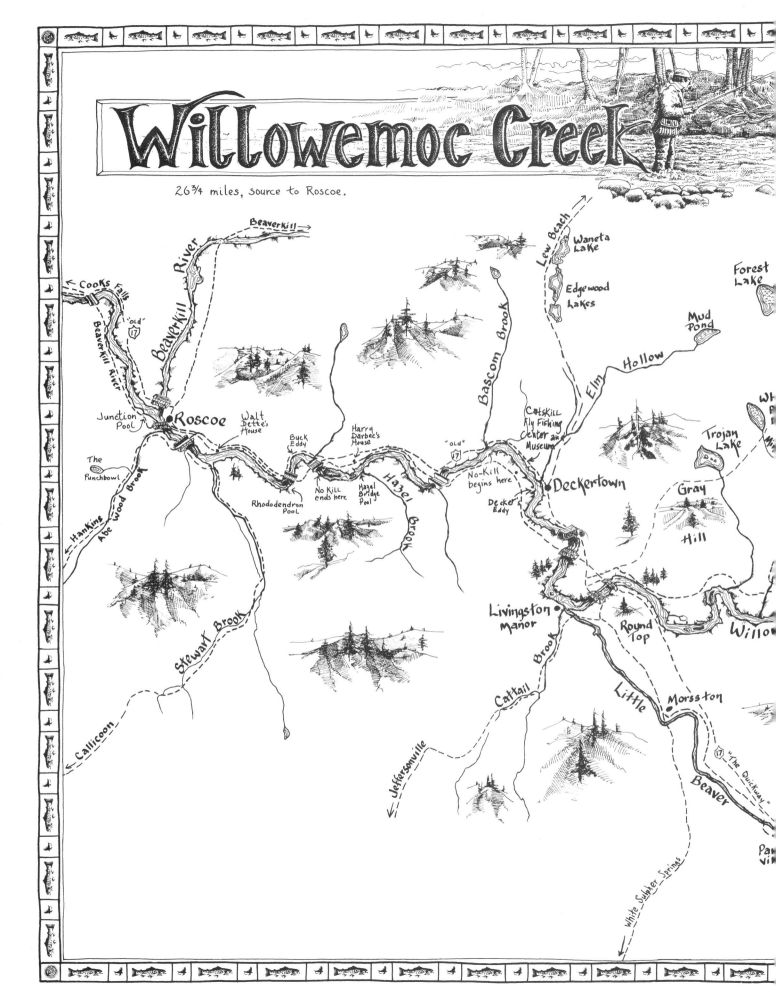

Willowemoc Creek

26¾ miles, source to Roscoe.

Beaverkill →

Beaverkill River

Cooks Falls

"old" 17

Beaverkill River

Junction Pool

Roscoe

Walt Dette's House

The Punchbowl

Hankins

Abe Wood Brook

Buck Eddy

No Kill ends here

Rhododendron Pool

Harry Darbee's House

Hazel Bridge Pool

Hazel Brook

"old" 17

No-Kill begins here

Decker Eddy

Catskill Fly Fishing Center and Museum

Deckertown

Stewart Brook

Callicoon

Jeffersonville

Cattail Brook

Livingston Manor

Round Top

Little

Morsston

Lew Beach

Waneta Lake

Edgewood Lakes

Bascom Brook

Elm Hollow

Mud Pond

Forest Lake

Trojan Lake

Gray Hill

Willo

Wh

17 "The Quickway"

Beaver

Pa vi

White Sulphur Springs

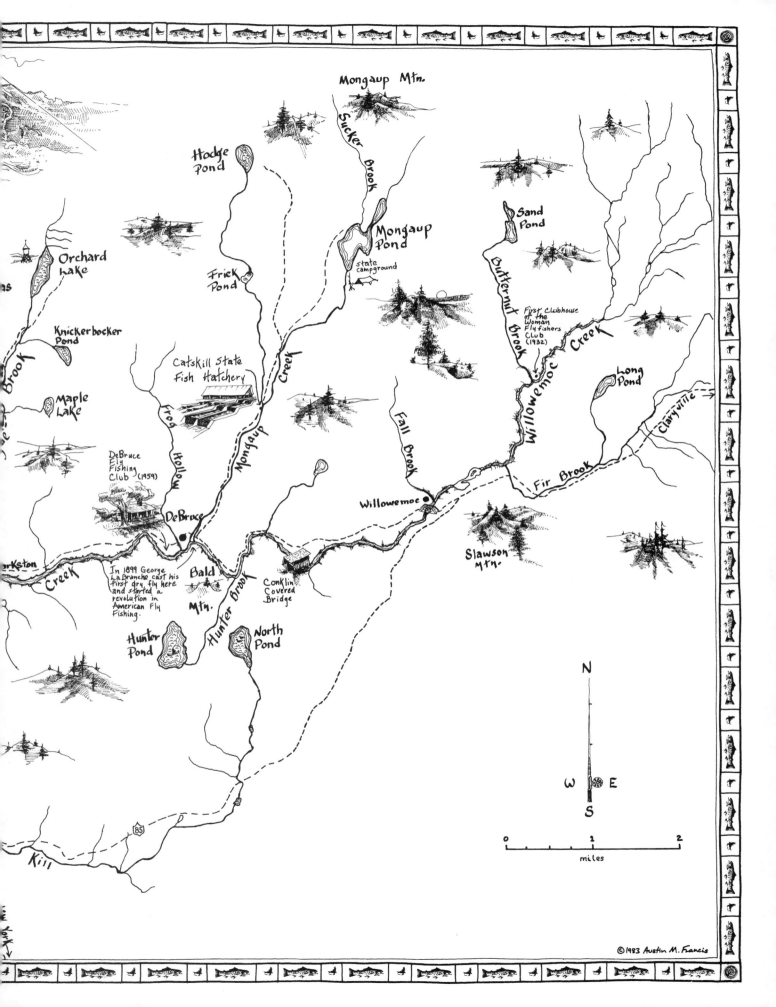

Big Rock Pool on the upper Willowemoc. Until recently the Willowemoc suffered an image problem when compared with the Beaverkill because so few of its pools were named. To overcome this deficiency, Beamoc Chapter of TU—imitating what Catskill Mountains Chapter had done for the Esopus two years earlier—collected or created names and published maps of the pools and access points for the Willowemoc and two of its neighboring streams. *Photo by Robert A. Cunningham.*

The middle Willowemoc actually steepens a little after its flat, boggy headwaters, falling about forty feet per mile until it reaches Livingston Manor. Throughout this fifteen or so miles, it ranges from twenty to fifty feet wide, with pools from two to four feet deep. The bottom consists of medium to smaller boulders and gravel. There is a good balance between fast water and silted eddies, the result being a nice accommodation of both burrowing and non-burrowing nymphs. Hatches, especially caddis, are frequent, varied, and heavy.

Fishing the middle Willowemoc usually produces about an equal number of brook and brown trout. These are smallish fish, running six to eight inches for brooks and nine to ten inches for browns. A twelve-inch fish is a good fish. Bill Kelly, state fisheries biologist, is puzzled as to why this section of the Willowemoc doesn't produce more and bigger fish. "It has all the right characteristics," he says. "Hemlock-lined banks, good bottom, plenty of insects. It's too bad it doesn't fish as good as it looks."

The theory that brook trout hit bright flies was tested one day on this stretch of the river, near the Conklin covered bridge, by Ed Van Put. "I was fishing with two wet flies, a Hare's Ear on the point and a Royal Coachman as a dropper and I caught eight or nine fish, browns and brookies. Every brown hit the Hare's Ear and every brookie hit the Royal Coachman. It was classic, by the book, fishing!"

Because of its many well-developed tributaries—Fir, Mongaup, Sprague, Little Beaverkill, Cattail, Stewart—one of the best ways to fish the Willowemoc is off the mouths of these feeder streams, especially when the trout are getting ready to go up them to spawn. The Department of Environmental Conservation shocked just below one of them in September a few years ago and counted two dozen fish fifteen to sixteen inches long. The pools above and below these tributaries are also good places to fish.

The lower Willowemoc between Livingston Manor and Roscoe opens up and becomes quite a good-sized trout stream. It varies from forty to one hundred feet wide. The wading is easy and there is a good mixture of riffles and pools. The pools are three to five feet deep, the notable exception being the Sherwood Flats pool. It appeared almost overnight when an ice jam forced the water beneath to dig out its fifteen-foot depth. Pools of this sort are of course ephemeral and a flood of only average proportions could fill it up as quickly as it got dug.

Bankside cover along these last seven and a half miles of the river thins out a lot. Stretches of completely open river alternate with stretches lined by maples, oaks, sycamores. The hemlocks are gone except on a few steep banks that slant sharply into the river.

The best fly fishing today on the Willowemoc is in the 2.4-mile no-kill section extending from Bascom Brook to the first highway overpass below Hazel Brook. Inaugurated in 1969, the Willowemoc no-kill is every bit as productive as the one established on the Beaverkill four years earlier. If there is a difference, it lies once again in the area of notoriety; the Willowemoc did not enjoy, as early as its more famous neighbor, the naming of its pools and runs. There used to be speculation, before most of the pools were named in 1982, that the Willowemoc no-kill angler was more secure, that he didn't need the recognition from being able to pull up to the Antrim bar and say, "The strangest thing happened to me this morning as I was fishing in the head of Cairns's . . . ."

The state conservation department ran a creel census the first and second years of the Willowemoc no-kill, comparing the effect of the new regulations—artificial lures only and no fish in possession—with those on the rest of the river. They found that four times more trout were caught by fishermen in the no-kill area in the first year alone. In the second year, both the number of fishermen *and* the trout caught per trip increased substantially, strong testimony to the success of these special regulations.

The best time to fish the Willowemoc no-kill is from April to June. In July and August, when the water warms up, the trout feed less and lose weight ("slink out," as Ed Van Put says). They reawaken when the stream cools in September but are already moving out to spawn. By October the mature fish are gone to the tributaries.

In the no-kill from April to June, you catch a lot of twelve- to fifteen-inch trout, a few in the 20-inch range. These are mostly hatchery fish, including holdovers—about 90% according to the 1969/70 creel census. In spite of a rich supply of stream insects, the lower Willowemoc depends on hatchery trout. The spawning tributaries are too far away from the no-kill for the young fish to come back with their parents in meaningful numbers.

In the second year of the Willowemoc no-kill, Ed Van Put ran his own test of the fishing conditions. "I fished down to Hazel Bridge one day, covering about a mile of the no-kill, swinging a pair of wet flies on about ten to fifteen feet of line, just to see how many fish I could catch. In two and a half hours, I caught fifty-four fish, lots of elevens and twelves, nothing over fourteen inches, but everything was right—temperatures, water flows, bugs on the water, time of day, and, luckily, the fish were on the bite!"

TEN

Neversink River

John Burroughs quickened his pace as he and three friends climbed up the valley of the "Big Injin" and crossed over onto the West Branch of the Neversink. On this June day in 1869, after a long absence, he had returned to his native Catskill rivers "to pay my respects to them as an angler."

They struck the river quite unexpectedly in the middle of the afternoon at a point where it was a good-sized trout stream.

It proved to be one of those black mountain brooks born of innumerable ice-cold springs, nourished in the shade, and shod, as it were, with thick-matted moss, that every camper-out remembers. The fish are as black as the stream and very wild. They dart from beneath the fringed rocks, or dive with the hook into the dusky depths, an integral part of the silence and the shadows.

They crept upstream. The spell of the moss was over all, and with noiseless tread they leapt from stone to stone and from ledge to ledge along the bed of the stream.

"How cool it is!"

Burroughs looked up the dark, silent defile, heard the solitary voice of the water, and saw the decayed trunks of fallen trees bridging the stream. All he had dreamed as a boy, of the haunts of beasts of prey—the crouching feline tribes, especially if at twilight with the gloom already deepening in the woods—came freshly to mind. They pressed on, wary and alert, speaking to each other in low tones.

Whether haunted or hallowed, the vaulted hemlock sanctuaries of this pristine stream were a place of reverence not only for itinerant anglers, but also for generations of Neversink natives. They made trouting their religion and could as easily fish while they worshipped as they could worship while fishing. This was borne out by one Claryville resident, Andrew Lang, who in 1894 confessed his Sunday weakness: "When I cannot keep the run of the sermon, I occupy myself by catching, in my imagination, large and lusty trout." And who could blame him, when on the church steeple, over his very head, was a weather vane in the image of an enormous trout?

The male population of Claryville were noted fishermen in those days. As soon as a boy got out of his cradle, he got into a trout brook; and by the time he arrived at the dignity of trousers, he knew more about catching trout than the city angler learned in a lifetime. It is told that, in the district schools, examinations on stream formation, location of pools, spring holes, and the like were regularly held, as well as trials of fly casting, and that the first problem in arithmetic began:

"If John has three trout and James has two, how many does the Yorker have?" The answer, of course, was "none."

For some men the Neversink was like a mistress. Its intimate beauty and seductive charm could overwhelm the beholder with an irresistible urge to possess, whether it took the form of outright ownership or just a little overnight poaching. One such man was Clarence Roof, New York importer of spaghetti and olive oil.

Roof came up regularly in the 1870s to the West Branch of the Neversink. He stayed at the "Parker Place," a small, informal hunting and fishing preserve. The proprietor, Martin Parker, was the first to stock and post this stream, but the local habitués ignored his signs and continued to fish it at will. Parker resisted, but the preserve was "poached by night and by day, the guardians were ill-treated and every effort was made to drive the members away or make their stay uncomfortable." Parker became discouraged and gave up, but not Roof. Infuriated, he wanted the poachers punished, and even more than that, he wanted the stream for himself. So he made Parker an offer he could not refuse. With the Parker Place as his centerpiece, Roof continued to buy surrounding farms until he had put together four thousand acres and five miles of trout stream. In one of the deeds he acquired, a former Indian owner had made a sign translated by a witness as "Wintoon." Roof liked the word so much that he chose it for the name of his Neversink preserve.

Under its new ownership, the West Branch of the Neversink became the setting for what the *Pine Hill Sentinel* billed as "The Great Trout Wars." It was Roof against the poachers, and he went after them with a vengeance. He had trespassers arrested and brought into court. He hired numerous lawyers to prosecute his cases. He pursued three young men for eight years through a series of trials and appeals only to have them acquitted. But overall he succeeded in his goal to create a private preserve for himself, his friends, and his descendants. The river has been in the family for more than one hundred years.

The Parker Place, a small hunting and fishing preserve on the West Branch of the Neversink, with a freshly skinned bear hide drying in the yard. The owner, Martin Parker, was the first to stock and post this stream in the 1870s, causing an uproar among local fisherman; the stream "was poached by night and by day, the guardians were ill-treated and every effort was made to drive the members away or make their stay uncomfortable." *Courtesy Frank Hovey-Roof Connell.*

Clarence Roof, new owner of the Parker Place, surrounded by his sporting equipment. Roof, a New York importer, bought out Parker in 1882 and cracked down on the poachers with arrests and lawsuits. He continued buying farm properties in the valley until he had assembled four thousand acres and five miles of trout stream. He named his new Neversink preserve "Wintoon." *Courtesy Frank Hovey-Roof Connell.*

Raphael Govin, one of Roof's lawyers from New York, shuttled back and forth from the city so often that he too fell in love with the Neversink. With Roof's help, Govin was able to buy several thousand acres of his own, including five miles of the East Branch, the last mile downstream on the West Branch, and Round Pond, which he renamed Govin Lake.

Govin took a different approach to protecting his section of the river. Perhaps he rejected a "total lockout" policy because an old woman in the middle of his new estate refused to sell, or he may have simply not wanted to be a prosecutor both on and off the job. Whatever his reason, he chose to hire Ira Irwin, the valley's best-known poacher, as the caretaker of his property, and to post only certain stretches of the stream. As a result, Govin had far less trouble with poachers than Roof.

For all their efforts to acquire the streams, neither of these men was a dedicated fly fisherman. Roof preferred riding horseback around "Wintoon," and Govin's only fishing was in his lake. He liked to be rowed around so he could troll for pickerel. The serious fly fishing at the time was being done a few miles farther downstream, on the main branch of the river, by a newcomer named Theodore Gordon.

Gordon moved to the Neversink in the early 1890s. It was there over the next twenty-five years that his fishing, writing, and flytying established him as the leading American angler of his day.

Gordon was a frail man, about 5′ 3″ tall, weighing ninety pounds, and a consumptive. These qualities undoubtedly influenced his choice of a solitary life and helped him, as John McDonald observed, "to put one thing only into his mind—the stream—and sustain it there unflaggingly for a great many years."

He was also a lonely man and it comforted him to write in his articles for fishing periodicals:

> It is a bitter cold winter's night and I am far away from the cheerful lights of town or city. The north wind is shrieking and tearing at this lonely house, like some evil demon . . . the wood-burning stove is my only companion. It is on nights such as these that our thoughts stray to the time of leaf and blossom when birds sing merrily and trout are rising in the pools. Spring is near, quite near, and it will soon be time to go fishing. We want to talk about it dreadfully. O for a brother crank of the fly-fishing fraternity, one who would be ready to listen occasionally and not insist upon doing all the talking, telling all the stories himself. But if we cannot talk we can write, and it is just possible that some dear brother angler will read what we say upon paper. There is some comfort in that idea, so here goes.

Gordon tried in the winter to break up his daily routine to avoid boredom but admitted that one day was much like another. "What victims of habit we become," he said. "I write for two hours, tramp in the country two hours, lunch, tie flies, tramp again, and read all evening."

In the spring, Gordon made trips to other Catskill rivers from his base on the Neversink, often staying a week or two at each one. On the Beaverkill he was welcome on the water of the Brooklyn Fly Fishers and up at J. L. Snedecor's stretch near Jones Mills Falls. His stooped profile and long rod bobbing along the streams was a familiar sight on the Neversink, Willowemoc, and Beaverkill.

Gordon never owned property in the Catskills and he never joined a fishing club. He mentions "our little club, the Fly Fishers," but all attempts to confirm his membership in clubs existing then have failed. Although he fished private water, and had many invitations to do so because of his fame, Gordon was philosophically disposed to public fishing. "Hard-fished, free water is a better test than a preserve where there are but a few fishers," he said, "but one must be liberal-minded enough to allow every mon to gang his ain gait and think and fish as he wishes."

On one occasion, a late June afternoon in 1909, Gordon was fishing a public section of the Neversink. He observed that there were thirty men on about 2½ miles of the stream:

> I met ten of them, and hearing that twenty more were coming down upon me, I confined my attentions to one long pool, until they began to appear at the top. Then . . . I fled homeward. First, however, I relieved my basket of its load of two fish, which I presented to the advance guard, as he had none; also, two flies with which he caught one trout.

Gordon rarely had companions on the stream. Other than his female fishing "chum," with whom his only fishing photographs were taken, he had three Catskill fishing companions. About Bruce Leroy, one of them, all we know is that he inherited a farm in the valley but preferred hunting and fishing to farming. The other two were Roy Steenrod and Herman Christian.

Steenrod went to work in the Liberty post office in 1904 and met Gordon by having to handle his mail ("ten to twelve letters a day") and through selling him foreign money orders with which to buy English fly-tying materials. Gordon taught only one person ever how to tie flies, and that was Steenrod, making him swear "on his honor not to tell anybody" the hints and tips he had been given. On his afternoons off from the post office, Steenrod used to walk the five miles from Liberty to Bradley and spend the afternoons with Gordon.

Herman Christian was an outdoorsman and backwoodsman in the old tradition. He trapped by his own secret methods, hunted, tied flies, and probably caught more trout than any other three fishermen in the Catskills put together. Christian fished regularly with Gordon, often showing him the lies of big fish. Gordon had great respect for his friend's fishing abilities. In a letter to Roy Steenrod, he wrote: "It seems to be an early season. Christian's getting those

In his later years Herman Christian lived in this cabin on his 176-acre farm next to the Big Bend of the Neversink. Essentially a backwoodsman, he lived off the land—bees, maple syrup, timber, a garden, trapping, hunting, fishing—"but my best crop is trout flies." *Courtesy The Anglers' Club Bulletin.*

twenty-six trout on wet fly shows that they are beginning to rise." And sometimes he showed a touch of envy: "I wonder how Christian got those sixteen trout? He used to be very strong with the minnow, and I know they will not rise as long as there is snow water in the streams."

When Theodore Gordon died of tuberculosis in Bradley on May 1, 1915, there was great sorrow in the world of angling. In an obituary published that summer in *Forest and Stream*, the editor called him the most proficient of American flytiers, adding: "He was a man known by nearly all the trout fishermen of the United States." By virtue of his twenty-five-year series of articles in the English journal *Fishing Gazette*, he was considered in that country to be the leading American angling authority. G.E.M. Skues, the great English wet-fly proponent, wrote at Gordon's death: "I have corresponded with many angling enthusiasts, but never with any so persistent and so enthusiastic as he." Gordon always enclosed a "little gift" in his letters to Skues—"a batch of summer duck breast feathers, samples of American woodcock hackles, or offers of some American squirrel or fox or hare." Said Skues, "I think he must have been one of the most generous of men."

George LaBranche, the American dry-fly expert, in a letter of eulogy, called Gordon "the greatest student of fly-fishing in this country, and without exception the best flytier I have ever known." LaBranche ended his letter:

In the great beyond there must be some little corner where anglers are tucked away, where one may hope to meet his streamside associates, and discuss again the old, old theories and experiences— at any rate, I believe there is such a place, that my friend Gordon is there now, and is rigidly reserving a seat next to his for me.

Three years after Gordon's death, Edward Ringwood Hewitt arrived on the Neversink to fill the vacuum. And if any man had the presence and self-esteem to think he could do so, certainly that man was Hewitt. The happy outcome was that he made just as valuable a contribution to angling as Gordon did, but in a marvelously different way.

Ed Hewitt was born into "good solid old New York money"—his grandfather Peter Cooper built the first steam locomotive in America—and was educated as a graduate chemist. He also had the natural talent of a mechanical engineer. Over his lifetime he was granted dozens of patents for a wide variety of inventions, including a black-fly deterrent, the felt-soled wading shoe, an opaque fishing leader, a fishing-line grease, a silent shotgun cartridge, a soap calculated to keep your hands warm in cold water, the bivisible fly (one both he and the fish could see), and a fishing reel that would come apart with the removal of one screw.

Given his abilities, his wealth, and a deep love for trout fishing, it was almost foreordained that Hewitt should become the greatest experimenter in the history of fly fishing. And his laboratory was to be the same section of the Neversink that Gordon lived next to and fished so often. In fact, before Gordon died, Hewitt and LaBranche used to drive up to fish Clarence Roof's water and have dinner with Gordon on the way home.

In 1918 Hewitt began accumulating twenty-seven hundred acres and four miles of river between the village of Neversink and Hall's Mills bridge. Herman Christian sold Hewitt the river frontage that included the Big Bend pool. On his new property, Hewitt enthusiastically set out on the twin projects of scientific trout-raising and stream improvement. Some of his experiments were quite ambitious. He imported salmon eggs from Norway to see if they could be established in the Neversink. He tried to increase the variety and quantity of trout food by bringing over nymphs and larvae of English stream insects. And in his waning years, as a ninety-year-old, when most men would have been vegetating, he sponsored an elaborate three-year project to bring impregnated Atlantic salmon eggs over from Scotland, hatch them, and plant the unfed fry in the river.

About 1933 Hewitt began to feel the effects of the Depression. "He'd lost a great deal of money, which he'd made from his inventions," said Mabel Ingalls. "He needed to turn his mind to other ways of making money, so he decided to rent out rods on his part of the Neversink." About 30 anglers took advantage of the privilege for $120 a year; they became known as the Neversink Rods, with headquarters in an old farmhouse located on high ground overlooking the river at the lower end of the property. It was an inspired answer to Hewitt's dilemma,

Molly's Pool in 1935, peak of the Never-sink Rod days when Ed Hewitt owned "five princely miles of that river." In the foreground is one of Hewitt's plank dams, engineering marvels designed to withstand the destructive force of Catskill ice and floods. Today, all of this is buried beneath the waters of the Neversink Reservoir. *Photo by Henry G. Davis.*

George M. L. LaBranche and Edward R. Hewitt on Hewitt's Neversink water around 1934. Fishing gossip has it that LaBranche used to kid Hewitt about fishing with bait and that a rift grew between them. When friends brought them together to fish and patch things up, each so distracted the other that neither of them caught any fish. *Photo by Henry G. Davis, courtesy Carolyn Capstick.*

for it not only paid for his experiments but also gave him a way of testing their effectiveness.

When his rods were in attendance, Hewitt spent his time showing them how to fish, making sure that any large fish they caught got released, and driving everyone around in an antique high-sprung sedan whose canvas top was aluminum-painted to reflect heat. A hole was pierced at the rear to serve as a rod holder. His rods called this vehicle the "mechanical goat," and he took them anywhere and everywhere in it at terrifying speeds.

When he was about eighty, Hewitt decided to change his Neversink camp from one with a yearly rod-rental basis to a fishing club for half a dozen or so permanent members. Contributing to his decision was the lower level of rod rentals that started during the car-and-gas shortage of World War II and persisted after the war was over. Another major influence was the imminent loss of over half of his river mileage to the Neversink Reservoir, which had been blocked out by New York City and was resuming construction after the war.

One of the benefits to Hewitt from this new arrangement was that he could turn the upkeep of his property over to the club members and continue to fish and pursue such experiments as importing salmon eggs, at the same time creating a self-supporting place of summer recreation for his descendants. Thus was born the Big Bend Club, which continues to this day.

Hewitt's Neversink experiences were the foundation and substance of several books on angling: *Telling on the Trout* (1926), *Hewitt's Handbook of Fly Fishing* (1933), *Nymph Fly Fishing* (1934), and *Seventy-Five Years a Fisherman for Salmon and Trout* (1948).

Besides his trout studies and books, Hewitt was also a consultant "on fishery matters for a large number of clients." Solving their problems added to a fund of experience which he felt was so much greater than anyone else's that he claimed: "I expect I know more about trout than anyone else in the country."

In an interview shortly before his death in 1957 Hewitt said that he wanted to have his ashes thrown into the Neversink. "That way," he said, "it will give the trout a chance to get even."

*   *   *

"The prettiest and crankiest river that I ever put a foot into is the Neversink. It is no baby of a creek, and did I say cranky—well, this river can rise higher and quicker, and fall in less time than any I have ever fished. It reminds me of nothing so much as a flurry in the stock market."

Robin Ruff, who said this in an 1893 article for *The American Angler*, really knew his river. Over the years, many who fished the Neversink, including Gordon and Hewitt, have observed that it is more volatile than other Catskill streams. There are stories of fishermen drowning in the Neversink because they did not pay attention to the water rising around their knees from an upstream thunderstorm.

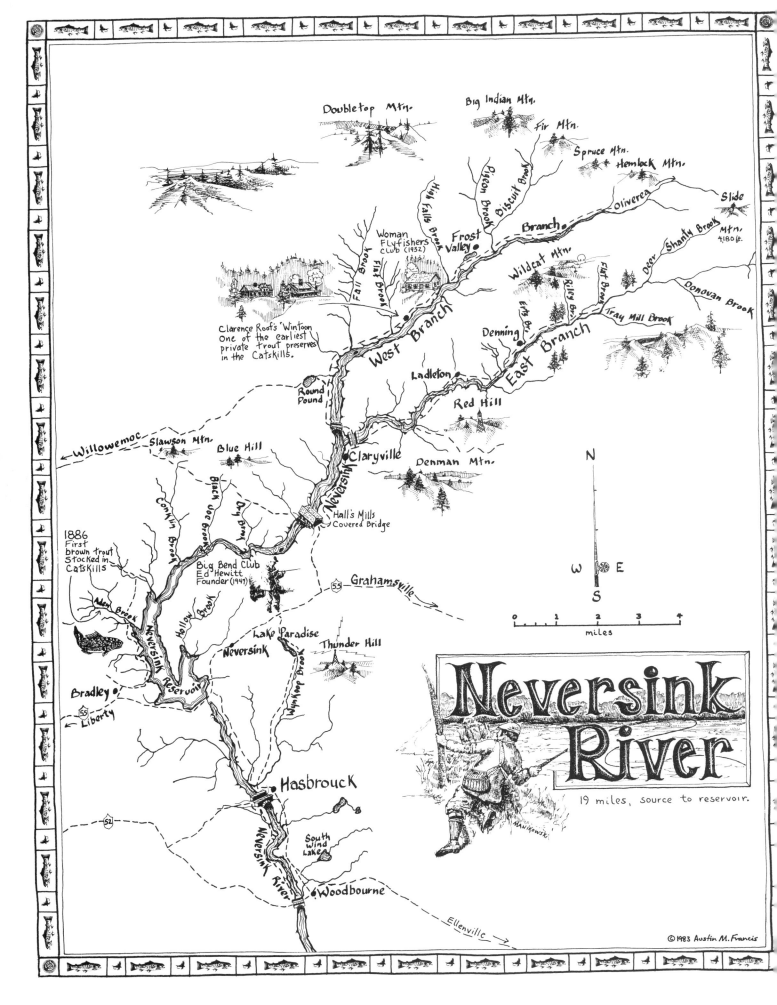

The Neversink River flows through a long, narrow valley, with steep-sided, rocky ridges. The name means "water between highlands" and it was well chosen by the Indians. It has fewer curves and eddies than other Catskill rivers. When heavy rains hit the valley, the river becomes a raging sluiceway and wreaks havoc with its banks and bed. Here is a report on an October 1924 storm from The Anglers' Club *Bulletin*:

> The Neversink suffered as much from the sudden and great rise of water in the early Fall as any of the other streams. The main road from the foot of Wyman Hill to the dugway, more than half a mile, was in many places entirely washed out, so that it was for a time impassable. Most of the camps along the stream were damaged—some almost entirely washed away. The famous "Pines Pool" was practically filled up, and the course and character of the stream for long stretches greatly changed.

These storms occurred often enough through the years to change continually the pools and channel of the main river. As Gordon remarked, the Neversink "is an ambitious river and wishes to occupy the whole valley. In the last few years it has carried away much meadow and other land when in flood. The consequence is that when the water level returns to normal, vast expanses of stones and gravel are exposed with a comparatively small stream flowing in the neighborhood."

This condition of unstable banks, loose gravel, braided channels—until the reservoir was built—affected the main river from Claryville down to Neversink village, about twelve river miles. Below that the valley broadens to dissipate the force of a flood. Above the fork, the East Branch has similar but less severe problems, while the West Branch is blessed with more stable banks resulting from ledgerock pools, large embedded boulders along the edges, and more overhanging hemlocks whose entrenched roots help keep the stream in place.

After the Neversink dam was completed in 1950, the reservoir filled to cover seven miles of river and completely changed the downstream conditions. Above the reservoir the river in spate behaves as it always did.

The east and west branches of Neversink River rise on Slide Mountain at elevations above three thousand feet. They are twins, but not identical twins, running parallel to each other two or three miles apart for fourteen miles to their junction in Claryville. In their first four miles they fall steeply, in excess of two hundred feet per mile. In their lower ten miles, they fall at a rate of approximately sixty feet per mile. They vary in width from ten to forty feet, in depth from one to four feet.

The main stem of the river to the reservoir falls more gently, at thirty-two feet per mile, and ranges from forty to seventy feet wide, from three to six feet deep. Below the reservoir for six miles the river falls at eighteen feet per mile until it reaches an elevation of twelve hundred feet at Woodbourne. Below there, the effect of the cold-water reservoir releases peters out, civilization crowds in along the banks, and the good trout fishing ends as far as the Catskills are concerned. Below Bridgeville, trout are again present in good numbers where the river steepens and cools as it flows through a privately owned gorge before joining the Delaware at Port Jervis.

As pretty and historic as it is, the fact is hard to accept that the Neversink is too cold and too pure to be an ideal trout stream. Because of its north-south, steep-sided valley, the river gets less sun. The normal water temperature in season ranges from 50° to 60°, rarely exceeding 70° even on the hottest days. Water this cold retards the growth of microscopic plant life, the first link in a trout stream's food chain. Said Gordon, "There is not a tinge of vegetable matter in its pellucid rifts or pools."

In water so clear, "as limpid as air," the smallest pebbles can be seen distinctly on the bottom of very deep pools. "Gin clear" was probably concocted by a hard-bitten Neversink Rod who proceeded once too often over his wader tops into a pool that looked much shallower than it was.

Neversink water tends to acidity, with a pH near 7.0 or below, and this indicates a lack of carbonates that fertilize the growth of tiny water plants. With so little to eat, the stream insects of the Neversink are less prolific than the Catskill average. In a 1951 study of this stream conducted by the state, caddis flies were the most common, mayflies were found in limited numbers, and stoneflies were very scarce. Hatch schedules are about two weeks later than in most other Catskill streams because of the colder water temperatures.

Wild trout are smaller and less plentiful in the Neversink than in most Catskill streams. However, because the colder water is more hospitable to trout, they make up a higher percentage of the total fish population than in the other streams. In the 1951 study, almost 60 percent of the Neversink fish counted were trout. That is unusually high. Of the trout, 78 percent were browns, 22 percent were brooks, and there were no rainbows. Incidentally, the first browns in the Neversink were put into Aden Brook, a tributary now of the reservoir, in 1886; they came from the state hatchery at Caledonia. The remaining fish counted in the 1951 study were sculpins, dace, suckers, and eels. Interestingly, there were no chubs—another indication of water colder than the Catskill average. There were very few large trout among the 574 counted. One brown measured twenty-two inches, one was fourteen inches, and the rest were under eleven inches. All brook trout were ten inches or less.

Neversink spawning conditions are acceptable, especially up the West Branch with its more extensive feeders. Brown trout run up the West Branch all the way to its source but tend not to go above Denning on the East Branch. Wild brook trout of six to eight inches are predominant in both branches, with a scattering of wild browns. On the main stem of the river, browns are more prevalent. A wild brown over twelve inches would be a rare catch on the Neversink. Tappen Fairchild in the mid-1930s caught a twenty-two-inch, 4¼-pound brown from a small feeder of the upper West Branch. After two seasons of stalking, he hooked "Grandma" on a motionless olive-green nymph and 3x tip. Having loaned his net, he finally lifted the fish with a finger through the gills after a thirty-minute fight. The Neversink king, however, is "Julius Caesar," and no one is sure how he got there. Taken by Karl Connell, Jr. from the West Branch in 1960, he measured thirty-one inches and weighed 10½ pounds.

As in Hewitt's time, Neversink fishing success, if measured by a goodly number of decent-sized fish, is dependent upon stocking. Because Hewitt had his own hatchery and strictly controlled the fishing, he was able to do rather well, as he tells in a 1935 letter to Harry Darbee:

> When you get a chance this summer drive over and see me and perhaps it will be so that I can ask you to fish if none of my rods are on the water. I want you to see what can be done in making trout fishing in our streams. I can get more big fish in a week than are taken in the whole Catskill country in a whole season. We get at least 50 fish over three pounds in the season and a number up to five pounds.

Hewitt's salmon-stocking experiments were founded on his conviction that the Neversink's ice-cold, simon-pure water made it very similar to the northern rivers where Atlantic salmon thrive. He also hoped the new reservoir would be their "ocean" in the same way that the Ashokan reservoir had been so hospitable to the imported rainbows of Esopus Creek.

After Hewitt stocked thousands of salmon fry in the Neversink's tributaries for three straight years, Red Smith told how only two were ever seen again:

> Lewis Madison Hull, fishing trout near the Claryville Bridge, rose, hooked, played in and released a 17-inch salmon. Fishing the west branch of the Neversink in the same period, Mrs. Sparse Grey Hackle tied on a fanwing Royal Coachman and sank the barb into a fish about 16 inches long.
>
> "Look what a broad tail it has," her husband said as she played the fish.
>
> "See how shiny he is," Mrs. Hackle said. When she brought it to net, they recognized it for what it was.
>
> "What shall we do with it?" Mrs. Hackle asked.
>
> "The stream needs it," Sparse said.
>
> The stream got it back, forever.

New York State has endorsed Hewitt's logic and, with some improvements, set out on its own salmon-management program for Neversink Reservoir. In 1971 and 1972, smelt from the Adirondacks were planted in the reservoir and its feeders to establish a source of food for the salmon. For three years, beginning in 1973, salmon smolts from the Grand Cascapedia were put into the reservoir and tributaries. None of these were seen again, and the best guess is that their seagoing instincts prevailed and they escaped over the reservoir's spillway.

Every year since 1975, landlocked salmon fingerlings from Little Clear Pond in the Adirondacks have been planted in the reservoir, and in 1978 Bill Kelly, the state's fisheries biologist who initiated the program, netted three salmon out of the reservoir, each about twenty inches long and 2½ pounds. The first Atlantic salmon taken by rod from the reservoir was caught by John D'Agata in May 1979 on a sawbelly. It was also twenty inches but weighed 3½ pounds. Its clipped fin identified it as one of the three-inch fingerlings stocked in October 1975.

So, Hewitt may not have had the correct formula, but he probably would have found it had he lived past ninety-one years.

*   *   *

The Neversink above its reservoir is essentially an all-private river. The uppermost few miles of the two branches, where they extend beyond the road climbing steeply to their sources, are on state land. The fishing there would be confined to backpacking in for small wild brook trout. There are two short public fishing areas on the West Branch above the Frost Valley YMCA Camp.

The state's salmon-stocking program is intended to create public salmon fishing from boats in the reservoir or from its banks. For either, a New York City permit is required in addition to a state fishing license.

Below the reservoir, extending for six miles to Woodbourne, the Neversink is experiencing a comeback that reveals a lot about the role of reservoir releases in making, or breaking, the trout fishing. The story behind this revival goes back to the time when the river flowed freely for sixty miles from Slide Mountain to Port Jervis. Fishing below the village of Neversink in those days was average, with a mixture of trout, bass, and chubs.

When the dam went in, a Supreme Court decision had just been handed down requiring a minimum volume of water to be released from the dams to be built in the Delaware watershed. Neversink Dam was the first of these, and by law New York City began sending 100 million gallons a day of cold water steadily coursing out of the reservoir. The warm-water species, mostly bass and chub, were sent scurrying downstream, and the trout fishing improved dramatically.

The next dam in the Delaware watershed was the Pepacton on the East Branch of the Delaware River. When it was completed in 1961, the city shifted the brunt of its releases to this much larger reservoir, and cut the Neversink releases to the "conservation minimum" of ten million gallons a day. Back came the bass and chubs and down went the trout fishing. As a local fisherman observed, "That really upset the people who fished this river. It was worse than before the dam. It was too warm and low for even smallmouth bass."

The lower Neversink ran at a permanently reduced fraction of its old levels until the mid-seventies when fishermen and their friends corralled enough support and, under the aegis of a group called Catskill Waters, succeeded in getting legislation passed to increase the levels of reservoir releases. The new releases began in June of 1977 and the amount of cold water coming out of Neversink Dam has led to the recovery of fishing at least as far down as Woodbourne. Added to this recovery has been the success of Ed Van Put, of the state's fisheries staff, in buying public fishing rights along this section of the river. From Woodbourne to the dam, in the last three years, more than two-thirds of the river has been opened to the public.

Today, it is possible to find trout rising all year long on this part of the river. It is tough fishing, made up of long, flat pools and shallow riffle areas. A long, fine leader and small fly are required. The wading is deep, and one or two casts are usually all you will get before the fish are put down.

The Neversink below the dam has very few spawning tributaries coming into it, so it is more dependent on stocking than, say, the East Branch of the Delaware, which also receives cold-water releases from Pepacton Reservoir. Thus the fish tend to stay where they are put into the river.

The river here is similar to a spring creek. The controlled flows and stabilized temperatures extend the hatches and feeding over much longer periods.

Looking at one of the pools, Ed Van Put said, "This is just like a hatchery raceway. With water coming from the dam at 41°, we could raise fish here all year long. It was a real fight to get the steady releases, but the river down here today is alive and well, and what you see is what will remain."

ELEVEN

Esopus Creek

The Esopus is the most hospitable of the Catskill rivers. Some who know its often muddy and turbulent waters may wonder why. Simply, the Esopus welcomes all comers.

It was home to the Algonquin tribe who chose its gentler valley over those of the Beaverkill, Willowemoc, and Neversink, into all of which they traveled to hunt. The name Esopus was given first to the stream by the Dutch settlers. It was their version of the Algonquin word for "small brook." The name was so successful—perhaps because it sounds so nearly like a stream itself—that Esopus became the name also of the Indian tribe and then of all the land in the valley.

As the most accessible Catskill river from New York City, Esopus Creek was the first to open its doors to visiting fishermen. In 1830, as sport fishing was just beginning to catch on in this country, the Esopus already had a boarding-house, run by Milo Barber in Shandaken, which catered to anglers from the city.

The nearness of Kingston on the Hudson River played a large role in the early development of Esopus Creek as a favorite of trout fishermen. To reach the Esopus in the mid-1800s, a fisherman boarded a steamboat in Manhattan and changed to a stagecoach at Kingston for the twenty- or thirty-mile trip to the villages along the river.

When railroads came into the Catskills, it was a Hudson River steamboat company, Romer & Tremper, that took advantage of its readymade market and in 1879 opened the first "railroad hotel" on the Esopus. Everything must have been up for grabs: the steamboat crowd installed Major Jacob H. Tremper as manager of the new Tremper House, had the name of the town changed to Mount Tremper, and the mountain behind the hotel renamed Tremper Mountain. To keep things in balance, an opposing peak on the other side of the river was given the name Romer Mountain.

Tremper House had many novel attractions as a resort hotel, including elevators, steam heat, bathrooms, and even a resident physician. Dr. H. R. Winter was an ardent fisherman "who often prescribed a course of trout fishing for businessmen wearied in the pursuit of dollars . . . and he was as ready with advice on trout flies and rods as he was with pills and powders."

Beyond Mount Tremper, the Ulster & Delaware trains made stops along the Esopus at Phoenicia, Shandaken, and Big Indian. It was so convenient that a fisherman could practically get on the train in his waders and pile right off into his favorite pool.

By 1900, Phoenicia had become the nerve center of the Catskills. "It lies at the cross-roads of Nature," said T. Morris Longstreth, "and is as snug in its valleys as a moth in a muff. For merchantry, it should be a strategic place to live. Every motorist who comes up the Esopus Valley from Kingston, or down the Esopus from the west, every traveler whose traffic delights the eye or dusts the nose of sellers of wares, must bisect Phoenicia."

Happily for anglers, the Esopus extended its hospitality to the rainbow trout. Although there are large wild rainbows in the Delaware, and stories of bygone runs of rainbows up the Willowemoc, Esopus Creek is the only Catskill river in which rainbows have thrived since they were imported from California in the late 1800s.

Theodore Gordon told a story about the Esopus rainbows that had been seen in the spring of 1902 jumping below Bishop's Falls, now covered by the Ashokan Reservoir:

> Precipitous walls of rock rise on both sides of the deep pool below these falls, the formation resembling a western canyon, and as no boat was available it seemed impossible to reach the fish. A mill is perched upon the cliff above the pool, and the miller conceived a brilliant plan of action. He baited a good-sized hook with a large helgramite and lowered it from the window of his mill down, down into the foam and spray far below. He struck a fish at once, and actually succeeded in hauling or reeling it up into the room in which he stood. It proved to be a fine specimen of the rainbow trout (*Salmo irideus*), eighteen inches long. I have not visited these falls for two years, but think the distance between the water and the window must have been about fifty feet. Lucky miller!

In 1906, before the Ashokan Reservoir or Shandaken Tunnel was built on the Esopus, Gordon observed in one of his *Forest and Stream* articles, "It is the only stream I know of where rainbow trout actually remained and multiplied for many years." He also noted in the same article that if you stocked Catskill streams with rainbows, "they might go to sea in the second year, but that is the risk one would have to run."

As if in answer to Gordon, the very next year New York City began building the Ashokan Reservoir, the first in its Catskill water-supply system, and when it was finished in 1915, the rainbows of the Esopus had their own little private ocean to run down to, feed, and grow in.

The Esopus was to have one more major physical change in order to provide New York City with water. In 1917, work started on Schoharie Reservoir, one valley to the north. To channel its water most efficiently into the supply system, the city hit upon an ingenious idea. It was customary to build an underground tunnel connecting two reservoirs; but someone noticed that Esopus Creek was directly in line between the Schoharie and Ashokan reservoirs, and the Shandaken Tunnel idea was born. By running the tunnel only two-thirds of the way, surfacing at Allaben, and using the Esopus riverbed to carry Schoharie water the rest of the way to the Ashokan, approximately ten miles of burrowing and construction were saved.

On February 9, 1924, the first water was sent through Shandaken Tunnel, twenty-six hundred feet beneath Balsam Mountain, and Esopus Creek became a unique trout river, certainly in the Catskills, if not in the entire country.

As all these physical changes to the river were taking place, trout fishermen were going through their own evolution. A group of them were relaxing after fishing one night in 1917 at Kincaid House in Phoenicia. Tom and Chester Mills were up from New York and their tackle store, William Mills & Son. Talk turned to fly patterns, a particularly engrossing topic especially if you were debating the pros and cons of dry flies and the dry-fly theories, say, of George LaBranche, who had recently written his landmark work, *The Dry Fly and Fast Water*. In the middle of the discussion, Tom and Chester got up and left the group. When they came back, they had a brand-new fly, the Fanwing Royal Coachman. Stephen Mills, Chester's son, quotes his father as saying, "Ninety percent of the trout I caught after that night were taken on the Fanwing." This pattern became immensely popular among fly fishermen, even beyond the Catskills, and continued to dominate most pattern selections until it was displaced in the 1940s by the more durable Hairwing Royal Coachman.

Just one year later, and only a few miles downstream, another influential group of anglers was fishing away on the porch of Susie Winchell's Four Maples at Cold Brook. They included A. E. Hendrickson, his fishing companion, banker George Stevenson, the custom rodmaker Jim Payne, and Roy Steenrod. Cecil Heacox later spoke to Steenrod who recalled, "We were talking rods and how they should have more pep. A.E. spoke up and said he had a three-piece salmon rod that might be right. We tried it, but it was too much rod.

"Then we tried using its second joint and the tip, and we decided that was much better than the rods we were using. Jim Payne said, 'I can make a better rod than that.' And he did."

Essentially, Payne put a handle on the top two joints of the salmon rod. The result was nine feet long and weighed about six ounces. "There was a lot more water in those days," Steenrod said, "so a longer rod helped to reach out. And very often we were into rainbows of eighteen and twenty inches."

Dr. George Parker Holden, left, and a friend fishing the Esopus in the 1920s. As a young doctor living in Kingston, Holden's first exposure to angling was on the Esopus around 1895. He later moved to Yonkers and established his reputation as an amateur rodbuilder, expert angler, and author of numerous articles and books including *Streamcraft* (1919) and *The Idyl of the Split-Bamboo* (1920). *Courtesy The Museum of American Fly Fishing.*

Payne, backed financially by A. E. Hendrickson, established his reputation building "peppier" rods based on those early prototypes conceived that day on the Esopus in 1918. They were among the first trout rods with a dry-fly action.

The Phoenicia Hotel was a popular hangout for angling notables in the 1920s. The Anglers' Club of New York held its "Annual Outing and Trout Fishing Championship" there in 1922, and its members often gathered there to fish and relax. They had such good times that one of the members felt disposed to write a pen-named article in the club bulletin describing the various ways members disported themselves on and off the stream. In it he referred to Phoenicia Hotel as the "Mattawan of the Esopus." Mattawan was a well-appointed mental institution in eastern New Jersey where acquaintances could sometimes be found if they let the market get too much with them.

Even without the self-inflicted distractions of its fishermen, the Esopus on its own power has always been a maddening trout stream. Its regulars can frequently be heard to say they love and hate it in the same breath. Almost without exception this frustration comes from the fact that the fisherman is often fishing in cloudy to downright muddy water. Deposits of fine-grained red clay peculiar to the Esopus and Schoharie drainages cause a lot of this "turbidity," a name preferred by the state's Department of Environmental Conservation and which, if it bestows an air of institutional resignation or inevitability to the condition, is most apt.

Any good rainstorm can force one of the Esopus's tributaries into a clay bank and it will run discolored for a year or more until that clay deposit is gone. One can go up the tributary and find exactly where the clay is, and above it the water will be clear. A deposit as small as a wheelbarrow can discolor the entire stream.

Shandaken Tunnel is the other main source of Esopus turbidity. It has come to be known as "the portal," connoting not so much a conduit from another watershed as a giant mouth that disgorges millions of gallons a day (mgd's) of water into the stream. Portal water is filled with silt and increases in opacity as the 600-mgd capacity of the tunnel is approached. It is believed that the source of the silt is a combination of a sediment layer on the bottom of Schoharie Reservoir, over ten feet thick near the intake gates of the tunnel, and the lining of the tunnel itself.

The portal has a tremendous impact on the Esopus. On the negative side, it adds to the discoloring problem already present in nature, and its heavier releases create very dangerous wading conditions.

Positively, the portal sustains the river with cool, full flows at times when other streams are warm and low. In midsummer, up to 90 percent of the flow below the portal is Schoharie water. And, best of all, mixed in with the inorganic silt from Schoharie Reservoir is a rich profusion of daphnia—tiny transparent water fleas—on which the native rainbows gorge and thrive. One other benefit is the presence of large walleyes that come through the tunnel and settle in the portal pool. It is no wonder that this pool is a favorite of bait fishermen.

From the time Shandaken Tunnel was completed, New York City water officials decided how the portal would run based on criteria oriented exclusively to the city's water requirements. Sometimes it would run "full pipe," causing the lower Esopus to roar down its course, discouraging any attempts to fish even with bait. Sometimes, immediately afterward, it would be shut off completely, leaving the river slack and the fish scurrying to get back into the main channel. This went on for more than fifty years.

Then, in 1974, two major fish kills occurred on the Esopus, and the fishermen were galvanized into action. In January and again in October, the portal got shut down abruptly, leaving thousands of trout and lesser fish stranded in the side channels of the river. Trout Unlimited and Theodore Gordon Flyfishers had already been fighting for improved release patterns, and now there arose a new group to lead the troops into battle. Frank Mele of Woodstock, New York, organized a coalition of anglers and friendly parties called Catskill Waters,

From this opening—known as "the portal"—up to 600 million gallons a day of Schoharie Reservoir water are emptied into the Esopus, having both good and bad effects on the fishing. When it runs heavily, the river discolors and becomes dangerous to wade. On the positive side, the portal sustains the river with cool, full flows at times when other streams are warm and low. These photos show, moving from the upper left downstream, how much difference the portal can make in times of low water. *Photos by the author.*

whose mission was to lobby for state legislation to balance the erratic reservoir releases affecting about 180 miles of prime trout water. Catskill Waters was officially launched in January 1975, with John Hoeko of Fleischmanns, New York, as its president and chief lobbyist in Albany. Financial support came from members of TU, TGF, and the Federation of Fly Fishermen, as well as from sympathetic individuals. Ogden Reid, DEC commissioner, convinced by Mele and Hoeko of the situation's urgency, backed their efforts and steered them to the state attorney general's office, whose staff offered advice and technical assistance in drafting an amendment to the conservation law.

In the summer of 1976, after many months of intensive lobbying efforts, and strong opposition by New York City, Title 8 of Article 15 of the Environmental Conservation Law passed in the New York Assembly by nineteen votes and in the Senate by a single vote, and, after a last-moment veto threat, was signed into law on July 28 by Governor Hugh Carey.

This law empowered the DEC to orchestrate reservoir releases, but not to change the aggregate amount of water flowing from the dams. This was fixed by a Supreme Court decree. In effect, the DEC was given "first hand" on the valve.

Rules were drawn, based on this enabling legislation, to govern the opening and closing of the intake gates at the Schoharie end of Shandaken Tunnel. However, although New York City is bound by the rules to cooperate with the DEC, the rules are binding only five months a year (June 1st to October 31st) and indeed are inoperative if their observance should cause the loss of water over the spillways of either Gilboa (Schoharie) or Ashokan dam.

Nevertheless, since the new release rules took effect in June of 1977, there have been pronounced improvements in the temperatures and water levels of the lower Esopus. A July 1978 survey in which temperatures were taken every day showed that the water below the portal averaged more than 13° cooler than above. Even as it flowed past the Cold Brook gauging station, eleven miles farther downstream, it was still averaging 4° cooler. And, instead of finding the river at flood stage one day and in drought conditions the next, rarely—because of the operation of the portal—is the river too high or too low. As a result, setting out to fish the Esopus is no longer the risky venture it used to be. Stream management has become a reality.

Even more significant than the improvements to Esopus fishing was the precedent that had been set. For the first time since 1907, when it annexed the Catskills into its water supply system, New York City had made a formal accommodation to the rivers affected by its dams. Many unsuccessful attempts had been made in the past to gain "conservation releases" from the three dams on the East and West branches of the Delaware and the Neversink. The situation on those rivers was far more complex, though, with several states involved and a federal river master in Montague, New Jersey. Thus it was harder to postulate the negative effects of curtailed flows and the benefits of conservation releases.

"But here it was dramatic," said one of the Esopus regulars, "with the extreme flows from the portal and the fish dying all over the place. That was what allowed us to get our hands on the city." And that was what paved the way for a series of release agreements for the other reservoirs that substantially improved many miles of Catskill trout fishing.

*   *   *

From the vantage of an eagle, Esopus Creek looks like a giant maidenhair fern. Its main channel and lacework of tributaries—from the source at Winnisook Lake, up, over, down, and back up its tributary Woodland Valley Creek to within a half mile of its beginning—form the fern's crown. The rest of the river to the reservoir is the stem.

Why the Esopus should have this almost symmetrical and circular shape to its upper waters is a mystery. All the other Catskill rivers, though they twist and turn along the way, flow in one direction unless they run into another river of equal force. Perhaps some highly focused geological event millions of years ago gave this river its unique whorl.

From the vantage of a trout fisherman, the Esopus has four distinct

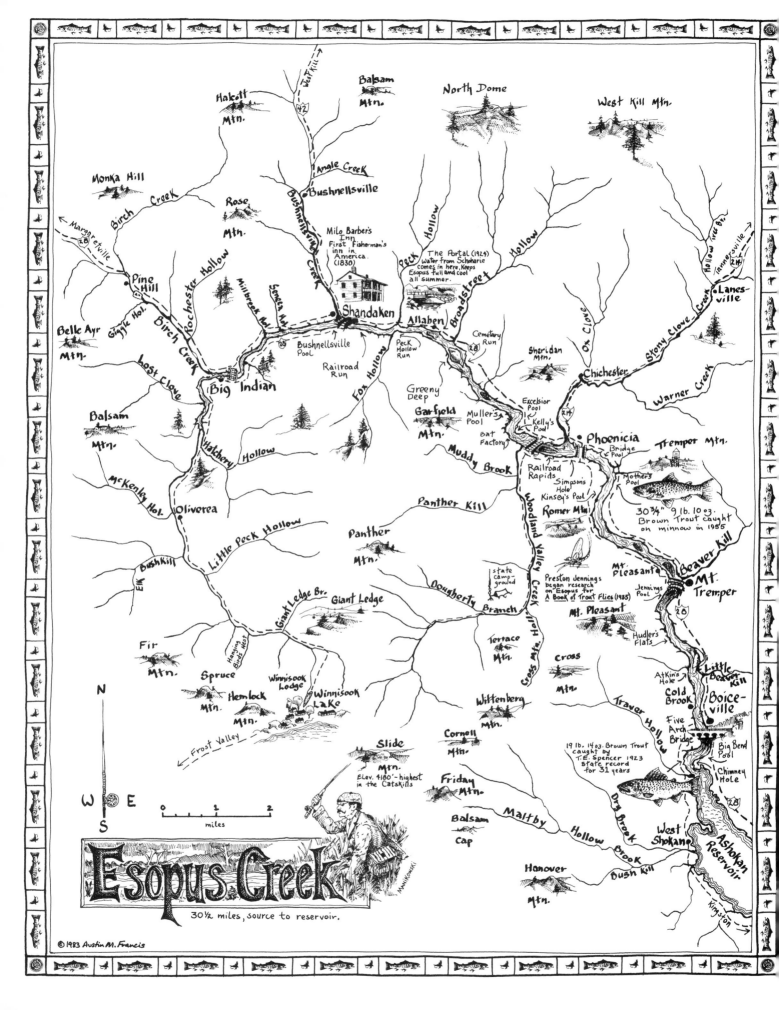

Esopus Creek

30½ miles, source to reservoir.

© 1983 Austin M. Francis

sections. Winnisook to Big Indian, its first 8½ miles, is steep, narrow, and shaded. In the mid-1800s, the name of this upper section was "Big Injin"; where it terminated, the "Esopus" began. Above Big Indian the cool waters are home to many small, wild brook trout and to larger browns and rainbows when they run up the river to spawn. This section of the river is mostly private and posted except for a few short stretches totaling about half a mile.

The river widens considerably at Big Indian, where the first major tributary, Birch Creek, comes in. This section, down to the portal at Allaben, is five miles long. The width ranges from fifteen to forty feet, the depth from one to three feet. The flow consists mostly of riffles, runs, and pockets, with a few scattered pools. The canopy begins to open up as the stream widens and the cover varies from mature overhanging trees to brush, to complete exposure where the highway closely parallels the stream and no trees line either bank. The deeper holding lies for big fish in this section are mainly within a few hundred yards of three large tributaries that empty into it—Bushnellsville Creek, Fox Hollow, and Peck Hollow. These tributaries themselves can yield good fish at spawning time. On November 30, 1980, the last day of the Esopus season, a twenty-two-inch brown was caught well up Bushnellsville Creek.

The river, in its lower three sections from Big Indian to the Ashokan, is 17 miles long. The rather gentle grade is 36 feet per mile, substantially less than the 172 feet per mile of the 8½-mile headwaters section. Highway 28 runs the full length of these 17 miles, passing through nine communities. A large number of restaurants, guest houses, gas stations, and other commercial establishments line the route. And although most of the river access is privately held, the Esopus is largely unposted and open to public fishing through the courtesy of hundreds of landowners.

The third section of the river runs from the portal to Stony Clove Creek at Phoenicia, a distance of 4.2 miles. The width now is from 40 to 80 feet with depths from two to five feet. There are more medium-size pools than above the portal, but most of the water is still riffles and pockets defined by a good number of large boulders. Streamside cover is intermittent. Stretches of undercut bank add to the hiding holes. The road runs farther from the stream over most of this section, making for quieter fishing. The deeper holes are again near the mouths of the tributaries—Broadstreet Hollow, Woodland Valley Creek, and Stony Clove Creek.

During the spring and at times of heavier portal releases, wading at Railroad Rapids and many of the rocky runs on down to the reservoir can be very challenging. When Lee Wulff lived in New York and fished the Esopus a lot in the 1930s he said he "loved to get in the water and wade upstream for the sheer exercise and joy of wading."

The lowest of the four sections covers 7.7 miles from Simpson's Hole at the mouth of Stony Clove Creek to Chimney Hole at the beginning of the Ashokan. The river varies from 60 to 100 feet wide and three to six feet deep. Cover is generally good but there are some bare gravel banks resulting from

A popular stretch of the river, from Excelsior Pool down to Bat Factory Pool; good holding water, two to five feet deep, with excellent riffles and pockets; better fishing in early season than the river below Phoenicia, using short line and weighted nymphs. *Photo by the author.*

The Esopus below Phoenicia from May until the fall is the best part of the river for fly fishing. Spawning rainbows are caught here as late as June. *Photo by the author.*

flood-control work after recent hurricanes and floods. This is the big-water Esopus, a brawny, bustling stream worthy of the highest rank in LaBranche's hierarchy of turbulence. Large car-sized boulders create big pool-like pockets and eddies, excellent holding water for the larger fish populating this section.

Theodore Gordon was familiar with this part of the Esopus. "It is a big stream," he said, "with pools big enough to hold the largest salmon. With a good stage of water it is very fatiguing to wade, and one often has to fish it as one would proceed on a salmon river. It is a grand stream in many parts and holds very large trout (up to 8 pounds or better). I have taken many up to 3 pounds, and cousins of mine who often fish it have killed 4-pounders on tiny flies."

Arnold Gingrich, fly-fisherman and editor of *Esquire* magazine, was very fond of the lower Esopus: "In the mile below Five Arch Bridge I could almost invariably count on one fish. There was no other part of the stream that I could approach with that much confidence." He also respected its "murderous currents," particularly after one November day when he ventured out following a rainstorm. Standing in the lee of one of the arches of the bridge, thinking of the new rod he was trying out, he absentmindedly took half a step forward into the rain-swollen current. He recalled, "I might as well have put one foot in front of a subway train. The river snatched me out of the protective patch of water where I had been standing, picked me up bodily and began rolling me downstream in the torrent, handling me as if I were a small piece of gravel. I must have been turned completely over somewhere between twelve and twenty times in the course of being carried downstream about the length of a football field, before I was finally plastered onto a large rock and held there, by the force of the current, like Shakespeare's 'alligarter on a wall.' "

Gingrich tells another story about an August evening in 1953 when he returned from fishing the same stretch below the bridge to have supper at the Rainbow Lodge in Mount Tremper. Overhearing his report of zero luck, a "thin florid white-haired man" at the next table pulled out a messy-looking nymph he had tied and suggested that Gingrich try it. Being polite and only a little condescending, he mumbled his thanks as the old man shuffled out with his wife.

Having tried everything else with no success, Gingrich went back to the stream the next day and tied on this "dark-red, gold-ribbed nymph with grubby whiskers." On the first cast he connected with a fourteen-inch brown. In the next forty minutes, he took eleven more trout, six of them rainbows, one brook trout, and four more browns, and all except the brook trout were over eleven inches.

Racing back to the lodge, Gingrich found out from the proprietor Dick Kahil that he had not encountered the patron saint of all fishers, as he was ready to believe, but Preston Jennings, author of *A Book of Trout Flies*. Jennings began the research for his book on the Esopus, ranging throughout the Catskills, Pennsylvania, and New England. He had given Gingrich a nymph imitation of the *Isonychia bicolor*, the most prolific of the Esopus insects, telling him to "fish it like a wet fly because it is the only nymph that swims."

In its last few miles before Ashokan Reservoir, the Esopus grows quite large. Theodore Gordon knew this part of the river. "It is a big stream," he said, "with pools big enough to hold the largest salmon." *Photo by Judd Weisberg.*

Five Arch Bridge, a river landmark and favorite fishing spot of many Esopus anglers. It was from behind one of these piers after a heavy November rainstorm that Arnold Gingrich got snatched by the current and rolled downstream end-over-end until he wound up "plastered against a large rock like Shakespeare's 'alligarter on a wall.'" *Photo by the author.*

The most popular pool along the entire Esopus is Jennings Pool, in Mount Tremper, named for this man to commemorate his substantial contribution to fly fishing.

*   *   *

Esopus Creek is one of the East's most productive wild-trout streams. On any given day there are over 100,000 wild rainbows and perhaps 10,000 wild browns throughout its length from Big Indian to the reservoir. One day early in March, Ed Van Put and I were driving next to the river just above Phoenicia when he looked out and exclaimed, "If you ever saw us shock this stream, you wouldn't believe it. It's absolutely loaded! I mean right *there* I would love to swing a couple of wet flies. Right *now* we would catch fish!" He was talking about the electro-fishing surveys conducted periodically by the state's conservation department. Two electrodes are placed in the stream with sufficient current to momentarily stun the fish; they are netted, tagged, counted, and released.

Besides wild fish there are hatchery browns, about 30,000 of them stocked in the Esopus each year. Of these, all but about 1,500 are fished out by the season's end. The survivors of "angling mortality," another state phrase, either die naturally or hold over to the next season. The permanent brown trout population concentrates in the reservoir where there is plenty of food and shelter. The really big ones tend to stay there, but have been caught in the river on rare occasions. A 30¾-inch, nine-pound ten-ounce brown was caught on a minnow out of Mother's Pool in 1955. And for thirty-one years the state record brown was a nineteen-pound fourteen-ounce fish caught in Chimney Hole, the first pool above the Ashokan, by T. E. Spencer in 1923.

Record fish notwithstanding, it is the wild rainbow that rules this river. Esopus rainbows spring from the same prehistoric sea trout as the Pacific Coast steelhead. The ancestral fish spawned in the brackish waters at the feet of glaciers and followed the ice inland when it receded and the rivers formed. Today, both the steelhead and in this case the Esopus rainbows begin moving upriver before it is time to spawn. We have known for some time that steelhead enter the Northwest rivers all summer long, not spawning until fall. But only recently was it discovered that Esopus rainbows do the same thing—from September until February, when their three-month spawning period begins.

Upon hatching, the young rainbows spend one to two years in the tributaries or main stream, growing to eight or nine inches, then go down to the reservoir. Some go down when they are only six months old. There they join the adult fish, grow up, and become part of the annual spawning run. After three years they reach about sixteen inches and at five years, beyond which very few live, they are over twenty inches and weigh up to five pounds. In a good year some three to four hundred rainbows over twelve inches have been counted in the creels of Esopus fishermen. Perhaps half again that many are caught and not counted. Most of these are caught at the very start of the season, even in the smaller tributaries. It is not rare to see fishermen in April walking next to the snow-covered banks of a tiny feeder with a string of twelve-inch to fourteen-inch rainbows.

Another demonstration of Esopus productivity is in pounds per acre. Other Catskill streams with good food and holding water produce about 75 pounds of trout per acre. In samplings of wild trout only, the Esopus has yielded 115 pounds per acre. A few years ago, one of the local conservation groups pressed the state to reduce the Esopus catch limit from ten to five fish on the widely accepted theory that any reduced limit automatically improves the fishing. After collecting enough information on Esopus fish populations to make a decision, the indication was that the fishing would probably be better with a 20-fish limit! In other words, by catching out more of the little "silver bullets," more room and food would benefit the remaining fish and result in larger fish in the creel.

No change was made to the ten-fish limit. However, for several years there has been no limit on how *small* a fish you can keep from the Esopus because of its wealth of rainbow fingerlings. As Van Put says, "You catch a *lot* of fish. You want action, you want pretty little wild fish? You get 'em here, oh man!"

Paul O'Neill fell in love with the little fish of the Esopus. He praised them eloquently in a May 1964 *Life* magazine article: "I am an eight-inch trout fisherman . . . I admire their beauty. I like the bulge a collection of them makes in my wet canvas creel. I like the way they taste, and when I wade into the stream, I am going after something special to eat.

"A great many fishermen are uninterested in small trout. But in most streams, and certainly in the Esopus, save for the spawning runs, there are very few fish of any other kind. Smaller fish, if they are fat, wild and freshly caught, have a tender and delicate taste which cannot be matched in the finest New York restaurants.

"They should be rolled in corn meal, sizzled for four or five minutes in bacon fat and served with a fresh salad and baked potato. The outside is crisp and gold; the inside, white, moist and of a flavor, subtle but poignant, to pierce the very soul."

He goes on with wood smoke, Martinis, and well-chilled Moselle, to end up in a state of mindless, motionless serenity that one is convinced cannot be attained in any better way.

The Esopus is an excellent wet-fly stream due to its plentiful fast-moving riffles and runs. A string of Leadwing Coachmen fished to rising fish during the *Isonychia* hatch will outperform any dry fly on the stream. An upstream nymph is also very effective in the pocket water. You throw it above the pocket, weighted, get it down, and the velocity is such that when the fish grabs it, you're going to feel him.

Because of the portal and its release patterns, Esopus fishing conditions vary a lot over the season. Above the portal is best from April 1 to early May because of the heavier natural flows and the presence of large spawning rainbows. It is easier then to wade closer to the bigger fish without spooking them, and weighted nymphs and wets are the favored tactic. In midsummer, the upper Esopus is usually low, warm, and very difficult to fish. By late September, water levels improve, spawning fish return, and conditions are good through the end of November, when the Esopus season closes.

The river from the portal to Phoenicia is best fished with weighted nymphs and short lines until midsummer, when the water velocity slows, permitting longer casts and a better float for dry flies. From Phoenicia to the reservoir is fairly muddy in the spring, and this section is better suited to bait fishing until the flows subside. Then, from May until the fall it is the best part of the river for fly fishing. Spawning rainbows are caught here as late as June.

Hatches on the Esopus are also affected by the portal. Above it they show pretty much as in other rivers of the area. Below the portal, hatches are affected by cooler water and do not conform to standard emergence schedules.

Although the Esopus is not as rich in nutrients as the Delaware, Willowemoc, and Beaverkill, it has a good representation of mayflies and caddis, and quite a strong hatch of stoneflies. Nymphs of the burrowing type are less prevalent because there are fewer slow sections where silt, debris, and organic matter can collect. The swimming nymph of the *Isonychia*, however, is prolific in the fast currents of the Esopus, and the *Isonychia* hatch is a major hatch lasting from mid-June to early September. Art Flick tied his Dun Variant to match this hatch on the Schoharie, just one valley to the north, and the Esopus rainbows love it.

*　　　　*　　　　*

The Esopus is a most egalitarian trout stream. Indeed, it has its own contingent of Frenchmen who fish none of the other Catskill streams. They use a strange-looking Pézon-Michelle rod that causes wonderment and disdain among other Esopus fishermen. The rod is made for dapping. It is fifteen feet long, relatively inflexible, with a large butt, a tiny reel, and a line that runs up the inside, exiting at the tip. They use one salmon egg and fish it like a nymph, throwing it out and following it down. When they connect, they just raise the tip and the fish comes right in.

Besides Frenchmen, the Esopus has a large following of orthodox bait fishermen. Not only is it the most accessible Catskill river to New York City, northern New Jersey, and Kingston, a city of thirty thousand only eighteen miles away; it also runs cold and cloudy a lot of the time, which puts fly fishermen off and suits the bait fisherman just fine. As a consequence—and particularly with so many easily caught pan-size rainbows—the art of minnow, worm, and spin fishing has reached a high degree of refinement on the Esopus. Where else would you find a pamphlet published by a local chapter of Trout Unlimited—that bastion of catch-and-release and fly-fishing-only—with advice on bait fishing including a detailed description and diagrams of how to make a minnow rig?

Adding to the égalité of the river, the Esopus is also home for a more recently developed sport known by its adherents as tubing, and by fishermen as the "rubber hatch." From a tuber's point of view, envision yourself on a hot summer's day, in an oversize inner tube with a six-pack of cold Genesee Cream Ale, borne down the river by the cool releases from Shandaken Tunnel. Unfortunately, when you're laying out a Dun Variant to a good fish and a tuber crosses right over your damn line, it is hard to see his point of view. There are several ways to avoid tubers: by fishing above the portal where the water is too slow, and below Five Arch Bridge where they are not allowed; and by fishing at dawn or dusk when they are not around.

A large percentage of Esopus fishermen are blue-collar workers from Kingston and northern New Jersey. One might jump to the conclusion that they are mostly bait fishermen, but if you scratch the surface of an Esopus fly fisherman, you are as likely to uncover a truck driver as a banker. More than 40 percent of Esopus anglers are from the home county, Ulster. Other Catskill rivers are fished by a much higher percentage of transients. This might help explain why it was Esopus fishermen who first won the battle over conservation releases. They are a fiercely dedicated and highly vocal group.

Where fishing legislation isn't a clear benefit to all of them, however, Esopus fishermen display their differing persuasions. When the state tried to improve brown-trout retention on a 0.8-mile section of the river by limiting their kill to three instead of five, the effort was fought bitterly and finally defeated by a group of local sportsmen. Obviously, the no-kill concept would not be welcome on the Esopus. Nor is it needed, with such great wild-trout reproduction.

Mile for mile, the Esopus is the most heavily fished river in the Catskills. Only the Beaverkill and Willowemoc no-kill sections get more fishing pressure. Aerial counts on the Esopus from 1975 to 1978 showed an average of about twenty thousand angler days per year. This popularity is due in part to the sixty extra days of open season after the normal September 30 closing. But mainly it is due to the huge success by man and nature in maintaining an outstanding trout stream.

TWELVE

Schoharie Creek

The crew from Westkill Tavern had quit fishing for the day and, heading back upriver, they stopped at Billy Boyd's. He was sitting in the back room, overlooking the stream, surrounded by his cats.

The boardinghouse, long since out of business, was now occupied only by eighty-year-old Billy, and as he sat there, bats flew in and out of the screenless windows picking off the evening's hatch as it circled above him around a bare bulb. Pointing to his attic, Billy grinned and bragged, "I keep bats up there!"

That was back in the early forties when the bass were so plentiful in Schoharie Creek that a special regulation favoring trout was passed allowing fishermen to keep as many bass as they could catch, regardless of size. And Billy Boyd was cut out for the job. Camped there next to one of the best pools on the whole river, he loved to catch bass, and his cats loved to eat them. His only problem was getting flies, and for that he had a novel solution.

Art Flick, proprietor of Westkill Tavern, always warned his guests to be on guard against Billy. But he was so full of himself and of stories and charm that they fell to him every time.

"Gosh, fellows, those bass are pretty bad out there, but I guess I don't have to tell you how *they* bother your flies," Billy would say.

"They sure are, Billy," one of his visitors would answer, "I wish we could do something about it."

"Well, I'd get quite a few of them," he would say, opening up one of those little blue Edgeworth tobacco tins with a single, well-chewed bucktail in it, "but I've just got this one fly."

At that point the guys from the tavern would fight with one another over the privilege of giving Billy some flies. As Art recalls: "George Newman, one of

Art Flick and Billy Boyd teamed up to cut back the excessive numbers of black bass in the Schoharie. Flick lobbied successfully for a no-limit regulation for Schoharie bass only, and Boyd took advantage of it by catching thousands of them out of the pool next to his house. Schoharie trout fishing improved dramatically as a result.

them who should have known better, said, 'Billy, we'll just take care of that.' And he runs up to his car, gets his big tackle box, comes down, opens it up, and says, 'Billy, help yourself!' And, of course, the old man always obliged them. I think he had more flies than all of our guests put together."

Bass were not always so bothersome to Schoharie trout fishermen. The problem started when Gilboa Dam was completed in 1926 and the waters of the reservoir rose to cover Devasego Falls, a forty-foot-high barrier to the fish of the lower river. A mile and a half downriver from Prattsville, the falls before then had divided the fishing into pike and bass water below and trout water above.

In a 1934 biological survey by New York State of the Schoharie watershed, it was noted that Gilboa Dam "has been responsible for the introduction of small-mouthed bass in the upper Schoharie, thereby doing great harm to the trout fishing. The bass have become very numerous in the section above the reservoir, having run upstream as far as Hunter." As one fisherman of that day put it, "The bass were just swarming up in this stream. After the water got up to fifty degrees you simply couldn't catch a trout. The bass were so thick in there that no matter what you threw in, even almost a bare hook, you got a bass."

That was the Schoharie in 1934 when Art Flick arrived fresh from New York City with his wife and two young sons. Leaving his job as manager of a Kinney shoe store, he took over the Westkill Tavern from his parents who had run it as an ordinary resort hotel since the early 1920s. His hope was to pursue a lifelong interest in fishing and hunting and turn the Westkill Tavern into a first-class establishment catering to trout fishermen and grouse hunters.

A major factor in Art's decision to become a professional innkeeper and outdoorsman was The Anglers' Club of New York's selection that year of Westkill Tavern as headquarters for its fourteenth Annual Outing and Trout Fishing Championship. Apparently, Ray Bergman's glowing reports of his visits in Westkill and of the local rivers had persuaded the Anglers' Club to come to the Schoharie for the first time, breaking a six-year string of outings at DeBruce Club Inn on the Willowemoc.

Only after being so auspiciously launched did Art find out about the bass problem. "Had I known I don't think I would have had guts enough to come into it," he says. But he *was* in it and there was no way out except to fight the bass. And in doing so, Art began a personal commitment to Schoharie Creek that has lasted almost fifty years.

Over those years the Schoharie has benefited from Art Flick's commitment in many ways. There was the barrier dam at Prattsville to keep more bass from running upstream, which he conceived and pushed through with the help of the Conservation Department. The state's condition was that Art find donors of land on opposite sides of the stream suitable for locating the dam. This he did, and the diplomatic effort it required soon spun off into one of New York's first public fishing rights acquisition programs. Shortly after the barrier dam was completed in 1938, Art lobbied successfully for the special bass-fishing regula-

Westkill Tavern, which Art Flick took over from his parents in 1934 as a country inn catering to trout fishermen and grouse hunters. It was centrally located, on the West Kill, for fishing the Schoharie and Esopus over in the next valley. Many well-known anglers, including Ray Bergman and Preston Jennings, considered this a favorite base of operations. In 1960 Flick sold Westkill Tavern and retired from innkeeping; three years later it was destroyed by fire. *Courtesy Art Flick.*

Barrier dam on the Schoharie at Prattsville, conceived and promoted by Art Flick, and built by the state in 1938. Its purpose is to keep bass from invading the upper reaches of the river. In combination with the special no-limit bass regulation, also spearheaded by Flick, the barrier dam has been a great boon to Schoharie trout fishermen. *Photo by the author*.

tion on which Billy Boyd and his cats thrived. In the first week after the new regulation took effect, more than 1,000 bass were taken by hook and line above the barrier dam. Gradually, the bass population dwindled in the upper river, and word got around that Schoharie trout fishing had improved tremendously. Art's fishing log bears this out: over the 14 years following the dam's installation, he averaged over 45 days on stream each year and over 13 trout per day for a total of 8,648 trout.

Besides the barrier dam, there are the willows Art and his sons planted each year, mostly along the West Kill, his home tributary of the Schoharie. They started planting them about thirty-five years ago, and Art still performs his early spring ritual with willow seedlings provided by the state. There always seems to be a new stretch of raw, begravelled bank in need of the holding power of the willows' water-seeking roots. They are planted simply by anchoring them with rocks on the bottom in about six inches of water so that when the stream goes down the roots will still have moisture. Once they are established, it is next to impossible to wash them out. Not only do they hold the bank, they also harbor trout among their roots and dress up an otherwise barren stream border.

And then there was the Westkill Tavern itself. Art thought of it and ran it as a private club. In its later years he even renamed it Westkill Tavern Club. To be a "member" you had to meet Art's personal standards as a proper sportsman, which meant that you fly fished or hunted grouse. Non-sporting guests were taken in as long as they were spoken for by a sportsman.

Fishermen staying at Westkill Tavern were encouraged to put back all fish under twelve inches, keeping the smaller ones only on their last day if they wanted to take some home to eat. "It was just something that I suggested," says Art. "They didn't have to do it. I was trying to keep fish in the stream, and it worked out quite well.

"As for our grouse hunters, I had them all trained to go and ask for permission. And for that reason we had no trouble whatsoever with the landowners. There were very few places where our guests weren't welcome. I always stressed the point, 'When you go up to ask permission, tell them you are staying at the Westkill Tavern.' So that after a while the owners got a pretty good idea of the kind of people we had."

Ray Camp, outdoor columnist for *The New York Times*, was one of them. He stayed at Westkill Tavern and fished the Schoharie regularly, and yet he never mentioned the river by name in his articles. Realizing that he could spoil a stream as fragile as the Schoharie, he always called it "West Kill" and he never exaggerated. Says Art, "He came up here so much he knew our people, many of them members of the Anglers' Club, and he knew darned well when he mentioned the West Kill, all the boys would realize he was talking about the Schoharie."

Chip Stauffer, a fly fisherman from Bucks County, Pa., who raised his own gamecock hackles, was another regular at the Westkill Tavern. One July day in 1934 he arrived with a newcomer named Preston Jennings who was immersed in a project that would change Art Flick's life and make Schoharie Creek an important contributor to thousands of eastern fly fishermen.

Jennings was compiling the first American trout-stream entomology to give reliable identification of natural insects matched with the correct artificial fly and its dressing. He talked Art Flick into becoming one of his main bug collectors for *A Book of Trout Flies*. In the process Jennings introduced Flick to natural dun hackles and taught him the "difference between a good and bad fly." Persevering in his stream studies and flytying, Art eventually became an expert in his own right. He went down to speak at the Anglers' Club in New York, and his longtime friend Ray Camp began hounding him to write a book himself. Camp finally won when he called the Westkill Tavern from an Italian battlefront: "I want to know if you're going to do that book!"

Arthur B. Flick, Dean of the Schoharie, fishes one of his favorite spots on the river. *Photo by Terry Ireland.*

The result, which came out in 1947, was *Art Flick's Streamside Guide to Naturals and Their Imitations*, and its distinguishing achievement was the substantial reduction of "must" patterns a fisherman had to have in his fly box. With its simplified emergence tables, identification system, and guide to selecting the "right fly"—based on Art Flick's Schoharie Creek research—this little book was "all the angler needed to know about trout-stream insects and their imitations." Since it was first published, *Streamside Guide* has sold over 75,000 copies.

Flick and his little book are still going strong, but the Westkill Tavern came to a violent, fiery end in 1963, three years after Flick had sold it and retired from innkeeping. Watching it burn just next door to his house, he said, "was like losing my own child."

*   *   *

Schoharie Creek is probably the most paradoxical of Catskill streams in its physical characteristics. Its broad valley and high surrounding peaks rank it an easy first for scenic beauty, and yet it is one of the smallest Catskill rivers. It rises at a comparatively low 2,500 feet, only 29 of its 85 miles are considered trout water, and it rarely exceeds 60 feet wide or three feet deep in its run from source to reservoir, below which is mainly bass and pike water. The Schoharie falls a steep 550 feet in its first mile and progressively flattens, with fall rates of 36½ fpm in the next 14 miles, 24½ fpm in the next 10 miles, and 14½ fpm in the last 4½ miles to the reservoir.

Perhaps the Schoharie's most distinguishing feature, sadly, is its high temperatures from about June 1 on until fall. This is the main reason this river has always been so hospitable to bass. Several factors are responsible. A wide, east-west valley with little stream cover allows the sun to have maximum effect. There is also a lot of dark, flat shale in the streambed; this absorbs the heat, transmitting it to the water. Temperatures in the mid-eighties are common all summer long. As a result, many Schoharie fly fishermen hang up their rods shortly after Memorial Day. After that, the alternative is to fish this stream at daybreak or from dusk on.

The lack of cover on the Schoharie goes back to the 1850s when all the surrounding hillsides were denuded for hemlock bark to feed the tanneries. More hemlocks were cut out of this valley than from any other in the Catskills. Before that, the Schoharie was a well-shaded, much cooler trout stream. Hardwoods now grow along the banks but not nearly to the degree that the hemlocks used to.

Of the six Catskill reservoirs built and maintained by New York City for its water supply, all except the Schoharie have improved the trout fishing above or below them, or both. The truth of this statement depends on the quality and continuity of the "recreational release" program, which has been threatened by dry weather in recent years.

Gilboa Dam, which created Schoharie Reservoir when it was completed in 1925, releases modest amounts of water to the lower Schoharie, but there is very little trout fishing below the dam anyway. Whenever Schoharie Reservoir

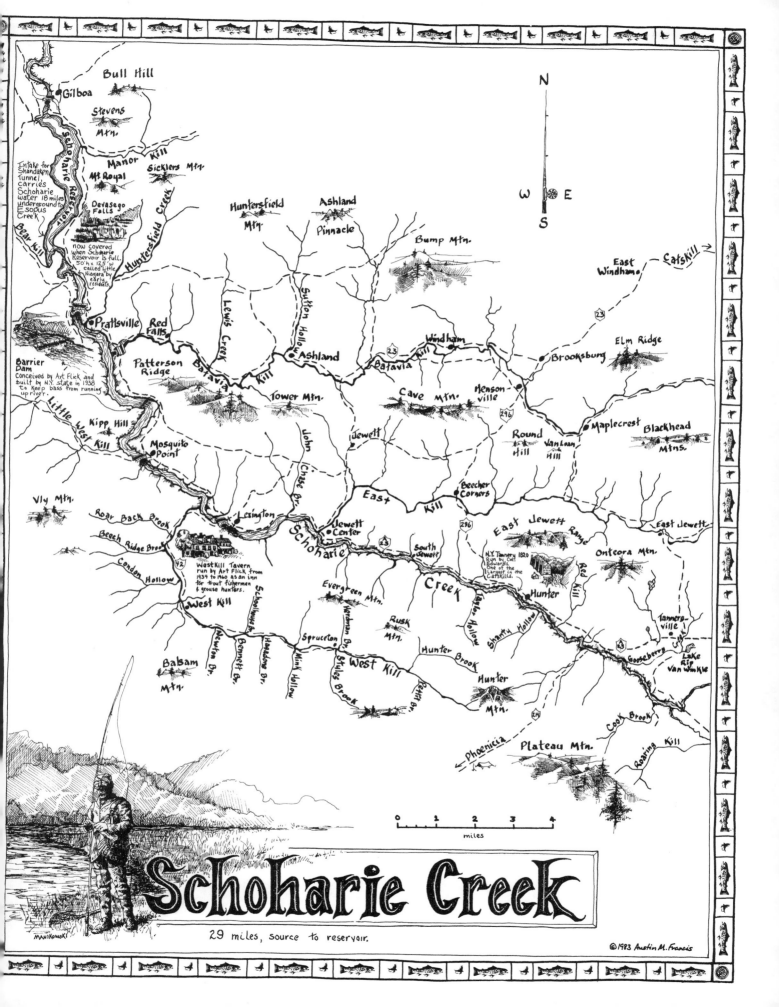

Schoharie Creek

29 miles, source to reservoir.

©1983 Austin M. Francis

Schoharie Creek has the broadest valley of any of the Catskill rivers, one of the causes of its higher temperatures after June 1st. Thus, the prime season for Schoharie anglers ends early. Said Wayne Elliot, one of its regulars: "If the Schoharie stayed like it is in April and May each spring, I would never fish any place else. It's just a gorgeous river!" *Photo by the author.*

even approaches being full—and it fills quickly due to its small size—the city diverts its water through the portal into Esopus Creek; this is done to the maximum allowed by law to keep from losing it downstream to the Mohawk, then the Hudson, and on out to sea. As a result, the reservoir's levels fluctuate dramatically, often as much as twenty to thirty feet in one day, and it is almost never full.

Upstream, when the reservoir is low, Devasego Falls is exposed, and its forty-foot drop prevents spawning trout from running up the Schoharie as they do out of Delaware, Esopus, Neversink, and Rondout reservoirs. Ironically, this falls, in the few times it is covered, is all the bass need to get upstream where they thrive without migrating. Art Flick's barrier dam at Prattsville has helped cut down the bass population some but has not eliminated it.

In a 1954 New York State fish population survey from Prattsville to Tannersville, Schoharie trout outnumbered bass two to one. The bass were found mainly below the junction with the East Kill, but some were counted up as far as Hunter. Another stream count showed the fall "standing crop" of trout at about 10 to 15 pounds per acre. This underlines the fact that the Schoharie has limited potential as a trout habitat. The Beaverkill averages about 75 pounds per acre, and the Esopus, with its myriad wild rainbows, averages 115 pounds.

One other problem the Schoharie has—but this is true to some degree of all freestone rivers—is that a number of the stream's long-standing pools are filling with gravel. Mosquito Point, still a very popular pool below Lexington, is now half its former size. Where the West Kill comes into the Schoharie used to be all water; it is now one-third gravel bar.

Some gravel movement is the natural result of storms and heavier seasonal flows, but the Schoharie has also been troubled with gravel that has washed into the stream from the roadbed when Route 23A was built from Prattsville up to

Tannersville in the early 1970s. Another source of gratuitous gravel has been the bulldozer activity by streamside homeowners attempting to keep their banks from washing away. According to one of the local fly fishermen, "They put a bulldozer in the stream, which is illegal in the first place, and push gravel and a few boulders up against their threatened bank. Then along comes the first big storm and all the gravel and boulders wash downstream into the next good-sized hole. And there goes another pool!"

Flash floods and the heavier flows of spring also dig out *new* pools, with the result that good pools still exist up and down the river. The net change on the Schoharie over the last several decades has been a reduction of larger pools and the creation of more pocket water. The river today is characterized by the alternation of riffle sections with stretches of pockets defined by countless block-shaped boulders and, every now and then, a pool.

Extremes of weather have probably done more damage to Schoharie Creek than to any other Catskill river. Over the 1980/81 season, it was subjected to a March flood, a summer drought, and heavy winter ice that broke up and gouged out the streambed. "It really wrecked the stream," according to a local fisherman. "The fly life and number of fish are down, many of the pools were damaged, and there's been a big drop-off in fishermen on the river."

For all its problems, the Schoharie has a cadre of anglers who love it and would never desert it. Wayne Elliot, state manager of fisheries for most of the Catskill rivers, is one of them. "If the Schoharie stayed like it is in April and May each spring, I would never fish any place else. It's just a gorgeous river!"

The waters of the Schoharie are readily accessible to visiting anglers, yet less crowded than other Catskill streams. Public fishing areas, totalling six miles, line the stream from the barrier dam to Dibbell's Dam. In addition, most of the main stream and a lot of tributary mileage is not posted and thus open to fishermen. In contrast to the angler population on public stretches of the Beaverkill, Willowemoc, and Esopus, aerial surveys have counted as few as one-half to one-third the number of anglers on the Schoharie.

Except for its upper five miles, where small brook trout abound, there are very few wild trout in the Schoharie. The torrential flows and high temperatures are just too much for a high-quality trout habitat. In a 1973 Schoharie creel census, 95 percent of the trout caught were hatchery browns, 80 percent yearlings, and 15 percent holdovers. The remaining 5 percent were wild browns.

The state's stocking policy for the Schoharie has changed over the years, recognizing that rainbows do not do well in this stream and that a lot of trout don't make it through the high temperatures each summer. From 1934 to 1954, rainbows were stocked from the barrier dam to Dibbell's Dam (Cook Brook), browns from East Kill to Dibbell's Dam, and brook trout above that. In 1954, it was decided that the brook trout needed no help, and that the hardier browns could survive warm-water spells better than the rainbows; so now only brown trout are stocked in the Schoharie.

In the past few years it has been found that if fingerling browns are stocked in the fall, by spring they are firm and broad, with long fins, and fight hard when hooked—essentially like wild fish. This refinement has now been added to the Schoharie's stocking program along with the spring complement of adult fish.

Rainbows do reproduce in the Schoharie but only in isolated sections. They have been seen in small numbers at Dibbell's Dam, above the village of West Kill, in the Little West Kill, between Hunter and Tannersville, and below Prattsville. The reality is, however, that almost no rainbows are caught anymore by Schoharie fishermen.

Special regulations have been tried on the Schoharie as a way of increasing the catch of big fish. In fact, the first no-kill stretch established in New York State was on the Schoharie near the Little West Kill. It lasted from 1962 through 1964 and was abandoned when the state's fisheries people determined that the trout were not surviving even with the no-kill regulation. Another special fishing area was established in 1974 from the junction with John Chase Brook upstream for 1.4 miles. The creel limit on this stretch was three fish 10 inches or better. This area too was returned to normal regulation status in 1981 when it was found that only in the best years for flow and temperature would there be an improvement in the late summer trout population.

*   *   *

Schoharie Creek never developed the large following of anglers typical of other Catskill streams. It was hardly ever mentioned in the early angling literature. It never had any private fishing preserves or fishing clubs, nor did it attract fly shops or other stores dedicated to fly fishermen. No acknowledged "headquarters" sprang up in shops or bars the way they did in Phoenicia, Roscoe, and Livingston Manor.

During the late 1800s, when other Catskill streams were contributing their part to the birth of American fly fishing, the waterfalls and cloves of Schoharie Creek and surrounding Greene County were being overrun by thousands of non-angling vacationers from the city. Tannersville was the first village in the Catskills to accommodate "summer people."

Anyone who fished the Schoharie in those days had to be pretty much of a loner, and even today this river appeals more to the individualist than it does to the majority of fishermen. Perhaps no one exemplifies the latter-day Schoharie angler better than Judd Weisberg, who eleven years ago gave up a college teaching job in Philadelphia to live permanently on the Schoharie. Now Judd mixes teaching locally with painting, sculpting, flytying (which he also teaches), overseeing an art gallery, and lots of fishing with his wife.

Being an artist, Judd describes himself as an "eclectic fisherman." What this means is that he changes his fishing methods frequently in order to spend as much time as possible on the stream. Summarizing his methods through a typical season gives a good idea of how one of the Schoharie's most dedicated anglers goes after his prey:

First few weeks after Opening Day. Big nymphs, bucktails, caddis pupae. Most productive pattern a heavily weighted Muddler Minnow. "This river's loaded with the big *Perlas*, so a large grey or black nymph works well. I bounce the bottom. I use between 21 and 28 turns of fuse wire in an average nymph, plus a wet tip to get it down."

Quill Gordon time to Memorial Day. Classic fishing to the hatch with traditional dry-fly patterns. Flick's *Streamside Guide* has very accurate hatch schedules for these flies. Important on the Schoharie, and more so each year, are the caddis and terrestrials. Recent years have been big for terrestrials, black ants in all sizes.

June first through the summer. River heats up, only decent fishing in evenings and at dawn, and middle of the night. Patterns: the old nineteenth-century originals, Rube Wood, Governor, Royal Coachman, big wets in sizes #4 and #6, three on a cast. *Potamanthus* a very reliable hatch on the Schoharie in the evenings from late June throughout the rest of the summer. They come off for a full hour at first, then the hatch period shrinks. Trout feed actively on this fly.

On the lower Schoharie, from about Prattsville to the reservoir, more of the deeper pools have bass, a number of them up to two and three pounds. And, as in Billy Boyd's days, they take flies—hair poppers and bushy patterns—just fine. Judd's best bass out of the Schoharie was a nineteen-incher he caught right below his house on a Golden Stonefly Nymph.

It was late one June afternoon and there were some stoneflies crawling on our kitchen window, so I figured since these flies mainly come off at night I would give it a try. I went down there, fished it real slow, *pow!* I get this hit, and it starts peeling line. The thing cartwheeled and I said, "I don't believe it, it's a bass!" It was almost dark, but I could just pick up its silhouette. Finally I got it in, and sure enough it was a smallmouth. I netted it, killed it, and took it home.

Judd agrees with those who see the Schoharie as an individualist's river, more attractive to single fishermen than to groups of friends. Groups fishing together prefer several other Catskill rivers. Summing up his feelings about the river, he explains why this is so:

When I think of the Schoharie in the abstract, it is a variable river, a river of mystery. It can't take as much pressure as other Catskill rivers because it doesn't have as many fish. So to get good fishing, you have to fish hard, early season, late at night, use stealth, and really work at it. You won't have competition except in the sense that you are competing with a river that gives up its treasures grudgingly. But if you fish it enough, and get to know it, you will have some excellent fishing."

THIRTEEN

Delaware River

To understand this river, a fly fisherman must view it as the sum of many parts and analyze each part separately. Otherwise, the Delaware is too big and complex a river to comprehend. From its source in the Catskills, it flows 330 miles until it widens and becomes Delaware Bay. Its upper tributaries are large rivers themselves—East Branch, West Branch, Mongaup, Lackawaxen, Neversink.

In the old days there were arguments over where the Delaware originated. "Some people denied that the Delaware has any true source at all," wrote Alf Evers in *The Catskills*, "but that it begins as a cooperative venture in which many streams share." They all seemed to agree however that it was a marvelous river for fishing.

Kit Clarke, New York jeweler, theatrical agent, and peripatetic angler, fished the Delaware for several decades spanning the turn of the century. Among his many talents, he was also a publicist for the Erie Railroad Company, writing a series of pamphlets for them entitled "Fishing on the Picturesque Erie." The Erie line ran from Hoboken, New Jersey, to Port Jervis where it joined the Delaware and followed its course to Hancock, then up the West Branch to Deposit before heading westward to Chicago. Completed in 1851, the Erie offered the earliest access by rail to Catskill fishing.

Considering the Delaware their province and a valuable resource, Erie management did everything they could to enhance and promote its attractions. They regularly stocked the many streams that entered the river along their right of way. In October of 1870, the Erie Railroad transported Ohio River black bass in a perforated basket made to fit the water tank of a locomotive and planted them in the Delaware. The bass took hold and within a few years could be caught

Photo by Larry Madison.

throughout the length of the main river and in many of its tributaries as far up as the warmer water prevailed. Said Kit Clarke, "The Delaware is loaded to the muzzle with this fish." He also praised their fighting qualities in one of his pamphlets:

> No sportsman ever yet held a gun that afforded him an iota of the glorious excitement which thrills a Delaware angler when one of these heavy bass makes a frantic rush and seizes the fly. I have seen men tremble in an ecstacy of agitation until the rod almost fell from their grasp.

Adding a plug for his employer, he said, "Fighting these big and burly black bass gives me the idea of having fastened my fly to the tail end of the 'Vestibule Limited.' " Generations of Catskill fishermen since have hooked onto these same Erie trains in their effusions over large Delaware bass and trout.

Clarke noted that many trout streams entered the Delaware that did not appear on any maps and described how he had stumbled onto one of them while fishing for bass. Returning the next day he filled his basket with the "gaudy, crimson-tinted finny fighters." On behalf of the railroad he cajoled: "Really good trout brooks, which are so accessible, deserve better patronage. Some day somebody will land on one of these streams and bring out a mess of big trout that will produce a paean of acclaim to make an oratorio seem like a little tin whistle."

The Delaware River was the setting for another fish-stocking experiment which failed. For three years beginning in 1871, the Fish Commission of New Jersey planted over 65,000 Atlantic salmon fry in the river. In 1877, 250,000 fry of the Pacific salmon were stocked at various points along the river.

"At last!" said an outdoor reporter in the April 13, 1878, issue of *The Country* as he described the first Atlantic salmon ever caught in the Delaware. It weighed 23½ pounds and was taken near Trenton. "The fish, which is undoubtedly one of the fry placed in the Delaware some six years ago, was in splendid condition. It was forwarded to U.S. Fish Commissioner Baird at the Smithsonian Institution, Washington, where it was viewed by the President and Mrs. Hayes, the Postmaster General and the Secretaries of War and the Navy."

Actually, according to a New Jersey Fish Commission account, seven salmon weighing eight to nine pounds each had been taken out of the Delaware the year before. In 1878, a total of eighteen salmon were killed, the heaviest weighing twenty-four pounds. That same year letters appeared in sporting journals complaining that gill nets set for spring-run shad, many of them illegal, were preventing the salmon from getting upriver in sufficient numbers to establish themselves. None of the correspondents acknowledged that salmon had never existed in rivers as far south as the Delaware. Whatever the cause, after 1878 salmon were never again seen in the Delaware.

An accidental stocking of the Delaware occurred in the 1880s when an Erie train was delayed by a wreck and happened to be carrying several cans of

"Black Bass Fishing" by artist A. B. Frost. The setting is a Delaware River eddy—long, deep pools so big and slow of flow that they appear to be mountain lakes. Robin Ruff described his 1889 summer outing in a flat-bottomed boat like this one: "Fortunate the angler whose boat nestles softly on the gentle bosom of any of these pools. His heart will be filled with gladness and his creel with fish, for they are the homes of the small-mouth black bass." *Culver Pictures.*

large rainbow trout. Dan Cahill, the brakeman on that run, was worried that the trout would die and persuaded his fellow trainmen to carry the cans a mile or so to Callicoon Creek and dump them in. The trout multiplied, and by 1900 Callicoon Creek was famous for its rainbow fishing.

On its main stem, the Delaware is punctuated by long, deep pools called "eddies." Some of them are so big and slow of flow that they appear to be mountain lakes. Looking upstream from an eddy, the river bends and a mountain seems to stand directly across the head of the "lake." A view down to the next bend unfolds a like effect; no outlet seems possible.

"Fortunate the angler whose boat nestles softly on the gentle bosom of any of these pools," wrote Robin Ruff in 1889. "His heart will be filled with gladness and his creel with fish, for they are the homes of the small-mouth black bass."

He went on to tell how "two good fellows, both being lovers of the rod and reel" put in part of their summer outing by taking a trip down the Delaware in a flat-bottomed boat.

Ruff and his friend set out from Hancock, having carried their boat up by train from Lackawaxen. For bait, they were supplied with a stock of 250 hellgrammites in one eight-quart tin pail and a mess of lamprey eels in another.

They drifted and fished along leisurely, anchoring at the bottom of a rapid so they could fish the upper end of an eddy before entering it. In one eddy they caught over 100 bass, ten of which weighed more than two pounds apiece. Ruff said their score should have been less but that his friend kept 15 to 20 under-sized fish.

Covering five or six miles a day, stopping at small river communities for the night, they fished on down to Lackawaxen where the Delaware and Hudson Canal Company had a dam that raised the river and formed what raftsmen called The Pond. Many "fine fellows" were continually caught from The Pond in spite of its popularity.

The fishing trip continued for another five or six miles to Handsome Eddy, "a big one and a dandy for bass." There, almost sixty miles below Hancock, the two fishermen got the canal men—"twenty-five cents will capture the canal chap"—to haul their boat up and place it on the canal boat for the trip back to their starting point.

> Now comes the slow and lazy ride back to Lackawaxen, while
> you lay off to enjoy the fine views and unlimited pipes of the weed.
> Any man that would ask for a lovelier trip than this from Hancock
> down would want the earth.

*   *   *

Everyone seems to want some of the Delaware's water, and therein lies one of the river's most disturbing complexities. Although it is a medium-sized river as American rivers go, it flows through and serves an area of over 50 million people.

Starting in 1925, the states of New York, Pennsylvania, and New Jersey tried to agree on the uses of the Delaware but failed. They tried and failed again in 1927. By 1931, mounting pressure from New York City for more water forced the issue into the United States Supreme Court which declared: "A river is more than an amenity, it is a treasure. It offers a necessity of life that must be rationed among those who have power over it."

The court decreed that the city could divert 440 million gallons a day from the Delaware, but that a flow of 1525 cubic feet per second had to be maintained past the gauging station at Montague, New Jersey. This came to be known as the "Montague formula" and was enforced by a federally appointed river master. The formula survived for twenty-three years until New York's growing water needs again forced a Supreme Court reckoning. The revised formula allowed an 800 mgd diversion provided that 1750 cubic feet per second was maintained at Montague. By this time the Neversink reservoir had been completed and the plans were well underway for dams on both branches of the Delaware. With these three "holding tanks," a greater reserve would be available so that everyone's greater thirst could be slaked.

And many are the "thirsty." Industries want and get by far most of the Delaware's water. Over 85 percent of it goes to sustain the processes in shipyards, steel mills, oil refineries, chemical factories, and paper plants from Port Jervis down to Pea Patch Island off Delaware City. Farms at the upper end of the river, especially along the West Branch, need water for irrigation and livestock. Power companies on the Neversink and Mongaup rivers want water for their turbines. Cargo ships use it to ply the river as far north as Trenton. New Yorkers use close to 1.5 billion gallons a day, most of it from the Delaware, to mix with their Scotch and flush their toilets.

The forces of recreation had to wait until 1961 to be formally recognized as legitimate users of the Delaware's water. That was the year President Kennedy and the governors of Delaware, New Jersey, New York, and Pennsylvania signed the Delaware Basin Compact. It was a "peace treaty" among all the water users, painfully hammered out over the four to five years preceding its acceptance.

To reach this milestone, it took the catalytic force of two devastating hurricanes in 1955, a $2 million Congressional appropriation for consulting reports, and the involvement of 19 federal agencies, 14 interstate agencies, 43 state boards, departments, and commissions, and over 250 public and private water-using companies. Within the framework of the Delaware Basin Compact all subsequent negotiations have taken place including those in the 1970s between the city and state of New York which led to recreational releases from the Delaware watershed reservoirs.

*   *   *

Around 1900, although fly fishermen were proliferating, the Delaware began losing its appeal among anglers; it was mainly a bass river, and the coming fashion was to fish with a fly for trout.

Shad were also abundant in the Delaware but they attracted a different kind of sportsman. The intelligence of the day on shad was that they refused to take any kind of bait and were seldom caught by anglers. Such theories were behind the organization around 1906 of the Delaware Shad Club of Binghamton. The club had about fifty members, and every year they would gather with an equal number of guests for a "great field day" on the river. Their method involved two sieves, one called a drag and the other a pocket sieve. The drag was deployed on boats across the head of an eddy, dropped into the water and drawn down slowly while several men held the pocket sieve at the tail of the eddy to prevent the shad from escaping downstream. The take on a successful draw would be from "two to three hundred beauties." Afterward, the remainder of the day was spent playing games, and ended with a huge shore dinner "that any red-blooded disciple of Izaak Walton would greatly enjoy."

Fishing interest in the Delaware, except for bass and shad, remained largely dormant until after World War II. Then, with angling pressure mounting

A Delaware River shad taken just below Hancock around 1935. Early shad sportsmen seined the river with nets; the Delaware Shad Club of Binghamton held an annual field day each year and netted several hundred fish for a big shore dinner that evening. In the last couple of decades the shad has become popular as a game fish—in some anglers' minds, "the poor man's salmon." *N.Y.S. Conservation Department 1935 Annual Report.*

on the central Catskill streams, the more resourceful fishermen started going to the East Branch and main stem of the Delaware to avoid the crowds. Sparse Grey Hackle in a 1948 letter to Harry Darbee called it "the last unfished water in reach of New York."

The decade of the sixties brought major changes to Delaware fishing. In 1961, the Pepacton Dam was completed at Downsville on the East Branch. It created a narrow, twisting reservoir of some seven-thousand acres, eliminating a little over twenty miles of river. It also took over most of the downstream releases from the Neversink to meet the Montague formula. These releases came from the colder, bottom layer of the reservoir and were sufficient to establish a cold-water trout zone all the way past Hancock down to Long Eddy, a distance of some forty-five river miles.

The lower stretches of this new cold-water zone—they were below Ed Hewitt's "trout minimum" elevation of 1,000 feet—had always been more hospitable to warm-water species. So, as the trout began to establish themselves lower down in the river, this new trout zone became a favorite place for the local experts to fish. Harry Darbee, Sam Hendrickson, Bill Kelly, Alan Fried, Joe Horak, and a select few of their friends from the city all used to fish this stretch. It had terrific hatches, good flow, cold water all the way down, and lots of one- and two-pound fish.

The Pepacton-created trout zone lasted for about six years until the West Branch dam at Cannonsville came onstream in 1967, and once again the release patterns shifted. Because the West Branch is subjected to greater pollution than the East Branch—it has many more farms and towns—its water is considered more expendable by the city water managers. Thus the Cannonsville Reservoir

The Pepacton dam under construction, October 21, 1950. A concrete core-wall, backbone of the earthen dam being built up on either side, spans the valley. The East Branch of the Delaware flows right to left through a diversion channel and tunnel cut through solid rock on the far side of the valley. *Courtesy Bureau of Water Supply, City of New York.*

Pepacton Reservoir, completed in 1961, is a narrow, twisting lake of some 6,500 acres that eliminated a little over twenty miles of the East Branch of the Delaware—once a superb trout stream. In the six years following, until Cannonsville Reservoir on the West Branch was completed, Pepacton was the principal source of cold-water releases to sustain flows and hospitable conditions for the river's trout and other fish. *Photo by Larry Madison.*

The Cannonsville dam looking downstream on October 10, 1963. Construction is nearly completed and the West Branch of the Delaware has been returned from a diversion channel at middle right to its old bed in the foreground. The bottom-release intake can be seen at the lower left where the river is interupted by the dam. The Stilesville Bridge is at the upper right. *Courtesy Bureau of Water Supply, City of New York.*

An early 1930s Delaware River eel rack. Looking upriver, from this trap of closely set slats, a V-shaped wall of rocks concentrates the river's flow into the trap. In the fall, when the eels leave the river to spawn, they are trapped by the slats, scooped out into holding tanks, and sold live or frozen by the rack owner. Today, only half a dozen licensed eel racks operate on the Delaware. *N.Y.S. Conservation Department 1935 Annual Report.*

was given the brunt of the downstream release requirements. For example, the last week of August 1982 showed the following split among the three reservoirs satisfying the mandated downstream flows: Cannonsville 84.6 percent, Pepacton 9 percent, Neversink 6.4 percent.

With the Pepacton and Cannonsville dams being thirty-three and eleven miles up their respective branches, releases from the Cannonsville dam pushed the cold-water zone even farther down the main river to Callicoon. And there it remains today with some seasonal and legally allowable fluctuations. Other dams have been planned for the Delaware watershed, but none of them has leaped all of the political and public hurdles necessary to become a reality.

                    *   *   *

The East Branch of the Delaware River rises on the side of Irish Mountain at an elevation of 2,400 feet and flows southwest for approximately seventy-five miles to join the West Branch at Hancock. It is interrupted from about its twentieth to fortieth mile by the Pepacton Reservoir.

Above the reservoir, the East Branch offers a little over eight miles of good trout fishing, up to Wawaka Lake at Halcottsville. Beyond Halcottsville, the stream diminishes to a slow-flowing, meandering brooklet of meadows and beaver ponds.

The upper East Branch and its tributaries, especially Batavia Kill and Bush Kill, have abundant fly hatches to support a large population of both wild and stocked trout, almost all browns. A moderate fall of fifteen feet per mile and above-average agricultural runoff contribute to the richness of plants and insects of the area's streams. Pools are nice and deep for a stream of twenty to twenty-five feet in width. The bottom is gravel, sand, ledgerock, and scattered boulders. Wading is easy, rarely calling for more than hip boots.

Brown trout are stocked in the East Branch above the reservoir but not in the tributaries, where wild browns tend to dominate. Catches of numerous small wild trout are common above the reservoir, with a fish over twelve inches being exceptional. A successful technique is to fish these small streams down with a wet fly or nymph, twitching them back up, switching to a dry fly only when there is surface feeding.

Browns from the reservoir run up most of the tributaries in the fall, including Tremper Kill, Platte Kill, Batavia Kill, Bush Kill, Dry Brook and Mill Brook. The last two are almost totally posted streams, but the others are generally open and unposted. Above the reservoir there is a total of about five miles of public fishing rights and about another sixteen miles of unposted water.

When the reservoir is down, several additional miles of river can be fished below Margaretville. In those stretches the East Branch has the appearance of many western rivers: it wanders a lot, is rather deep, and has sandy, grass-covered banks with few trees on the immediate flood plain. There are also fewer boulders and almost no shelf rock.

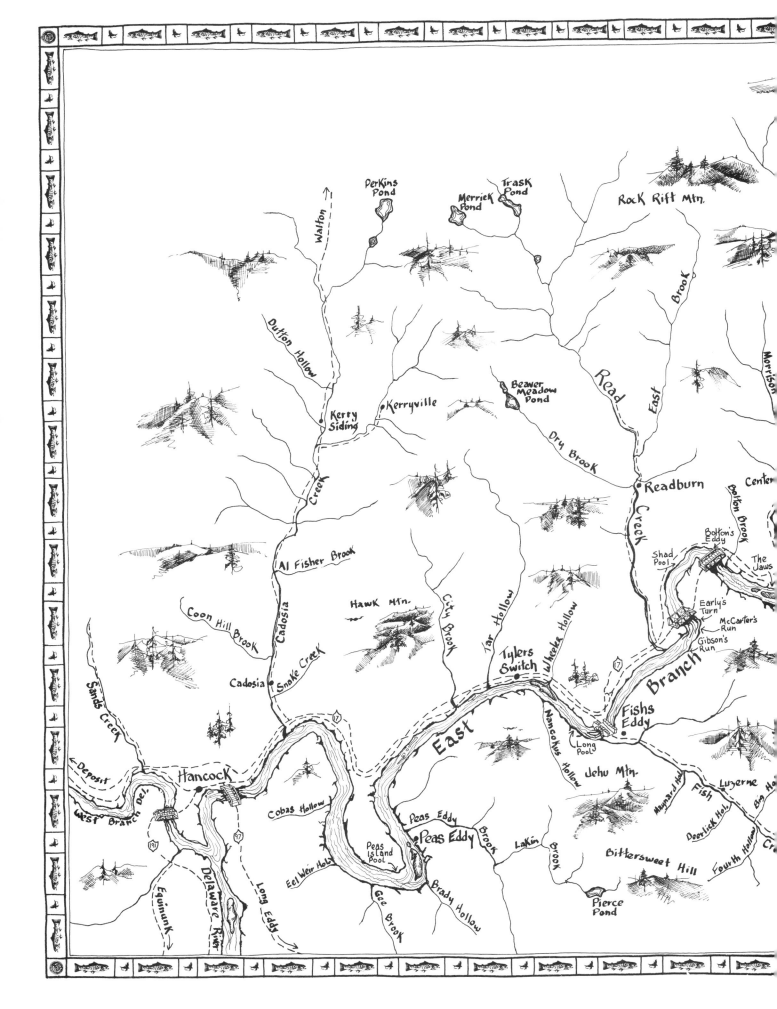

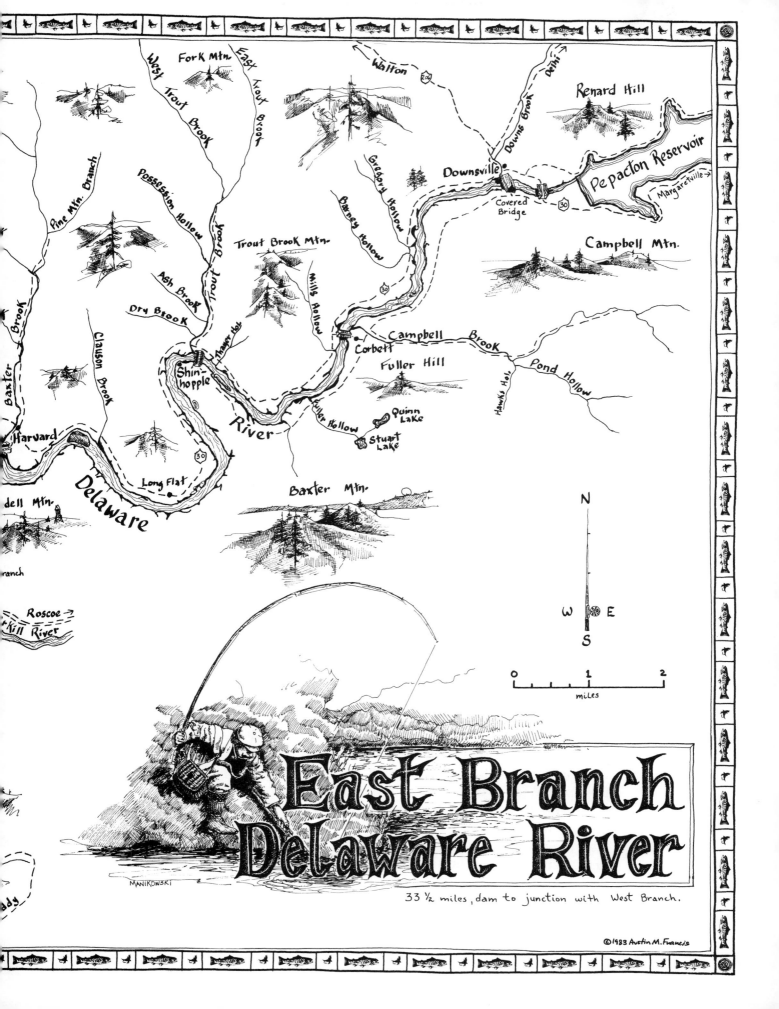

East Branch Delaware River

33 ½ miles, dam to junction with West Branch.

©1983 Austin M. Francis

In its last thirty-three miles downstream from the Pepacton Reservoir, the East Branch is very different above and below its junction with the Beaverkill. The upper section, of some sixteen miles, is a series of long pools and shallow riffles, falling at a rate of six feet per mile. This stretch of the river is unnatural in that it is maintained by the releases coming out of the reservoir. The original river cut a bigger channel than it presently occupies. Therefore, the pool flows are slower and the depths throughout shallower than in a natural stream of the same capacity. The only time the East Branch fills up now is when the reservoir spills over.

The river varies along this section from 75 to 150 feet wide. The bottom is fine gravel, sand, and silt with very few boulders. Wading is not hard, but many of the pools are too deep to cross.

Brook trout in the 10- to 12-inch range are caught in the East Branch near Downsville. They come out of Downs Brook. The water is so cold coming out of the reservoir that they will come down and stay in the larger river. The rest of this part of the river is mainly brown-trout water. It gets stocked with browns, and browns spawn in the tributaries. With the long growing season there are browns here of fourteen to fifteen inches and larger, in excellent shape—plump, fat fish.

The entire East Branch from the Pepacton Dam to Hancock is unposted with the exception of a few short stretches, so the whole river is open to the public through the courtesy of owners or state-owned fishing rights. A fisherman who knocks and asks permission to fish the river behind someone's house is rarely turned down. It is also easy to find campsites along the valley which cater to fishermen.

There are certain advantages that come from the controlled flows on the East Branch. The 40-degree water released from the bottom of the reservoir maintains cool, even stream temperatures all year long. This helps create a more stable environment, like a spring creek, and gives the trout a longer growing season. Examine the East Branch below Downsville and you will find lots of weeds, loaded with little fresh-water shrimp, and a rich variety of insects.

Because of the even temperatures and distribution of food, the fish feed throughout the length of these flat, glassy pools, instead of the heads and tails of pools as they would on the Beaverkill and Willowemoc. The only problem with that is they are very tough to catch. One-quarter of the way down the pool you run out of drift and the fish have too much time to look at your fly and leader. These conditions defeat most fishermen. The fish are there but you have to find the flows, and with the riffle sections so short and infrequent, you can drive for a mile past water where you would be unwise to fly fish.

Ed Van Put says that many times he has seen thirty to forty fish rising at once on these pools and that one cast had put them all down. Five to ten minutes later they were all rising again. "I know you could catch more and larger fish over here than you could on the Beaverkill," he says. "The river simply holds more fish. You'd just have to work damn hard to do it. That's the challenge of this particular river."

A typical stretch of the lower East Branch in the last seventeen miles below its junction with the Beaverkill. Of rather stony, unstable bottom, its pools and runs change dramatically from year to year. During seasonal high flows, the undammed Beaverkill contributes most of the lower East Branch's water. Likewise, when the Beaverkill is low, so is the lower East Branch. *Photo by the author.*

Below its junction with the Beaverkill, the East Branch resumes the character of a mountain freestone stream. In one of its typical stretches, the fast water comes in, hits the bend, forms a pool, breaks, turns into a riffle, then into another pool that tails out before rounding the next bend. During seasonal high flows, the undammed Beaverkill contributes most of the lower East Branch's water. Likewise, when the Beaverkill is low, so is the lower East Branch.

Thus, throughout the remainder of its seventeen-mile run to Hancock, the East Branch is a river of fluctuating levels and temperatures. Because of its stony, rather unstable bottom its pools and runs can change dramatically from year to year. The river here varies between one hundred and two hundred feet wide and pools range from three to eight feet deep. Trees overhanging the water are rare and even when they do the river is wide enough so that it gets plenty of sun.

The best months to fish the lower East Branch are April through June and again in the fall. In July and August you usually need to fish it at dawn and dusk, or at night, to get decent water temperatures. By contrast, the East Branch up to the Pepacton is often best fished around noon, even in midsummer, after the dam water has warmed up a few degrees. This is an area where a thermometer is helpful; if the water is above 75°, the fish would be bunched up off the tributary mouths.

Hatches on this section of the river are fairly typical of the Catskills, plus green drakes, dobsonflies, and an abundance of large stoneflies. Harry Darbee used to fish at daybreak between East Branch village and Fishs Eddy with a cutdown version of the Edson Dark Tiger bucktail to imitate these big stones. One nineteen-incher he caught had eaten several hundred of them. The peak of the hatch, when Harry fished it, lasted only two or three days and came right after the green drakes.

The dobsonfly and its carnivorous nymph, the hellgrammite, are present in this part of the East Branch and in almost no other Catskill rivers because they like warmer water. On the main Delaware, where they used to thrive, they have dwindled in numbers since the Cannonsville releases began. They can still be found in fair numbers below Callicoon. The dobson is so large that when dusk falls it is often mistaken for a small bird. It is the eastern equivalent of the salmon fly out West, but does not play so important a role for fly fishermen.

As a live bait for walleyes, the hellgrammite sees plenty of service along the East Branch below Fishs Eddy. Also used are lampers, junebug spinners, minnows, and night crawlers. The walleyes in this part of the river run sixteen to eighteen inches but have been found dead as big as thirty-six inches and weighing twelve pounds. They are found in growing size and number the rest of the way down the river, but they do not respond well to flies and are rather sluggish on the rod.

Wild rainbow trout begin to show up near Read Creek and are caught all the way down into the main river to Callicoon. Read Creek is a spawning stream for brooks, browns, and rainbows, a distinction not many other Catskill streams can claim.

Brown trout are stocked in the lower East Branch. They also reproduce well in the tributaries. Compared with the upper East Branch, there are fewer but bigger browns in spite of a shorter growing period, because there is a lot of food and the river holds bigger fish. As a result, fishermen have a better chance of catching browns up to twenty inches and better in the lower East Branch.

There is a story about Bill Kelly and a secret fish he had located on the lower East Branch in the late fifties, before the four-lane highway was completed. Kelly had spotted a really big brown down there and mentioned it to Elsie and Harry Darbee, but didn't say where it was. One night the Darbees were driving along the river and spotted Kelly at the mouth of one of the tributaries, just sitting on the bank and staring into the water, so they knew his fish was right off this tributary mouth.

Kelly tied up a six-inch-long muddler and had worked hard for several days to catch this fish. One day he had it on, but he lost him; the next night Kelly came back and another fisherman was there showing off the fish, a beautiful seven-pound brown. He had caught it on a minnow.

Below Fishs Eddy down to Peas Eddy the river widens, shallows out, and gets more sun. The fishing along that section is not as good as it is above and below.

In the Hancock Diner, there used to be a big trout on the wall that came out of Peas Eddy. Harry Darbee and Ed Van Put often stopped there when they fished the Delaware. On the windows of the diner would be all the hatch of that day and the night before. It would be simply loaded with flies. Harry used to tell Ed: "Look outside the bars on the window glass and you'll see what's hatching, or when you get to the river in the evening, put your inside car light on with the windows open so the stuff will come in, and you can see that way." Harry rather favored the bar approach.

Below Hancock a lot has changed since Robin Ruff's flat-bottomed-boat-and-black-bass days. It is still the same river, but the fashion now is chest waders, dry flies, and wild rainbow trout.

The "Big Delaware" flows 255 miles to the sea but it is the first 27 miles that interest fly fishermen. This is the river's artificially maintained cold-water zone; when releases are in progress it has the same "spring creek" characteristics displayed by the first sixteen miles of the East Branch below the Pepacton Dam. It differs from the East Branch in that its riffle sections are longer and deeper. This is important because the riffles are the aerated, food-producing sections of the river. They are also the most productive of trout because the fly fisherman can wade to his fish and get a nicely paced, bouncy float over it with his fly.

The riffle sections of the Delaware are usually two to four feet deep and several hundred feet long. The flow when dam releases are in progress and abetted by the six-foot-per-mile fall is challenging but not dangerous to wade. The riffle bottoms are gravel and grapefruit-to-basketball-sized stones with occasional submerged large flat boulders, interspersed with water weeds.

Also productive are the heads of pools before the force of the riffle runs out. Sometimes the tail of a riffle will push a gravel bar well down into a pool, creating an extended "casting jetty." The pools themselves give up trout but they are harder to fish. For example, the pool might be four hundred feet wide, you can wade out seventy-five feet, and if the fish are rising out in the middle or on the other side, you need a canoe. As far as fly fishing goes—with many of these giant, slow-flowing eddies running to six hundred feet wide, from six to twenty feet deep, and stretching on up to a mile long—there is not much action between the riffles.

Water temperature is the single most important factor in determining the quality of fly fishing in the Hancock-to-Callicoon trout zone. Therefore the regularity of Cannonsville releases is watched closely by Delaware anglers. Ed Van Put explained how the fight in a fish is directly related to the water temperature: "You get a Delaware River fish when the water is 66°, it's like hooking onto that *train!* You set the hook and they *explode*—jump and run, down and across, into the backing on one run sometimes. You catch the same fish when

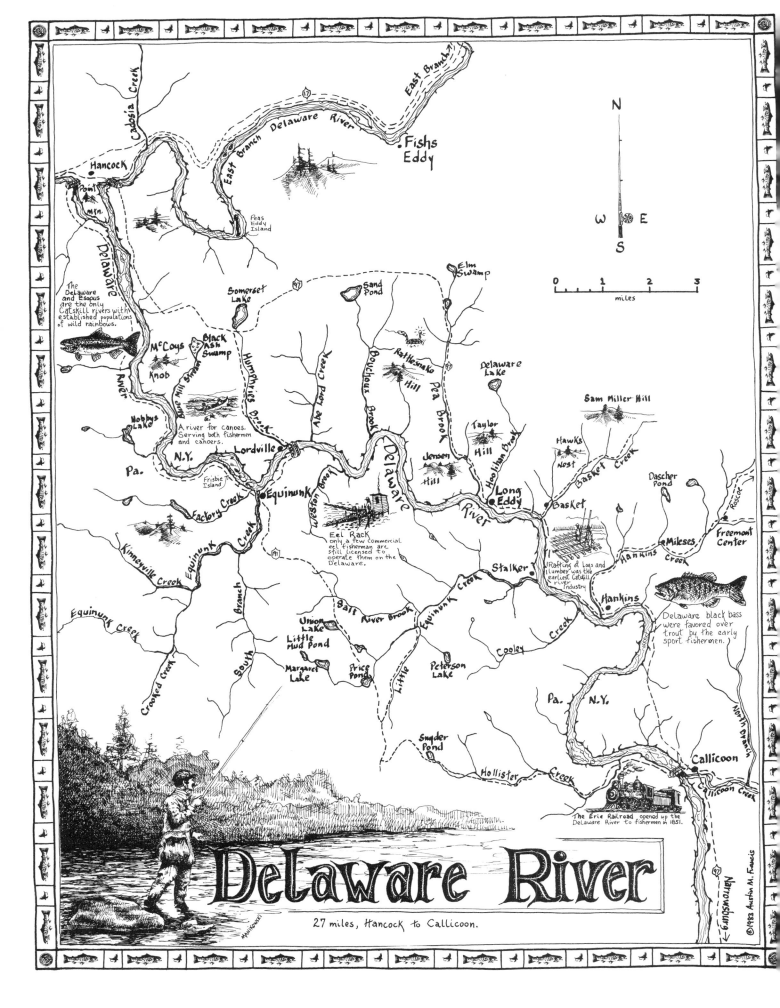

Delaware River

27 miles, Hancock to Callicoon.

The Delaware and Esopus are the only Catskill rivers with established populations of wild rainbows.

A river for canoes. Serving both fishermen and canoers.

Eel Rack only a few commercial eel fisherman are still licensed to operate them on the Delaware.

Rafting of logs and lumber was the earliest Catskill river industry.

Delaware black bass were favored over trout by the early sport fishermen.

The Erie Railroad opened up the Delaware River to fishermen in 1851.

©1983 Austin M. Francis

it's 72°, and it's a *big* difference. It's hard to believe those few degrees give the fish so much more energy."

These fish also feed best when the temperatures are between 45° and 66°. The hatches they feed on are probably the most plentiful in the Catskills in terms of variety of species, size of an individual insect, and density per square foot of streambed or water surface.

An interesting effect of water temperature is the size of a given insect species—the warmer the water the larger the fly. In the upper East Branch where water flows are artificially controlled but the average temperatures are lower, the same species will be a good hook size smaller. The farther you go downriver from Hancock, the larger the flies get. They have longer growing seasons. Warm water also tends to encourage greater hatch density.

In the lower reaches of the trout zone, beginning near Callicoon, there is a fly that hatches in August called, appropriately, the "August Fly." Only recently has it been included in stream entomologies. It is a big, white mayfly, size 12, with a little brown spot on the thorax. "It hatches here in such numbers," says Ed Van Put, "that when I have been fishing they were plastered along my rod from getting on the line and getting squashed when I stripped them through the guides. The greatest hatches of any fly I have ever seen. You could close your eyes and hold out your hand and you would believe it is snowing!"

The trout zone of the Delaware is also home to a rich variety of other fish. Black bass are less plentiful now with the cooler water, but they are still present in the eddies, will take flies readily, and have often saved a dull day from defeat when the trout were not working. Bass caught on the rod average eight to twelve inches with an occasional fish up to eighteen inches and three pounds. Walleyes are here too; they seek the warmer flows, respond mostly to bait, and are far better on the plate than on the rod. They run sixteen to twenty-four inches, but rare catches are reported of walleyes exceeding thirty inches and ten pounds. Chubs are here, though not as many as there used to be before the latest flow agreements took effect in the mid-seventies. No one keeps records about large chubs.

Two more species, the American eel and the American shad, share the Delaware in a very interesting fashion. Eels run out of the Delaware in late fall evenings to spawn in the Sargasso Sea. Shad come into the Delaware in early spring, spawning up as far as Harvard and Shinhopple on the East Branch, in some years entering the lower Beaverkill. The shad run varies a lot from year to year, but fisheries biologists have estimated the Delaware's potential shad run at one million fish. Indeed, the *American Journal of Science and Arts* reported in 1837 that fishermen with shore and drift nets in the lower Delaware caught an estimated 1,500,000 shad annually, and that occasionally more than 10,000 were taken in a single haul.

Eels are harvested on the Delaware by angling from boats, spearing, and by a handful of commercially licensed "eel racks." To spear eels, you must wade the shallows at night usually in September or October. Armed with a strong light and a stout spear, you can spot the eels foraging as they work their way down the river toward the sea. Eel racks are essentially tiers of closely set slats positioned at the point of a huge downstream-pointing "V" bulldozed into the riverbed to concentrate the flow into and through the rack. The eels are trapped by the slats, scooped out into holding tanks, and sold live or frozen by the rack owner. One owner said that his all-time, one-night record was just under three thousand eels. On a very slow night he might get thirty eels.

Shad reach the upper Delaware toward the end of April and continue pressing upstream as the fishermen take their toll. Most of the shad are caught by boat and from the banks on a small lead jig called a shad dart, but fly fishermen have created their own version of the dart, a fluorescent/optic wet-fly pattern that works very well. On light tackle, the shad's acrobatic leaps and runs have earned it the sobriquet of "poor man's salmon." After shad have spawned, they respond more readily to dry flies.

The Delaware is the only major Catskill river not stocked with trout; all its trout are wild. From Hancock to Callicoon, browns and rainbows far outnumber the brook trout. Starting with about an equal number of each, the farther down you go in the 27-mile trout zone, the more rainbows there are caught for every brown until the ratio gets as high as ten to one. The tributaries moving down toward Callicoon carry progressively higher concentrations of young rainbows. Most of them live in the tributaries for a year or two and then come down to the big river.

Only two major rivers in the Catskills have established populations of wild rainbows—the Esopus and the Delaware. The rainbow's heritage is that of a sea-run fish; it must have big water to grow up in. On the Esopus, this is the Ashokan Reservoir. On the Delaware, the river itself serves this purpose.

Access to Delaware fishing is a real problem. Although it is the most public river in the Catskills—because it is a navigable interstate waterway all the way up to Hancock—the land bordering the river is private and usually posted. Except at public boat-launching sites, bridge crossings, and a few other places, permission from owners is required to get onto the river. Once you have access, however, you have full run of the river up to its high-water mark.

Canoes on the Delaware—and there are thousands at times—can be a curse or blessing depending on your point of view. Landowners view them mostly with disgust, which accounts for the high degree of posting along the river. The small percentage of canoers who carouse and litter when they stop overnight have ruined the reputation of all the rest. Fishermen tend to like canoes if they are using them to reach the fishing, whereas they dislike them if the canoes are putting their fish down. And, of course, canoers love canoes, especially when gliding down this wild and beautiful river.

The Delaware is Ed Van Put's river. He has fished it so intensively and continuously for the past fifteen years that as a fisherman, you might say he owns it. Gardner Grant bestowed on Ed the title "Admiral of the Delaware," and no one has risen to challenge him. Even Daniel Skinner, the original "Admiral" of the early 1800s, would most likely be pleased to share the title with his successor.

In his peak ten years of fishing the Delaware, Ed averaged 100 days on the river in a 160-day season, and caught 240 to 260 trout a year. This may seem like awfully few fish to anglers accustomed to 10- and 20-fish days. And therein lies the true character of the Delaware: it is a tough river to fish.

"It would be hard for publicity to spoil the Delaware, because it's such a difficult river," says Ed. "You don't come over here and slaughter them. I get wiped out often enough on this river, and most fishermen don't like getting wiped out."

One of the difficulties with Delaware rainbows is they do not hold position like browns do, even in a good hatch. They rise and move and rise and move right by you. One of their patterns is to move steadily upstream, rising all the way, then to drop back and do it all over again. "If you see a rise," says Ed, "go to that fish. Don't expect it to be there even a minute from now. Get your fly over it as soon as you can."

Dry flies are by far the best choice when the Delaware is being maintained at bank-grass levels. It is such a big river with so few protruding boulders that the flow in riffle sections appears to be much slower than it is. Wet flies, even with sinking lines, sweep by, at the most a foot below the surface. It is three to four feet deep in the riffle sections and the velocity is too great for you to get the flies down. Nymphs and lead will get down but then you have to fish close, and the Delaware has a *lot* of water to cover. Nymphs will work better in the fall when the riffles tend to be half of their spring depth.

Because the Delaware trout are all wild, they display great individuality and unpredictability. Hatchery fish from the time they are hatched are fed all at the same time and on a regular schedule. They learn that their food always comes from above so they are trained to look up.

"Delaware trout feed when they're going to feed," says Ed. "You can be in Kellam's Bridge pool tonight, with a good hatch, and maybe a dozen fish are working. You come tomorrow night and there'll be a hundred, the next night, three hundred! Most fishermen would guess very differently how many fish were in the river based on these different nights.

FOURTEEN

Catskill Rivers Today

T he Beaverkill and its sister streams have known the presence of man for only the tiniest fraction of their two-million-year existence. From their pristine days—in the short span of just two angling lifetimes—they have served many masters and survived a relentless series of abuses to emerge as some of the world's most popular trout rivers.

When Thad Norris and other early American anglers began fishing in the Catskills, the rivers were already supplying the needs of the first in a long line of competitors for their limited resources. Of course, in the early and middle 1800s there was hardly a sense of competition because everything seemed so plentiful.

The river raftsmen did not believe that the white pines lining the Delaware could ever give out. The tanlords looked up the valleys and saw endless stands of giant hemlocks waiting to give bark to tan hides into leather. Their tanneries used the clear Catskill waters to fill vats, run machinery, and carry wastes downstream. Sawmillers harnessed the streams to power up-and-down saws and likewise floated their sawdust downstream. Wood acid factories devoured miles of "four-foot" hardwood and leached corrosives into the streams.

These early river industries were located on or in the rivers and each one damaged or changed the fishing. They took away the virgin forest cover and raised the temperatures of the streams. The brook trout still around after the massive overfishing of the 1870s and 1880s retreated to cooler feeders and headwater reaches. The hardier brown trout took over and thrived in former brook-trout habitats.

There were very few insects and fish living downstream from the tanneries, mills, and acid factories. These had collectively, for several generations, polluted most of the mileage of the major rivers throughout the Catskills.

Gradually, the old river industries died out as their markets and technologies changed or as their raw materials were consumed. Slowly, from about 1885, the rivers cleared, microscopic plants returned, then the bugs, and finally the trout. However, the competition for river resources, far from diminishing, only shifted to new kinds of competitors.

Over the years since 1900, the interests of a very diverse group of individuals and organizations have had both good and bad effects on Catskill rivers. They have given up gravel to roadbuilders and for aggregate in mixing concrete. Such use is now illegal. They have also received unwanted gravel from nearby excavations, especially new roadbeds paralleling long stretches of river. When Highway 23A went in along the Schoharie, gravel washed into and in some cases eliminated a number of its best pools.

The most renowned and resisted highway in the Catskills is four-lane Route 17, also known as "The Quickway." It was fought bitterly by fishermen and conservation groups from the mid-fifties to the early sixties. They succeeded only in getting a few changes in its alignment and a few added contract specifications to reduce stream damage during construction. They failed to get eliminated even one of the twelve bridges that carried the new highway back and forth across the most fished sections of the lower Willowemoc and Beaverkill, through or next to such famous pools as Barnhart's, Hendrickson's, Cairns's, Wagon Tracks, School House, Painter's Bend. A new legion of anglers has come along who do not remember the river before the highway, but a lot of the old-timers hung up their rods or found other rivers to fish.

Then there were the gypsy moth sprayings with DDT in the 1950s when C47s flew down the valleys of Fish Creek, Basket Creek, the East Branch and main stem of the Delaware, and the Neversink below its dam. Sparse Grey Hackle described the result:

> It killed the gypsy moths, all right; it also took incalculable bird life, eliminated from the area the honeybees upon which so many plants depend for fertilization, and indiscriminately killed off both stream and land insects to such an extent that it was years before the standard stream insect hatches regained their normal size and order of emergence. To this day, the grasshopper has not returned to its former abundance.

Dairy and chicken farms were a major source of Catskill river pollution in the 1920s. Their numbers have fallen off sharply since then, but the state in 1922 listed hundreds of them in a special report of stream pollution. Milk wastes and manures were the chief offenders. Harry Darbee raised chickens and knew how serious the problem could be:

> The chicken "eggeries" spoiled the fishing in Callicoon Creek. They shoveled the chicken manure into the hollows, and it leached its way into the stream. Now that's terrible stuff, and I ought to

know. It's almost pure nitrates, and it burns everything it touches, be it soil, humans, or fish.

There have been many other influences on the health and welfare of Catskill rivers through the years. Nature has flooded and ice-gouged them, shifting their sinuosities and pools back and forth since the beginning of time. They have been used as a conduit for waste, especially by towns and residential developers to get rid of sewage effluent. Streamside owners have altered their beds and banks in the name of beautification or flood control.

The hottest competition over the rivers has come from those who want the water itself, including the fishermen. Attractive trout water is as close to gold as the natural resources of the Catskills can get, and fishermen have fought to own it, lease it, or just to find a quiet stretch of it on which to fish. Farms have diverted Catskill rivers for livestock and crops; industries, for cooling and processing.

The biggest users of Catskill water are power companies and downstream municipalities. Most of Mongaup River, a tributary of the Delaware, was eaten up in the 1920s by three hydroelectric dams built for the Tenney System. Through a 1931 Supreme Court decree, Philadelphia is guaranteed enough fresh water moving down the Delaware to keep salt water from being sucked into its municipal water intake.

By 1967—when the last of New York City's Catskill reservoirs was completed—approximately 58 miles of six principal rivers had been consumed in stages by their reservoirs. Other reservoirs have been planned but were cancelled or delayed for various reasons. Among them are Hawk Mountain Dam, which would create a thirty-mile-long reservoir flooding all but two miles of what remains of the East Branch of the Delaware between Hancock and the Pepacton Reservoir, with a five-mile-long arm extending one-third of the way up the Beaverkill beyond the village of East Branch; Willowemoc Reservoir, four miles long, extending from a point one mile above Livingston Manor upstream past Parkston almost to DeBruce; and Beaverkill Reservoir, four miles long, extending from just below Jersey Brook past Lew Beach up to Beech Hill Brook.

The reservoirs have been both bad and good for the Catskills and its rivers. The first effect of each dam as it went in was the emotional trauma of residents and longtime visitors as they realized that their valleys were being terminated, that they were being evicted en masse, and that their villages were losing not only their identities but also the bodies of their dead.

Bishop's Falls on the Esopus was one of these communities. For years a gristmill had stood beside the falls, operated by a famous blind miller named Bishop. Villagers and summer boarders reveled in the beauty of the old mill and the falls cascading down next to it. Imagine their feelings when, around 1910, they realized the full extent of the city's plans for the Ashokan reservoir, graphically envisioned by Alf Evers:

Bishop's Falls would disappear behind the longest dam of its kind then existing anywhere in the world. The inhabitants not only of farms but also of seven hamlets would be forced to flee. They would be joined by the bodies of almost three thousand people who had been quietly awaiting the judgment day in thirty-two Esopus valley cemeteries, for New York's almost twenty-four square miles of the valley would be scraped clean of every vestige of its former inhabitants and their works before fastidious New Yorkers would drink the Ashokan Reservoir's water.

After the initial wounds had healed, there were the long-term effects of the city's reservoirs. Six large lakes had been created in a region previously known among anglers almost exclusively for its stream fishing. These lakes in general have become the home and feeding grounds for large rainbow and brown trout as well as other species, and can be fished with a city permit from bank or boat. Upstream, they provide the spring and fall spawners that give stream fishermen a chance at larger-than-average trout. They have also been the source of bass and other warm-water species running up into trout territory.

Downstream, the reservoirs have been the focus of intense fighting over New York City's water-release practices. After many years of "mud or flood" stream conditions below the dams, in 1976 a group of fishermen and conservationists, backed by the state, succeeded in getting legislation passed that gave control of the dam releases to the state's Department of Environmental Conservation, provided that the city would continue to get the same amount of water as before.

Since June 1977, when the new water-release program took effect, stream flows below the affected dams have been more regular and cooler in the summer months, and the fishing has improved in these downstream sections. However, the release program has been disappointing to its advocates, who contend that even better stream conditions could be achieved within the limits of the new legislation. The main limitation, of course, is that only so much water may be released by all the reservoirs combined. Asking for more water down one river just takes away from what can be sent down the others. Said Ed Van Put, "It's like punching holes in the hose."

Unfortunately for everyone who legally shares the Catskill rivers—the farms, industries, cities, power companies, canoers, and fishermen—the amount of water that would satisfy all of them is more than the rivers can produce.

*　　　*　　　*

In spite of the persistent competition for their resources, Catskill rivers have survived and are today running clean and full of trout. They are just as fragile and changeable, but they are being fished by more anglers than ever before in their history. Whenever there is a new threat to the fishing, friends of the rivers in growing numbers are joining ranks to fight. Among recent encounters have been these:

Hunter Highlands

This project would have resulted in a condominium development on Hunter Mountain which would have withdrawn water from Schoharie Creek and discharged sewage into it. Catskill Mountains Chapter of Trout Unlimited and Theodore Gordon Flyfishers opposed the project. It went to court three times with the result that substantial modifications have been made in the way Hunter Highlands will use the Schoharie.

Prattsville Pumped-Storage Project

This has been a major fight involving some forty chapters of Trout Unlimited, Theodore Gordon Flyfishers, Catskill Center for Conservation and Development, and Phoenicia Fish & Game Association, all of whom joined to form the Esopus Legal Defense Fund. The fight has been going on for over eight years in an effort to prevent the Power Authority of the State of New York from building a giant pumped-storage generating plant on a mountain above Prattsville. ELDF contends that the plant's operations will seriously damage both the Schoharie and Esopus fisheries and that PASNY has acceptable alternatives for its power needs.

Titan Project

This is a recreation-vehicle and summer-home development at Tennanah Lake for one thousand families, with original plans to dump sewage effluent into the Beaverkill near Junction Pool, principally in the summer months when the river is lowest and warmest. Two funds, the Beaverkill Legal Defense Fund and Save Our Beaverkill, were organized by Roscoe residents Bob and Rose Mary Bock. The funds got support from many fishermen and conservation groups and have thus far caused Titan to avoid the Beaverkill and attempt to run its pipes in the other direction toward Callicoon Creek.

Support to protect the Catskill rivers has come from many sources, among whom are a number of well-established conservation groups:

Phoenicia Fish & Game Association
Rte. 28, Phoenicia, NY 12464

Organized in 1929, P.F.& G.A. is the oldest sportsmen's group in continuous operation in the Catskills. Approximately 250 members stock fish and game in the area, encourage and protect unposted land, and support conservation causes. Past president Chuck Schwartz is active and a very knowledgeable Esopus fly fisherman. Meetings are the second Monday of every month in the P.F. & G.A. clubhouse two miles south of Phoenicia on Rte. 28. Annual turkey shoot in the fall.

Theodore Gordon Flyfishers
24 East 39th Street
New York, NY 10016

Although based in New York City, this group is named after the Catskills' most famous fisherman, and many of its seven hundred members fish the Catskill streams. Founded in 1962, TGF is one of the strongest, most active angling conservation groups in the country.

Catskill Mountains Chapter of Trout Unlimited
P.O. Box 285, Lake Katrine, NY 12449

Founded in 1962, Catskill Mountains was the first TU chapter in New York State. It donated members to nearby chapters as they were born, including Beamoc, Mid-Hudson, and Croton. With about 175 members, Catskill Mountains/TU "looks after" an area that includes the Esopus, Schoharie, Bush Kill, and the upper East Branch of the Delaware. This chapter has been extremely successful in raising money to defend its rivers, due in good measure to the hard work over many years of its widely known member Ed Ostapczuk.

Beamoc Chapter of Trout Unlimited
P.O. Box 138, Livingston Manor, NY 12758

Founded in 1975, Beamoc/TU took the name of the old Beaverkill-Willowemoc Rod and Gun Club's mythical mascot, a two-headed trout that lives in Junction Pool. Carolyn and Kenneth Hobbs guided the chapter in its early years. The 75 members published a set of river maps showing public access and pool names for the Willowemoc, Little Beaver Kill, and North Branch of Callicoon Creek.

Catskill Fly Fishing Center & Museum, Inc.
P.O. Box 1295, 5447 Old Route 17, Livingston Manor, NY 12758

Founded in 1981 as the successor organization to the Catskill Fly Fishing Museum, of which the late Elsie Darbee was first president. Under the direction of president Dr. Antonio LaSorte, CFFC has approximately one thousand members. It is located on the Willowemoc between Roscoe and Livingston Manor in a cluster of buildings that includes a museum, education center, administrative offices, shop, outdoor pavilion, and casting pond. It continues to grow steadily and is widely known as a gathering place for Catskill fly fishermen, and as a museum of artifacts and memorabilia of Catskill angling. The museum is now under the direction of Lisa Lyons.

The Catskill Center
for Conservation and Development, Inc.
Arkville, NY 12406
914-586-2611

Incorporated in 1969, The Catskill Center includes the welfare of the rivers in its broader purpose of balancing the forces of conservation and development in the Catskills. With more than 2,500 members, this organization has been an effective force in helping to conserve and enhance the region's manmade and natural resources. One example of this commitment is the center's participation in the Esopus Legal Defense Fund, an effort to resist the building of a pumped-storage power plant near Prattsville by the Power Authority of the State of New York.

Catskill river conservation fights are typically triangular: in addition to the defendant—often a developer or industrial company—and the plaintiff conservation group(s), there is the government body with jurisdiction over the rivers, the New York State Department of Environmental Conservation, known familiarly as the DEC.

The plaintiff identifies the issue, initiates legal action, generates publicity, lobbies for votes and political support, and in general organizes the campaign. The DEC acts as moderator and issuer of permits; it conducts public hearings, provides information, and in the end issues or withholds the permit to a developer or company involved in a project that affects the environment, in this case water quality and the rivers.

The DEC, in its ongoing role outside of conservation fights, can be thought of as a manager of the rivers. It conducts resource surveys to help determine the "management strategy" to protect and improve the rivers. Among its duties, the DEC runs hatcheries, stocks the streams, enforces fishing regulations, and conducts creel censuses, angler censuses, and fish population surveys. It also buys public fishing rights, as well as administering the issuance of permits under the Stream Protection, Wetlands, and Pollution Discharge laws.

Two DEC offices have jurisdiction over Catskill rivers: Region III, 21 South Putt Corners Road, New Paltz, NY 12561, and Region IV, Jefferson Road, Stamford, NY 12167.

*   *   *

If you are a beginning fly fisherman, where do you go to get started? If you are a veteran angler, and you've just caught a trophy trout, where do you go to show it off, or—if you put it back—to let the news out? In either case, you most likely go to a tackle shop. Tackle shops not only offer the flies and other necessaries to go forth with confidence onto the stream; they also are the best places to get advice, meet people, and generally to immerse yourself in the fullness of angling.

Many of the Catskill fishing tackle stores are "mom and pop" businesses. In fact, the moms are often home tying flies and minding the store while the pops are out fishing. That was the case with Elsie and Harry Darbee, whose fly and tackle shop was so vividly described by Sparse Grey Hackle:

Fishermen come in for their needs, remain to tell their experiences, get into conversations, and finally constitute a voluble, vociferous, constantly changing, nonstop seminar with the participants standing crowded together and all talking at once.

Other Catskill tackle shops share this wonderful combination of characteristics: they are combined emporiums and forums, extensions of the collective psyche of their customers, the gregarious half of a half-solitudinous sport. They are good places to know and to visit.

Al's Wild Trout Ltd.
Box 666
Shinhopple, NY 13755
607-363-7135
Al Carpenter

Beaverkill Angler
Stewart Avenue
Roscoe, NY 12776
607-498-5194
John McCullough

Darbee House Fly Shop
R.D. 1, Box 163
Livingston Manor, NY 12758
607-498-5791
Martin Redcay

Delaware Fly Shop
Route 191
Hancock, NY 13783
717-635-5983
Harry Batschelet

Dette's Flies
Cottage Street
Roscoe, NY 12776
607-498-4991
Winnie and Mary Dette

Donegal's
6 Stewart Street
Roscoe, NY 12776
607-498-5911
Paul Filippone

Esopus Fly Fisher
261 Van Kuren Avenue
Pine Bush, NY 12566
914-361-5069
Bob Ewald

Folkerts Brothers, Inc.
Main Street
Phoenicia, NY 12464
914-688-9936
Anneliese and Herman Folkerts

Fur, Fin & Feather
DeBruce Road
Livingston Manor, NY 12758
914-439-4476
Sue and Rich Post

Poul Jorgensen
Cottage Street
Roscoe, NY 12776
607-498-4509

Kuttner's Fly Shop
Beaverkill Road
Livingston Manor, NY 12758
914-439-5590
Frank Kuttner

The Little Store
26 Broad Street
Roscoe, NY 12776
607-498-5553
Bob Bock

McFadden's Fly & Tackle Shop
Route 97
Hankins, NY 12741
914-887-6000
Joe McFadden

Old Glory Fly Shop
Rockland Road
Roscoe, NY 12776
607-498-4567
Ralph Graves

West Branch Angler
150 Faulkner Road
Deposit, NY 13754
607-467-5525
Harry Batschelet

*   *   *

The power of Catskill rivers to make friends is as resurgent as their riffles and runs. With each advancing season, newcomers join the ranks of those who are putting back more than just their fish. They are caught in the spell of these rivers and they become involved in helping them endure. Who are some of these friends?

Kris and Art Lee moved to Roscoe in 1973. Kris is an outdoor and angling photographer whose work has appeared in *National Geographic*, *Geo*, *Fly Fisherman*, and numerous other publications. She can often be found on the Beaverkill or Willowemoc capturing her favorite subject, her husband, in the act of netting a large trout. Art is a contributing editor to *Fly Fisherman*, author of many fishing articles and the recently published *Fishing Dry Flies for Trout on Rivers and Streams*. From their base in Roscoe, the Lees reach out around the Catskills, photographing and writing about the fishing, combining the talents under one roof of a p.r. firm for the rivers.

Ed Van Put grew up fishing bluegills in New Jersey and progressed in a normal manner up the fisherman's ladder to trout and the dry fly. He made his first trip to the Catskills in the late 1950s where he met Elsie and Harry Darbee, who taught him to tie flies and took him fishing. By 1965, the streams had taken so powerful a hold on him that Ed left a promising career in construction management and moved up permanently to make Catskill streams and fishing the organizing force in his life. After four years of odd jobs, he landed a job with the fisheries staff of the state's Department of Environmental Conservation. Today, after fourteen years of total immersion in Catskill trout streams, both on and off the job, Ed has become one of the best-known angling personalities of the Northeast, both for his dedication to protecting and improving Catskill angling conditions and for his own fishing prowess.

If a contest were held to pick the Catskills' most dedicated and persistent angling conservationist, Phil Chase would be an odds-on favorite. Phil was born in Port Jervis, where the Neversink joins the Delaware, and he has grown up fishing and fighting for his home rivers. A full-time high school science teacher, Phil has over the years given an awesome amount of his time to the welfare of Catskill rivers. He originated with Jim Gilford the Water Watchers Program for Fontinalis Flyfishers and the Federation of Fly Fishermen in the late 1960s; for 13 years he wrote a freelance conservation column for *The Middletown Record*; he served as vice president of Save the Delaware Coalition, an effort involving 55 conservation organizations fighting to stop Tocks Island Dam from being built on the Delaware; he has testified since 1965 in almost 100 public hearings on reservoir releases and other Catskill river issues; in 1970 he was named Man of the Year by the Federation of Fly Fishermen for his work on dam releases and the Water Watchers program. Reflecting on his many encounters, Phil said, "You have to realize in a conservation fight that it takes a lot of people working together to win, and these are only battles; the war is continuous because there is always some new threat looming just around the bend."

Gardner Grant fell prey to the magical powers of the Delaware and the Beaverkill in the early 1970s and gave up his fishing base of operations on one of Pennsylvania's classic trout streams to become a permanent Catskill angler. This was a lucky break for Catskill and New York State anglers generally, because Gardner is a mover and a shaker. No sooner was he resettled than he went to work on behalf of his newfound rivers. Among his achievements, he has helped clarify the applicability and enforceability of New York's Stream Protection Law; he also helped draft and lobby for New York's Wild and Scenic Rivers Law. In each case, Gardner worked with long-time friend and environmental attorney Stan Bryer to develop an effective legal and political strategy to realize their objectives. In his continuing role as president or director of numerous national angling organizations, Gardner has acquired the contacts and credibility to become a leading champion of the rivers.

Joan and Lee Wulff, considered the world's best-known husband-and-wife angling team, came to the Catskills in 1979 and opened a fishing school on the upper Beaverkill. It was a first for the Wulffs and the Catskills and has been mutually rewarding for both. Now in its fifth season, the Wulff Fishing School offers courses on trout, Atlantic salmon, and fly casting. The casting course is the only course dedicated entirely to casting that is given by any fishing school. Joan especially wanted to offer this course so that students could benefit from her record of 16 years as national or international women's casting champion. Her record cast is 161 feet. Lee is one of the top salmon anglers in the world and author of several books including *Lee Wulff On Flies* and the recently updated and republished *The Atlantic Salmon*. Joan and Lee personally teach each of their students. Courses run from early May to late July. More information on the current course schedule can be obtained by writing or calling Wulff Fishing School, Lew Beach, NY 12753, 914-439-4060.

Hoagy Carmichael also came under the spell of these rivers, but he went even further and surrendered to the spirit of a man. Soon after meeting rodmaker Everett Garrison, Hoagy realized that he was fated to carry on the Garrison tradition of exquisitely crafted bamboo rods. What this meant was years of study and effort to understand Garrison's highly technical approach to rodbuilding, to master the skills of an ultra-precise craft, to begin a book with Garrison, and to go on after the old master died to finish the book and build the rods. Fifty years ago, Garrison sent the first rod he designed up to the Beaverkill for testing; today, Hoagy fishes both Garrisons and Carmichaels on the Beaverkill. It would be hard to find a better symbol of the strength and continuity of the Catskill angling tradition.

Indeed, in the century-and-a-half since Washington Irving "sallied into the country" with his "stark mad" fishing friends, Catskill angling has been remarkably constant throughout the upheavals and changes that have occurred within the region.

The Catskill angler has arrived at his fishing ground via stage coach, train, bus, automobile, and now, in rare cases, helicopter; his streams were originally open to all, then heavily private, then gradually more open and state-controlled until today a mix of all these prevails; his adversaries have been tanneries and acid factories, dams, power companies, modern industries, and developers; his shelter began with and progressively included tents, farmhouses, clubhouses, fishing hotels, motels, vacation homes, campers, and recreation vehicles.

Through all these changes there has been preserved in the Catskills, especially in its deeper reaches, a remote wilderness of pristine beauty. The angler of today retreats to these streams, is drawn back in time, and—even with his modern equipment and methods—could easily be a Burroughs, a Norris, or a Gordon.

Selected Bibliography

Five libraries or private collections have been the source of most of the secondary research for this book: The New York Public Library; the Carl Otto von Kienbusch Collection and the Kenneth Rockey Collection, both at the Firestone Library of Princeton University; the library of The Anglers' Club of New York; and the private collection of Harry A. Darbee.

American Angler, A Weekly Journal of Fish, Fishing and Fish Culture, The. William C. Harris, editor. New York: The Anglers' Publishing Co., vols. I–XXX, 1881–1900.

American Angler, The. Enos Post, editor. New York: vols. I–V, 1916–1921.

American Fly Fisher, The. Austin S. Hogan and Paul Schullery, editors. Manchester: The Museum of American Fly Fishing, vols. 1–9, 1974–1982.

Anglers' Club Bulletin, The. The Anglers' Club of New York, vols. 1–60, 1920–1982.

Anglers' Club Story: Our First Fifty Years, 1906–1956, The. The Anglers' Club of New York, Privately printed, 1956.

Brown, John J. *The American Angler's Guide.* New York: D. Appleton and Co., 1857.

Burroughs, John. *In the Catskills.* Boston: Houghton Mifflin, 1910.

Conservationist, The. Published by the New York State Department of Environmental Conservation. Albany, NY: vols. I–XXXVII, 1946–1982.

Cross, Reuben R. *Tying American Trout Lures.* New York: Dodd, Mead & Co., 1936.

Darbee, Harry, with Mac Francis. *Catskill Flytier: My Life, Times, & Techniques.* Philadelphia: J. B. Lippincott, 1977.

DeLisser, R. Lionel. *Picturesque Catskills, Green County.* Northampton, MA: Picturesque Publishing Co., 1894.

———. *Picturesque Ulster, Townships of Denning and Hardenbergh.* Kingston, NY: Styles & Bruyn Publishing Co., 1896.

Evers, Alf. *The Catskills: From Wilderness to Woodstock.* Garden City, NY: Doubleday, 1972.

Flick, Arthur B. *New Streamside Guide to Naturals and Their Imitations.* New York: Crown Publishers, 1969.

Garrison, Everett, with Hoagy B. Carmichael. *A Master's Guide to Building a Bamboo Fly Rod.* Katonah, NY: Martha's Glen Publishing Co., 1977.

Gerow, Joshua R. *Alder Lake.* Liberty, NY: Fuelane Press, 1953.

Gill, Emlyn M. *Practical Dry-Fly Fishing.* New York: Charles Scribner's Sons, 1912.

Gingrich, Arnold, editor. *The Gordon Garland, A Round of Devotions by His Followers.* New York: The Theodore Gordon Flyfishers, 1965.

———. *The Well-Tempered Angler.* New York: Alfred A. Knopf, 1966.

Hackle, Sparse Grey. *Fishless Days, Angling Nights.* New York: Crown Publishers, 1974.

Hewitt, Edward R. *A Trout and Salmon Fisherman for Seventy-Five Years.* New York: Charles Scribner's Sons, 1950.

———. *Better Trout Streams.* New York: Charles Scribner's Sons, 1931.

Hogan, Austin S., editor. *American Sporting Periodicals of Angling Interest.* Manchester: The Museum of American Fly Fishing, 1973.

Irving, Washington. *The Sketch Book of Geoffrey Crayon, Gent.* New York: C. S. Van Winkle, 1819–20.

Jennings, Preston J. *A Book of Trout Flies.* New York: Crown Publishers, 1970.

Keane, Martin J. *Classic Rods and Rodmakers.* New York: Winchester Press, 1976.

Kudish, Michael. *Vegetational History of the Catskill High Peaks.* Unpublished doctoral thesis, Syracuse University, 1972.

LaBranche, George M. L. *The Dry Fly and Fast Water.* New York: Charles Scribner's Sons, 1914.

Longstreth, T. Morris. *The Catskills.* New York: The Century Co., 1918.

McDonald, John. *The Complete Fly Fisherman: The Notes and Letters of Theodore Gordon.* New York: The Theodore Gordon Flyfishers, 1970.

———. *Quill Gordon.* New York: Alfred A. Knopf, 1972.

Marbury, Mary Orvis. *Favorite Flies and their Histories.* Boston: Houghton, Mifflin and Co., 1892.

New York State Conservation Commission. Annual Reports, 1911–1965.

New York State Fisheries Commission. Annual Reports, 1869–1895.

New York State Fisheries, Game & Forest Commissions. Annual Reports, 1895–1909.

Norris, Thaddeus. *The American Angler's Book.* Philadelphia: E. H. Butler & Co., 1864.

Pelton, Frank Curtis. *Eel Rack: An Epic Narrative of the Delaware.* Philadelphia: The Ferguson Press, 1921.

Quinlan, James Eldridge. *History of Sullivan County.* Liberty, NY: G. M. Beebe and W. T. Morgans, 1873.

Rhead, Louis. *American Trout-Stream Insects.* New York: Frederick A. Stokes Co., 1916.

Roosevelt, Robert B. *The Game Fish of the North.* New York: G. W. Carleton, 1862.

Tiffany, Lena O. B. *Pioneers of The Beaverkill Valley.* Laurens, NY: Village Printer, 1976.

Tuscarora Club's Forty-Year History, 1901–1941. Privately printed, 1941.

Woman Flyfishers Club Bulletin, The. The Woman Flyfishers Club. New York: vols. 1–22, 1937–1982.

Important Dates in Catskill Angling

1830
First known fisherman's boardinghouse in America, established by Milo Barber in Shandaken, on Esopus Creek.

1851
Erie Railroad completed along the banks of the upper Delaware River, offering the earliest access by rail to Catskill fishing.

1856
Bill Hardie of Shin Creek, responding to an offer of five hundred dollars by showman P. T. Barnum, caught a five-pound brook trout and delivered it alive to Barnum's aquarium in New York. Barnum hedged when he saw the fish's poor condition, but Hardie devised a country remedy and collected his reward. The trout died the following morning.

1860
John Burroughs, native Catskiller and famous naturalist and writer, made his first fishing trip to the Neversink and Beaverkill. Hiking in over Big Indian mountain, he found "a mountain brook born of innumerable ice-cold springs, with fish as black as the stream and very wild."

1864
Publication of *The American Angler's Book* by Thaddeus Norris, first important American book on angling, dedicated to the "Houseless Anglers," a small group of Catskill fishermen.

1868
New York Fisheries Commission established. Seth Green appointed first superintendent of fish culture. Green's private hatchery in Caledonia was bought by the state and served as the official hatchery for Catskill rivers until 1895. It was the first American hatchery and is still operating today.

1870
Black bass from Ohio planted in the Delaware by Erie Railroad. They established themselves up and down the main river and in warmer tributaries to become a prized game fish.

1871
First year of Atlantic salmon-stocking experiments in the Delaware River. Pacific salmon were also stocked in 1877. Both experiments failed because the river is too far south to be a natural salmon river.

1872
A significant date in Catskill angling. Two railroads were completed just ten miles on either side of the headwaters of the Rondout, Neversink, Esopus, Willowemoc, and Beaverkill rivers. From 1872 forward, Catskill trout fishing flourished.

1873
Founding of Salmo Fontinalis on the Beaverkill, the first private stream club in the Catskills.

1875
First rainbow trout stocked in the Catskills. Brought in from California by Seth Green's Caledonia hatchery, 260 of which lived to become the breeders that supplied not only New York but much of the East.

1880
First wood acid factories opened on Catskill streams around this date. These factories made wood alcohol, acetate, and charcoal through the process of destructive distillation of hardwoods. This industry peaked during World War I.

1881
First issue of *The American Angler*, published in New York City until 1900 by William C. Harris, considered the most important to fishermen of nineteenth-century American periodicals.

Hiram Leonard moved his rod shop from Bangor, Maine, to Central Valley, New York, on the threshold of the Catskills, where he perfected his rod designs and distinguished himself as "the father of the modern split-bamboo fly rod."

1882
Clarence Roof bought the "Parker Place" on West Branch of Neversink and began assembling four-thousand-acre "Wintoon," the first major private fishing preserve in the Catskills.

1883

Balsam Lake Club founded on the headwaters of the Beaverkill.

First brown trout arrived in America on February 24 as eighty thousand impregnated eggs were shipped from Germany to Cold Spring Harbor Hatchery on Long Island. Half of the eggs were sent on to the Caledonia hatchery where they were hatched and then stocked in the Catskills.

1885

Erie Railroad train carrying cans of large rainbow trout was delayed by a wreck near Callicoon Creek on the Delaware around this date. Brakeman Dan Cahill had the fish planted in Callicoon Creek so they wouldn't die. They thrived and the creek became famous for its rainbow fishing.

Catskill Forest Preserve established when New York State acquired title to a large tract of Catskill land that had been abandoned because of overdue taxes.

1886

First stocking of brown trout in Catskills, in Aden Brook, a tributary of the Neversink.

1887

Jay Davidson began operating Trout Valley Farm as a fishing hotel in the village of Beaverkill. Fred Banks bought it in 1922 and continued running it until 1963, a seventy-six-year tradition of angling hospitality.

1890

On February 22, Englishman Frederic M. Halford sent fifty of his favorite dry-fly patterns to Theodore Gordon, and "the dry fly winged its way to the New World." Gordon used them as the model and inspiration for new American dry-fly patterns.

George J. Gould bought 550 acres on Dry Brook, headwater tributary of the East Branch of the Delaware, the beginning of a three-thousand-acre estate with twenty-six-room log home "Furlough Lodge."

1892

Founding of The Fish and Game Protective Association of Sullivan County, N.Y. Theodore Gordon was one of the incorporators of this group, which placed its own wardens on the Neversink, Willowemoc, and Beaverkill to help the state enforce game laws and stop predatory fishing practices.

1895

Fly Fishers Club of Brooklyn incorporated by a group of wealthy Brooklyn brewers setting up their headquarters in Ben Hardenburg's log cabin on the Beaverkill.

First women anglers reported on Beaverkill and Neversink; one of them was the fishing "chum" of Theodore Gordon. They wore wading boots under their long skirts.

First hatchery established in the Catskills, on the Beaverkill two miles upstream from Junction Pool. It was shut down in 1901 because of a lack of an adequate year-round supply of cool water.

1898

Edward F. Payne established the E. F. Payne Rod Company in Highland Mills, two miles up the road from his old employer and mentor, Hiram Leonard. Son Jim Payne took over in 1914 and ran the company until 1968.

Raphael Govin, prosecutor of poachers for Clarence Roof, began assembling his own thousand-acre estate on the East Branch of the Neversink.

1900

Beaverkill Fishing Association organized on the Beaverkill below Lew Beach, merged in 1910 into Beaverkill Trout Club.

1901

Tuscarora Club founded on Mill Brook, tributary of East Branch of Delaware.

1904

Last known Beaverkill log raft was run from Spooner's Eddy at Horton to a Callicoon sawmill on the lower Delaware.

1906

Delaware Shad Club of Binghamton organized with about fifty members. They held an April "field day" each year near Hancock and seined several hundred shad for a huge shore dinner on the banks of the river.

1908

William Keener caught an 8½ pound brook trout in The Punchbowl, near Roscoe. It is *still* the state record.

1912

Publication of the first American book on the dry fly, *Practical Dry-Fly Fishing*, by Emlyn M. Gill, who fished mostly in the Catskills, especially on the Willowemoc.

1914

Publication of *The Dry Fly and Fast Water* by George M. L. LaBranche, establishing the author as the leading American authority on dry-fly angling. LaBranche cast his first dry fly in 1899 at the mouth of Mongaup Creek on the Willowemoc.

IMPORTANT DATES IN CATSKILL ANGLING

1915

Theodore Gordon died on May 1 in Bradley on the Neversink, mourned by many at the time as America's leading angling authority.

Ashokan Reservoir completed, damming Esopus Creek—the first New York City reservoir in the Catskill water-supply system.

1916

Publication of *American Trout-Stream Insects* by Louis Rhead, based on insects collected by the author on the Beaverkill. Ambitious but misguided, this book was the first attempt to create an American stream entomology.

1917

Tom and Chester Mills, New York fishing-tackle dealers, created the famous Fanwing Royal Coachman fly pattern while fishing with Hiram Leonard in Phoenicia on Esopus Creek.

1918

Edward R. Hewitt began assembling his twenty-seven-hundred-acre, four-mile river estate on the Neversink below Claryville. There he built his trout laboratory and became America's leading authority on fish culture and stream improvement.

Roy Steenrod, fishing the lower Beaverkill with his friend A. E. Hendrickson, ran into a tremendous hatch of mayflies and created an artificial to match it. Later named the Hendrickson, it has become perhaps the most popular brown-trout fly in America.

Jim Payne developed one of the first dry-fly actions in a trout rod while fishing with A. E. Hendrickson, Roy Steenrod, and several other friends on Esopus Creek.

1919

Repeal of the old Blue Law of the New York Penal Code which made it a misdemeanor to fish on Sunday. Law had been disregarded since late 1800s.

1923

H. S. "Pinky" Gillum began his rod-making business in Ridgefield, Connecticut. Harry Darbee's fly shop in Roscoe was Gillum's only "official" retail outlet. The Gillum rods are among the finest bamboo fly rods ever made.

T. E. Spencer caught a nineteen-pound fourteen-ounce brown trout in Chimney Hole, the first pool on Esopus Creek above Ashokan Reservoir. This fish was a state record for thirty-one years.

1926

Gilboa Dam completed on Schoharie Creek, creating the second of New York City's Catskill reservoirs. A tunnel delivers this water into Esopus Creek at "the portal" in Allaben.

1931

United States Supreme Court ruled that the water of the Delaware River was a limited and valuable resource that had to be rationed among the four states through which it runs: New York, Pennsylvania, New Jersey, and Delaware.

Publication of *Better Trout Streams* by Edward R. Hewitt; the first American book on stream improvement, based on the author's Neversink experiments.

1932

Incorporation of the Woman Flyfishers Club on the West Branch of the Neversink, the only female angling club in the world.

Everett Garrison officially went into the custom rod-making business with two eight-footers. One went to John Alden Knight, the other to Garrison's close friend Vernon Heyney, who was in a Depression-induced retirement on the Beaverkill.

1934

Art Flick gave up a New York City job and moved to the West Kill, a tributary of Schoharie Creek, where he ran an inn for fly fishermen and became an influential conservationist.

1935

Publication of *A Book of Trout Flies* by Preston Jennings; America's first stream entomology to identify scientifically the principal eastern stream insects and match them up with effective imitations. Jennings began his insect collecting on the Esopus and concentrated on Catskill streams.

1936

Publication of *Tying American Trout Lures* by Reuben R. Cross, Catskill flytier and pattern designer. This book was a major influence on American flytiers of the thirties and forties.

1946

Publication in the May issue of *Fortune* magazine of comprehensive article by John McDonald on American angling and flytying, highlighting the contributions of Theodore Gordon and his disciples.

1947

Publication of *Streamside Guide* by Art Flick, based on his insect collections on Schoharie Creek. This book was hailed by anglers as a "practical classic" because of its simplified approach to identifying trout-stream insects and their imitations.

Ed Hewitt converted his Neversink river property into the Big Bend Club.

1949

Opening of the DeBruce Hatchery at Toad Basin Spring on Mongaup Creek. Described at the time as "the most modern fish-culture facility in the world," the DeBruce state hatchery today serves most of the public stocking requirements in the Catskills.

Founding of The Beaverkill-Willowemoc Rod and Gun Club of Roscoe, N.Y., Inc. Fred Ackerly, Walt Bock, and Harry Darbee helped organize the group, whose main purpose was to fight the damming of Catskill streams.

1950

Dams completed on the Rondout and Neversink rivers, creating the third and fourth of New York's six Catskill water-supply reservoirs.

1952

Fly-fishing-only sections were tried on the Willowemoc and several other New York streams. The experiment failed because it was seen as an elitist regulation, and because it could not be proved that the regulation produced more and bigger trout.

1953

On September 10, the O&W Railroad—after 82 years of transporting fishermen and fish to and from the Willowemoc, Beaverkill, and East Branch of the Delaware—made its last scheduled passenger run out of Sullivan County.

1961

Downsville dam completed on the East Branch of the Delaware, creating Pepacton Reservoir, the fifth of New York City's reservoirs.

1962

First no-kill section in New York established on the Schoharie near the Little West Kill. Section was abandoned after two seasons when it became clear that high water temperatures were killing the trout in spite of the no-kill regulation.

1965

First no-kill section opened on the Beaverkill. Its success led to extensions and to a neighboring no-kill section on the Willowemoc, giving a total of 6¾ miles of no-kill fishing in the Roscoe/Livingston Manor area.

1967

Dam for Cannonsville Reservoir completed on West Branch of the Delaware, the sixth and last reservoir to date in New York City's Catskill water-supply system.

1976

Catskill Waters, a special-interest group formed by Frank Mele and John Hoeko, succeeded in getting state legislation passed that gave control to the Department of Environmental Conservation of water releases from Catskill reservoirs owned by New York City.

1981

Founding of Catskill Fly Fishing Center, organized to provide a riverfront center as a gathering place for Catskill fly fishermen and a museum of artifacts and memorabilia of Catskill angling.

Index

Note: page numbers in *italics* refer to material in illustrations or captions

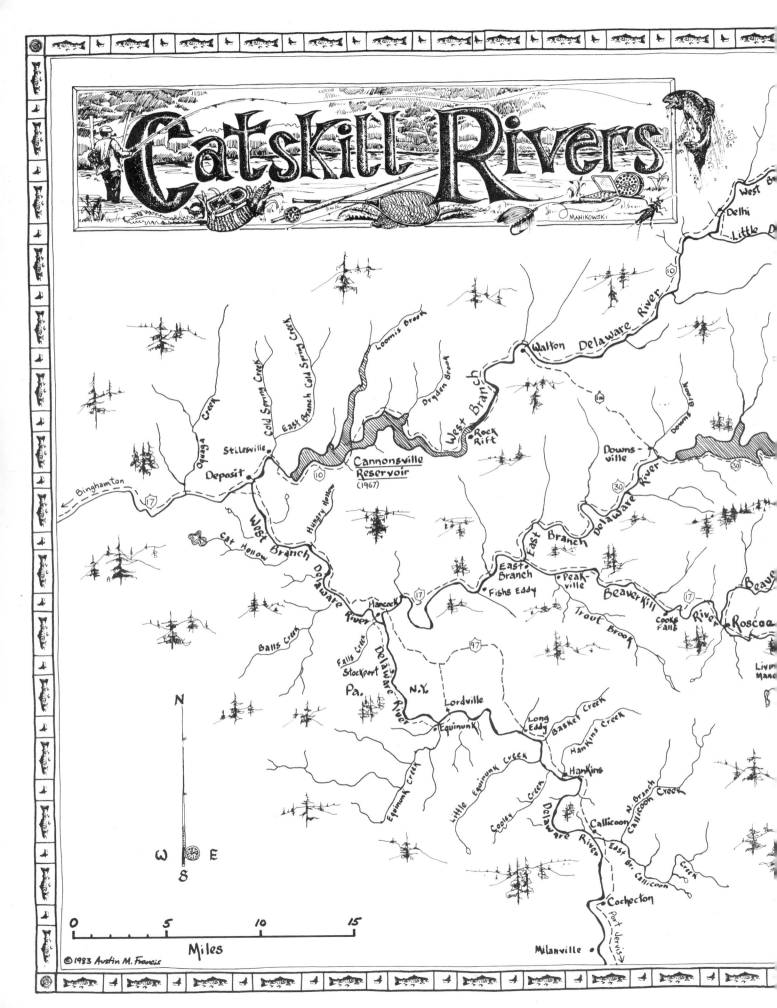

Catskill Rivers

MANIKOWSKI

West Br
Delhi
Little D

West Branch
Loomis Brook
Dryden Brook
Walton   Delaware River
Rock Rift
Downs
Downsville
Cannonsville Reservoir (1967)
East Branch   Delaware River
Beaver
Oquaga Creek
Stilesville
Cold Spring Creek
East Branch Cold Spring Creek
Deposit
Binghamton
West Branch
Hungry Hollow
Cat Hollow
Delaware River
East Branch
Fishs Eddy
Peakville
Beaverkill
Trout Brook
Cooks Falls
River   Roscoe
Livin
Man
Balls Creek
Hancock
Falls Creek
Stockport
Pa.
N.Y.
Delaware River
Lordville
Long Eddy
Basket Creek
Hankins Creek
Equinunk
Equinunk Creek
Little Equinunk Creek
Cooley Creek
Hankins
Delaware River
N. Branch Callicoon Creek
Callicoon
East Br. Callicoon
Creek
Cochecton
Port Jervis
Milanville

N
W   E
S

0   5   10   15
Miles

© 1983 Austin M. Francis